PERSONAL AND INTERPERSONAL APPRAISAL TECHNIQUES

Personal and Interpersonal Appraisal Techniques

For: **COUNSELORS**
TEACHERS
STUDENTS

By

M. A. KILEY, Ed.D.

Professor of Education
Towson State College
Baltimore, Maryland

CHARLES   C   THOMAS   ·   PUBLISHER
Springfield · Illinois · U.S.A.

Published and Distributed Throughout the World by

CHARLES C THOMAS • PUBLISHER

Bannerstone House

301-327 East Lawrence Avenue, Springfield, Illinois, U.S.A.

*With THOMAS BOOKS careful attention is given to all details of
manufacturing and design. It is the Publisher's desire to present books that
are satisfactory as to their physical qualities and artistic possibilities and
appropriate for their particular use. THOMAS BOOKS will be true to those
laws of quality that assure a good name and good will.*

Printed in the United States of America
C-1

Library of Congress Cataloging in Publication Data

Kiley, Margaret A.   1928-
    Personal and interpersonal appraisal techniques for
counselors, teachers, students.

    1. Personnel service in education. 2. Teacher
participation in personnel service. I. Title.
[DNLM: 1. Counseling. 2. Interpersonal relations.
3. Psychology, Educational. 4. Self-concept.
5. Students. 6. Teaching. LB1027.5.K48p]
LB1027.5.K52   371.4   74-16447
ISBN 0-398-03219-X
ISBN 0-398-03240-8 (pbk.)

PERSONAL AND INTERPERSONAL APPRAISAL TECHNIQUES

Relevant material is contained in this volume for public school counselors and teachers who are searching for improved methods of helping students adjust to the pressures of maturing, obtaining an education and making realistic choices for the future.

Assisting students in personal, academic and career decision-making is viewed as a cooperative effort between counselors, teachers, students and parents. The most effective counseling can be accomplished when well-trained counselors, using a variety of approaches for appraising student potential and achievement, are aided by empathetic teachers who have strong rapport with their students. Methods for developing greater self-understanding on the part of the student through a variety of self-appraisal and analysis techniques are also presented.

In this text, experienced teachers who disapprove of the widening gap between faculty and students will find useful ideas for assessing classroom climate and improving peer group dynamics and teacher-student relationships. Those preparing for and recently entering the teaching field, often confident of their subject but unsure of how to communicate with students as people, will gain insight into the human side of the teacher-student relationship. Counselors-in-training and newcomers to the profession will find valuable material for understanding the team relationship between teacher and counselor, while the experienced counselor, overburdened by excessive counselee loads is offered practical suggestions for involving teachers in guidance techniques in the classroom setting.

ENTS
T ME

PREFACE

IF, AS CRITICS CHARGE
    "schools induce alienation"
  "teachers teach subjects not students"
  "counselors are too busy to counsel"
how can schools provide an atmosphere where students can not only *survive,* but *succeed?* Admittedly, there are schools where counselors and teachers are guilty as charged, but thankfully there are also many others throughout the nation where the faculty understand and communicate with their students and foster pupil self-development as well as stimulate academic growth.

What is the secret that enables these counselors and teachers to reach their students while others grow increasingly disenchanted until, admitting defeat, they leave the profession or, worse, refusing to change, grimly remain in the school, living proof of the critics' fears? First, obsessive concern with "content" must yield to mutual respect and empathy between teachers and students. Next, counselors must recognize that the facts in their files are insufficient for effective counseling and utilize the insights of the teachers about students. Teachers can make valuable suggestions in the areas of appraisal, placement, and evaluation, as well as supplying information, even counseling, on students' personal problems. Often a student will talk with a trusted teacher before confiding in the remote counselor. Counselors can become more effective if they go into the classroom "where the action is"; working with teachers, observing students as they cope with the pleasures, pressures and frustrations of learning. Teachers can become more responsive and effective if counselors enlist their support in dealing with student concerns and in seeking solutions to students' problems. There must be a joint acceptance by all the faculty of their mutual responsibility to provide a humanistic setting within the school facilitating the development of a positive self-concept in each student, of personal identity vital to achieving satisfaction and fulfillment.

This book presents methods for developing greater student self-understanding through a variety of self-appraisal and analysis techniques. Persons taking introductory courses in guidance, in analysis of the individual, and techniques of counseling will find the material valuable. Student teachers and new teachers, confident in their subject field but apprehensive of dealing with students as "people," will gain insight into the human side of the teacher-student relationship. Thus, this book can prove a useful supplement to texts used in teacher education programs. Re-examination of these techniques by experienced counselors and teachers may reveal opportunities for cooperative efforts in the classroom. The counselor, overburdened and often overwhelmed by excessively high counselee loads, by effectively involving the teacher can use many of the techniques in the classroom setting. Experienced teachers who deplore the widening gap between faculty and students will find useful suggestions for assessing classroom "climate" and improving peer group dynamics and teacher-student relationships.

FORMAT OF THIS BOOK

Chapter 1 examines the changing, complex, demanding world of the student and the need for counselors and teachers to aid pupils in their individual search for identity, while Chapter 2 challenges the reader to examine his or her own attitudes and biases which will affect teaching and counselor effectiveness. Subsequent chapters focus on the specific techniques which counselors and teachers can appropriately use in guiding students to better self-understanding. Attention is given to interpretation and use of the student's permanent personnel file, the autobiography, questionnaire, fact-finding conferences, observations and anecdotal records, sociometric devices, rating scales, and the case study as well as examining the use of standardized test results as a means of evaluating student potential and achievement.

Chapters include actual samples of devices so that the reader will have an opportunity to examine and analyze them, noting the limitations and possible dangers inherent in each, as well as understanding the positive results of their use.

Such appraisal devices, correctly used and interpreted, can en-

Personal and Interpersonal Appraisal Techniques

FOR: COUNSELORS
TEACHERS
STUDENTS

M. A. KILEY, Ed.D.

Professor of Education
Towson State College
Baltimore, Maryland

CHARLES C. THOMAS • PUBLISHER
Springfield • Illinois • U.S.A.

CONTENTS

PERSONAL AND INTERPERSONAL APPRAISAL TECHNIQUES

CHAPTER 1

IF YOU'RE NOT PART OF THE SOLUTION, YOU MAY BE PART OF THE PROBLEM

ARE YOU PREPARING to become a counselor, or looking for some magic to teach increasingly difficult classes of adolescents? How successful will you be? Will your counselees question values which you, too, might begin to doubt? Can you teach the present curriculum so that it makes some sense to your students, or will you find yourself impatient with some of the "required" material? Can you prepare your counselees or your students for the world they will soon inherit? Can you even anticipate what kind of world will be theirs? Along with the B.A., B.S. and M.A. degrees, should we demand all teachers and counselors be certified in clairvoyance so that on a "clear day" they can see "forever"?

Ask most teachers what their most important function is and invariably they will reply "to teach students *how to think.*" Question counselors as to their chief objective and they will emphasize facilitating their counselees' ability *to make decisions.* Developing these abilities places a responsibility on teacher and counselor far beyond explaining the textbook and maintaining students' files.

Can we speculate on the kinds of decisions today's students must make after the books have been put away and counseling sessions concluded? Will they not have to select a compatible lifestyle? Will their education show them how to differentiate between the real and the spurious in determining what will be most satisfying to them? Will they choose whatever their friends choose or take an independent path, with its uncertainties, frustrations, and disappointments, or opt for the security of the collective, computerized society? What kind of work will be "right" for them? No work at all? Life in the half-world of the drug culture or searching for answers in the communes? Students cannot elect a life-style

3

until they come to grips with the questions of "Who am I?" "What kind of person am I now and what kind of person do I want to become?" "What kind of world do I want and how can I make such a world?"

As teachers and counselors, we must offer students an education sufficient to meet the challenge of their tomorrows. They will find their answers from the world in which they are presently living; from their social and educational environments; from personal experiences, physical and psychological; from the examples of adults and peers; from the media which continuously bombard them. It takes time and active involvement to build an integrated personality. Psychiatrist Bruno Bettelheim[1] voiced concern for youth who seduced by TV develop a passivity which discourages them from facing life's problems actively; who wait for the voice from the TV tube to tell them how it all comes out. But in order to design an educational program which will develop a base upon which students can build their values, we must first understand the reality of their world today.

And how do we *see* their lives? Like this, perhaps?

A FATHER OF TWO TEENAGERS: "Good grief, they live in a perpetual playground, a wonderland. Cars, plenty of spending money, trips to Europe, clothes, parties; we never had it so good."

A MOTHER OF FIVE, AGES ELEVEN TO EIGHTEEN: "They don't want to do anything. They surround themselves with noise so they won't even have to think. Do you know my eldest will plug those earphones into the stereo and sit for hours, staring into space, listening."

A PHYSICAL EDUCATION TEACHER: "Physically, many of them are a mess. They eat nothing but 'junk' food, baby themselves, avoid all forms of exercise. I hate to think of what they'll be like in ten years."

A COUNSELOR: "Some of these kids have so many attractive offers they don't know which one to choose. Here's one of my top students whose parents can afford to send her anywhere. Acceptances from Radcliffe, Stanford, Mt. Holyoke, Michigan, and yet

---

1. Bruno Bettelheim, *The Informed Heart* (New York, Avon Books, 1969), pp. 55-56.

she says no matter which one she chooses, she knows she won't be completely satisfied."

AN ASSISTANT PRINCIPAL: "I don't know what gets into these kids. I could understand if they were from our poorer neighborhoods, the ones where kids really do have a tough time trying to get an education and get a break in this world. But they aren't. Yet they tell me that their parents don't understand them; I don't understand them; no adult does. That the world's corrupt, so why not 'turn on and tune out.' What kind of life are they going to have with brains scrambled by drugs?"

A SUNDAY SCHOOL TEACHER: "It's a wonder they have any values or sense of morality at all the way violence, perversion, sex, and pornography are shoved at them from all sides. Really these kids are very ethical; they have very high standards. They are disgusted by adults who preach decency and then patronize X-rated movies, evade their taxes, and cheat on their spouses. Society's double standard really sickens them. No wonder they are anti-establishment."

AN ENGLISH TEACHER: "These students are getting lazier every year. They practically refuse to read or do any homework; you don't dare assign a term paper because you know they will just go and buy themselves one. All the classics have been explained, outlined, and critiqued so they won't have to do any thinking at all. And now our school is going to try a 'pass/fail' grading system. So who's going to bother putting out any real effort as long as everyone is going to receive the same grade?"

A DOCTOR: "You know, it's pathetic to see some of these girls come in and want the pill so they'll be safe if they and the boyfriend decide to go 'all the way' some fine evening. I warn them about VD; I try to tell them what promiscuous premarital sex can do to their chances of building a deep, lasting relationship later, and they look at me as if I were insane. How can I hope to counteract those Hollywood skin-flicks which promise the next love affair will be more exciting than the last?"

A PROBATION OFFICER: "Can you really put all the blame on them? Of course, I know it's wrong when they steal, but let's admit that some of these kids aren't ever going to have a chance at the 'good life.' Discrimination isn't going to disappear tomorrow.

They are already disadvantaged and deprived because of the neighborhoods they live in, the schools they go to, and the second-rate education they get. How much of that could you take before you decided to grab a little for yourself? I don't know the answer. How can I tell them tomorrow will be better when I'm not really sure it will be?"

A SCIENCE TEACHER: "My sophomores pleaded with me to set up a field trip to the biological research laboratory, and frankly, I had my doubts. I thought they just wanted to get of class. Yet their enthusiasm, questions, and comments so impressed the research staff that several of their scientists volunteered to come to the school to talk about their work. After listening to the students talk about their science fair projects, the lab staff offered some free materials and the use of their equipment. Honestly, I was so proud of those students."

A CAREER COUNSELOR: "When I suggested offering some 'hands-on' job experiences and group seminars on careers to college-bound students, I never dreamed we would get such response. Our regular vocational-technical work-study program for non-college students where the student is in school a half-day and on a school-supervised job for the remainder of the day has always been popular, but I wasn't sure that college-bound students would be as interested in exploring jobs. Despite the fact that we were obliged to set up the visitations on the students' time, not regular school time, we were swamped with requests. The kids often get so excited telling about their experiences it was hard for anyone to get a word in during the seminars! Business and professional men who cooperated on the project have been so impressed by the effort and enthusiasm of these students they have offered several of them part-time jobs. Who says all today's teenagers are lazy?"

A SOCIAL STUDIES TEACHER: "Those kids are fantastic. I thought I would have to use a club to get them to study the required unit on local government. But once they saw how government affects their lives, I couldn't stop them. So far, they have interviewed the mayor, director of the budget, and several city councilmen. The superintendent of schools was so impressed with a research report done by three students, he invited them to appear at future school board meetings as 'consultants.' When students see value in learning, they really work at it."

Contradictory views? Which are accurate? Could it be that there is some truth in each of the statements quoted? Looking at the world we have learned to accept, a world that we are not necessarily happy with, you must admit that it is often a brutal place. From East Asia to the streets of any big city, life is valued cheaply. Brotherhood seems an illusive myth. People of all ages, colors, and creeds exist at a poverty level in this, the richest country in the world. Young people sickened by these evils of modern society who would like to be able to turn to the school for solutions frequently find a curriculum which evades today's problems. Some teachers are more anxious to cover the Civil War than civil rights (and in some instances this is the kind of curriculum endorsed by school boards and parents); while some counselors are too preoccupied interpreting college board scores to find time to discuss options other than going-to-college. The purpose of school seems to be self-perpetuating. One goes to elementary school so that he can go on to high school. Complete high school, son, so you can go to college, and on to graduate school. But what will all this learning do for you? Will it broaden your outlook; deepen your sense of humanity toward your fellow man; help you to understand your role as a citizen in today's world; teach you how to live happily ever after? If not, why not?

In today's overcrowded schools, students find it more and more difficult and frustrating to retain a sense of positive self, as daily they are submerged into a sea of anonymous faces which floods our classrooms. Who can enjoy being pushed and shoved through crowded corridors only to reach classes where the teacher records your presence by noting there is a body in Row 2, Seat 5, and then proceeds to recount life in the days of King Arthur. Sometimes disruptive behavior is a call for attention, a cry for someone to notice.

Once a teacher has achieved a degree of empathy with students, designing a relevant curriculum becomes easier. Teaching strategies can be devised to achieve greater student involvement and participation. A classroom atmosphere will result in which students are unafraid to test their opinions, question the views of others including the teacher, and make up their own minds on the issues. Consequently, teaching becomes easier, yet more challenging and exciting, for both teacher and students. Learning consequently becomes more stimulating, worthwhile and relevant to the here-and-now, and the future.

Although the counselor does not see his counselees for the concentrated periods of time as teachers do, he is faced with the similar problem of establishing a bridge of communication and understanding before he can help the 250, 400, or 800 students assigned to him. The counselor's prime concern should be the personal growth of the student, to assist in developing the student's capacity to analyze and solve his own problems based on a realistic evaluation of his strengths and limitations. Counselor involvement is crucial to counselor effectiveness. The counselor cannot permit himself to be trapped by the mountain of forms that consistently demand attention or isolate himself so that students believe he can be seen "by appointment only." The counselor must be a familiar face, one who has time to laugh with students during the lunch hour; who drops into classrooms; attends sports events; arranges informal sessions to discuss colleges, jobs, or whatever the students suggest; who encourages parents to visit the school to discuss problems, realizing that knowing the parent will aid immeasurably in understanding the child. Although a good percentage of time is spent in individual counseling, the counselor will also provide for small group sessions to consider problems of common concern. Teachers having problems with a specific class must also find the counselor willing to offer assistance. "Availability" should be the counselor's byword. To be effective with students, the counselor must try to see the world through their eyes and develop strategies to learn how the student operates in the classroom, how he perceives his relationships with his peers and with adults, and how they relate to him. Counselors must enlist the support of teachers and parents in studying and interpreting student behavior. Specific techniques for collecting and analyzing information to achieve these ends are discussed at length in the following chapters.

What kind of practical help can a counselor offer a boy he has never seen before who drops into his office and asks, "What's the use of studying anyway? College isn't such a big deal; who needs it? You can make good money without a college degree. Why not have some laughs now; who knows, tomorrow may be the start of World War III?"

Or to the girl confused about what she wants from life . . . "three of my girl friends are engaged already. I know Tom loves me, but I'm not sure I want to get married right away. With my typing and shorthand, I know I could get a good job; Tom's working at the auto repair shop after school, and they've promised him a full-time job as soon as he graduates. So we could afford our own apartment and buy furniture right away. My Mom was only seventeen when she and Dad got married. Yet sometimes I think maybe I'd like to go to college or be a stewardess and travel a lot. I don't know, what do you think?"

How effective can a counselor be in such a situation if the only things he knows about these students are facts typed on permanent record cards? Even lesser issues, such as "Should I drop Spanish?" "Why take an honors English course?" "Can I get a job with only one year of metal-shop?" cannot be dealt with effectively unless the student's home situation, potential, and future plans are known to the counselor. Students pressured by parents to major in a certain specialty; those thinking of getting a job or joining the service after graduation; those debating about dropping out of school all need someone to talk to, an adult who can empathize and understand their problems. The counselor should be one of those people. Frequently, a favorite teacher will also be asked for advice by students searching for answers. The information given is dependent on how well the counselor or teacher knows the individual student; the greater the knowledge, the more realistic the suggestions given the student for consideration.

Decision-making is an essential component of maturity. Each one of us has had to make many decisions about our educational, personal, and vocational lives, and we will continue to do so as long as we live. Some decisions are easy; some seem insurmountably difficult. At one time or another, we have all needed help in making realistic choices. Now, as counselors and teachers, we must accept the responsibility for providing the tools and knowledge to our students so they may better understand themselves and those around them and develop strategies for making effective choices.

This new Renaissance of understanding between faculty and students will come only when both sides begin to talk *with* each other, not *at* one another; when teachers and counselors listen to students and encourage them to seek new answers to the old questions, both academic and personal. When this happens, students will begin to believe that the school cares about each of them and wants them to succeed. School then becomes a place where they are important; where there is work they are able to do which will further their personal goals.

There are concrete ways in which teachers, counselors and students can work together to break down the barriers now separating them and get some positive interaction going. Curricular reform may provide one avenue of approach. Self-appraisal and analysis by students in cooperation with their counselors and teachers is another. But it must be remembered that techniques for self-study by students or analysis of group behavior by counselors or teachers will be effective only to the extent that certain basic assumptions are accepted by all those who use them. Failing to recognize the limitations of the data found in the student's permanent record; misinterpreting standardized test scores; misusing the student autobiography, questionnaire, or rating scale will seriously hamper the student in his efforts to better self-understanding and can only weaken the teacher or counselor's effectiveness in aiding his search.

Briefly stated, these assumptions are
1. Every student is a unique individual, worthy of respect and dignity.
2. Every individual shares similarities and differences with his peers.
3. Every individual develops emotionally and socially as well as intellectually while in school.
4. Every individual is searching for his identity, his sense of self, of personal worthwhileness, while in school and throughout life.

5. Every student needs help in his search for intellectual and emotional maturity.
6. The faculty should be willing to assist each student as he develops intellectually and emotionally.
7. The faculty should be available to help students in making realistic personal, educational, and vocational choices.
8. The faculty are models for students as they search for values and answers.
9. Appraisal and analytical techniques provide only small samples of behavior or performance; they should not be considered as "absolutes."
10. Faculty using appraisal and analytical techniques should be given training in the use and interpretation of specific devices.
11. Faculty using appraisal and analytical techniques should be fully aware of the limitations and dangers of each specific device.
12. Any techniques used for individual self-appraisal and analysis must meet the tests for validity and reliability.*

SUMMARY

If teachers are to do their jobs successfully they must realize that teaching is not solely fact-finding, testing, and grading. There are many important lessons to be learned before the adolescent becomes an adult, and not all these lessons are contained in textbooks. The student must learn how to accept and value himself and his immediate society as well as the world around him. Counselors working with students in making personal, educational, and vocational decisions recognize that such choices require careful introspection and self-evaluation. Only after the student believes his parents, teachers, and counselors accept him as a worthwhile individual can he develop a self-concept strong enough to make such judgments successfully.

In the following chapters, specific ways in which counselors and teachers can assist students in their quest for a positive personal identity will be explored.

---

* See Chapter 11, "Glossary," for definitions of these terms.

SUGGESTED READINGS

Borton, Terry: *Reach, Touch and Teach—Student Concerns and Process Education.* New York, McGraw, 1970.

Describes techniques to reach students at basic personality levels; to "touch" them as individual human beings, and yet to teach them in an organized fashion.

Ginott, Haim: *Teacher and Child.* New York, Macmillan, 1972.

A beautifully perceptive view of the best and worst in the teacher-student relationship; "must" reading for everyone in education.

Greer, Mary, and Rubinstein, Bonnie: *Will the Real Teacher Please Stand Up?* Pacific Palisades, Goodyear, 1972.

A primer on humanistic education, visually and verbally defining the goals of today's education.

Hamachek, Don E.: *Encounters With the Self.* New York, HR&W, 1970.

A clear examination of the ideas of the self-concept, including self-consistency, growth and development; focuses on behavior of the individual through the eyes of the person doing the "behaving."

LaBenne, Wallace D., and Greene, Bert I.: *Educational Implications of the Self-Concept Theory.* Pacific Palisades, Goodyear, 1969.

Application of the self-concept theory to the issues of intellectual functioning, ability grouping, promotion, grading, and discipline. Measurement of the self-concept as well as developing a healthy self-concept are also examined.

Psychological education. *The Personnel and Guidance Journal, 51:*9, 1973.

Entire issue devoted to psychological, affective, and humanistic education, focusing on counselor involvement for greatest effectiveness.

Simon, Sidney B., Howe, Leland W., and Kirschenbaum, Howard: *Values Clarification: A Handbook of Practical Strategies for Teachers and Students.* New York, Hart, 1972.

Practical strategies for teachers to use in guiding discussions on values; would be equally effective used by counselors in group sessions on values clarification.

CHAPTER 2

HOW BIASED ARE YOU?

M OST OF US CONSIDER ourselves fair, unbiased, and objective in our treatment of all students. But is this really true? Bias can be so subtle that its influence may exert itself unrecognized.

WHO'S BEING FAIR TO MY SUSIE?

Looking back on my high school counseling days, I remember conversations with colleagues concerning those pretty, vivacious, but not-too-bright young ladies every one of us numbered among our counselees. With a smile, we tacitly agreed as long as they were attractive, it didn't matter if they weren't smart; they'd get a husband and live happily ever after. Let's concentrate on those who really needed our help–those always-in-trouble boys and the "plain" girls.

When girls discussed their future with me, most of them would preface any remarks with "well, you know, it's just until I get married," assuming that on that happy day when Prince Charming (or some reasonable facsimile) walked down the aisle to meet them, all worries and decisions on their part would magically cease. In the true Hollywood tradition, they would walk off together into the sunset. Even assuming this traditional pattern of education-then-marriage, many women will still look forward to twenty years on a job. Given this possibility, I encouraged my female counselees to consider preparing for a career that would interest them. Such a suggestion was often received with (1) disbelief, (2) scorn, (3) horror, sometimes all three. "Job," "work," "career," had definite unpleasant associations for most female high school counselees. Working evoked the grim spinster toiling in the library, department store, or the public schools; alone, unloved, financially dependent upon her own resources, waiting desperately for someone to rescue her by putting that gold wedding band on the third finger of her left hand. That one might get bored with cleaning, cooking, washing, and the other aspects of keeping house; that raising children was oftimes fatiguing and frustrating; that the traditional vine-covered cottage was more apt to be a cramped one-bedroom apartment were thoughts too demoralizing to be considered.

To a limited extent this attitude is changing today. Yet many girls and women still have definite stereotypes about themselves and what roles they should fill in order to find happiness.

Mr. Darvel, whose student teaching included a twelfth grade class in "Problems of Democracy," was listening to his seniors discuss the unit on "Sex and Family Living." Students had been debating premarital sex, trial marriages, teen-age marriage, and divorce. Phyllis, seventeen and wearing an engagement ring, had commented that "if you don't know your own mind about someone, a trial marriage isn't the answer. Although everybody expects to get married, you shouldn't do it if you both don't think you can make it last."

As he listened, he realized that every girl had expressed a belief that she would marry. The boys, he noted, were not as convinced that marriage was so essential to their happiness. He later commented to the Department Chairman, Mr. Ellender, that all the senior girls expected to marry and compared their attitudes with those of his female college friends, some of whom had no immediate plans for marriage, and a few were quite undecided about getting married at all.

"Well, that just goes to show you what a college education does to some women," Mr. Ellender retorted, "what else should girls do but get married?"

The place of women in the minds of some adults (both men and women) is as stereotyped as in the minds of some females themselves. A girl gets the first indication of her "place" when she meets that happy pair, Dick and Jane, in her first grade reader and learns how strong Dick is; what glorious adventures he can have (which are forbidden to Jane because she is only a girl). Our first-grade female also learns that girls can't become doctors (the unwritten but unmistakable implications being girls aren't smart enough); nor should they climb trees (a great shock to many a girl who has been enjoying tree-climbing tremendously). All the "Janes" grow up to be mommies and live in the kitchen happily ever after (no options or alternatives allowed!). TV and movies endlessly tout husband, home, and marriage as *the* only fulfillment for a woman.

It is not surprising that the daughter who hasn't married by twenty-nine is a source of grave concern and embarrassment to her family (quite likely to herself, too). She is a failure in the eyes of the world. All her friends will wonder "what's wrong with Ellen (or Mabel or Bernice)?" The single state cannot be a matter of choice; rather it must be the result of being unchosen, says the world.

The women's liberation movement with its demands for equality on the job, in the schools, in the home, and in the courts have caused some rethinking by women (and men) as to the real role of women. Attacks by such fervent women-libbers as Betty Friedan, Germaine Greer, and Gloria Steinem against women for their passive acceptance of injustices suffered by their sex have stirred other women, content with home and hearth, to denounce, rebuke, and confound the issues. The airwaves and newsstands exploit the controversy as women search to find where they "belong." In counseling college women, this searching is evident; in talking with high school girls, it is far less discernible. Working women who have felt employment bias champion the "equal pay" plank of the women liberation platform. Many, however, see no need for an identity as a unique, separate individual, above and beyond the partnership they enjoy with their husbands. Their jobs most frequently are a means of augmenting the family income, and they see working merely as a means of maintaining their home. Those women who enjoy their jobs sometimes admit to a feeling of guilt about their careers.

Yet more and more girls and young women are combining marriage and career, not because of economic pressure but by choice and are seeking entrance to professions and fields usually restricted to men, but not without problems! In planning post-high-school education with girls, bias against women applicants cannot be ignored. Those who wish to consider medicine, law, or most of the professions soon become aware that even today some professional schools rate women a poor risk. Their admissions personnel and teaching faculties are unwilling to include women in the classes since they feel women will doubtless marry and leave the profession to raise a family. Women seeking the Ph.D. degree are frequently discouraged for similar reasons; education would be "wasted" on them; better give their place to some deserving male who will loyally remain in the field. Although women may interrupt their working for brief periods because of raising their families, the majority return to the world of work. Professions which require long training periods are sometimes not favored by girls' parents who feel that so much time devoted to studying may keep their daughters from the more important pursuit of finding a husband. Some parents are also fearful of those jobs which seem to be unfeminine.

Maureen dropped by Mr. Ellison's office, her senior counselor, to discuss her application for college. As she handed him the completed forms, he looked up and said, "Are you kidding, Maurie?" "This is for State Polytechnic."

"Yes, that's right, Mr. Ellison, I want to study architecture."

"Architecture? a girl?"

"Well, why not," she said, "I've had straight A's in four years of math; my quantitative score was 670 on the SAT and I'm getting an A in physics, too. During the summer, I worked for Scriber and Wolman, Architects; I really like that kind of work."

"But, Maurie, a girl in architecture—who's going to hire you when you graduate, a woman architect?" Mr. Ellison asked her.

"That's just what my parents say, but I really am serious about this," she replied.

"O.K., I'll complete the application and send it in for you, Maurie, but don't be surprised if State Poly refuses."

Later, Mr. Ellison commented to the other counselors, "You know, it just doesn't seem right, that cute little girl in such an unfeminine job. Can you imagine a woman architect, Maurie, building skyscrapers?"

P.S. Maureen was accepted, the first girl accepted into that college's architecture program. She did superior work, graduated, and landed a good job.

Maureen was an exception; most girls accept strong stereotypes about the appropriateness of the subjects they should study if they hope to achieve the status of the ideal girl. Girls who excel in math and science are definitely not considered feminine; English and foreign languages are, however, permissible interests. How vivid the stereotype of the bird-brained wife who can't balance a checkbook or understand why the car won't start. The cliché that the brainy female will be a social outcast is still operating. Even today girls are careful not to boast of their intellectual abilities, fearing if the fact they have any brains becomes known, their social acceptance will decline proportionately.

How smart *are* girls? How smart do their teachers and counselors think they are? How smart do they, themselves, think they are? In *The Feminized Male,* Patricia Sexton, who surveyed an entire school system of some 12,000 students, presents some startling statistics, beginning with the charge that "though run at the top by men, schools are essentially feminine institutions. . . . Women set the standards for adult behavior, and many favor students, male and female, who most conform to their own behavior norms –polite, clean, obedient, neat and nice ones."[1]

Although teachers and counselors profess to treat every student alike, in actuality their treatment of boys and girls shows marked differences. The sex-neutral school is a fiction. Sex differences do exist; bias against boys and girls is exhibited by the faculty. Counselors, for example, in many schools will not permit girls to register for mechanical drawing, metal shop, or industrial arts while boys are not permitted to enroll in home economics. The only boys encouraged by some counselors to take art are those who couldn't "make it" in an academic course and need an "easy" credit.

When report cards come out, girls frequently have higher marks than boys. Sexton[2] found girls received better grades in every course but physical education in the schools surveyed. Yet on

---

1. Patricia Sexton. *The Feminized Male* (New York, Random House, 1969), p. 29.
2. Ibid., p. 63.

standardized *aptitude* tests, boys scored somewhat higher than girls. "Boys," Sexton reported, "are far more likely than girls to be underachievers, that is, to score higher on aptitude tests than on teacher ratings."[3] Among seniors in the highest decile on aptitude tests, 90 percent of the girls got A's and B's on their report cards. Only 79 percent of the top aptitude boys got such high report card averages.[4] Girls consistently do better than boys on almost all paper and pencil tests of achievement and cognitive skill. Yet other statistics indicate boys are smarter than girls. These contradictions can perhaps be traced to the tests themselves. The SAT and the Graduate Record Examination are said to favor males because of the number of items requiring advanced math.[5] It is difficult to prove sex bias in test items or whether tests designed by men (as is the case of most standardized tests) could have unconscious bias in favor of males by using vocabulary and examples more easily understood by boys than girls.

Although the charge that girls receive higher grades from their teachers than boys is more easily proven, the reason behind the higher marks for girls is not so easily discovered. Is it that girls *are* smarter, or are their papers neater, more legible? Do they follow directions better? Or do they know how to please the teacher better than boys so when their work is graded, the teacher is consciously or unconsciously influenced by these intangibles?

Despite evidence of their "smartness," girls do not seem to have a very high opinion of their intellectual abilities or of themselves as individuals. In counseling girls, negative feelings toward themselves are quite evident. Many girls believe themselves worthwhile only if someone else values them. This attitude of "reflected glory" might be called the "Behind-every-great-man-stands-a-woman" syndrome. Girls are rarely in leadership positions in the schools; the student council president is invariably a boy, so too, most class and club presidents. When encouraging girls to run for school offices, particularly in the senior high school, the girls would tell me they simply couldn't see themselves in the leadership

3. Ibid., p. 63.
4. Ibid., p. 87.
5. Ibid., pp. 106-109.

role. To be in such a position was unfeminine, aggressive, an indication of latent bossiness (a characteristic particularly disliked by men), and for most high school girls, *the* most important ingredient for happiness in school was being liked by the boys. Any attempt by girls to compete against boys was shunned. If they received higher grades than the boys, it was some kind of unpleasant accident; one not to be dwelled upon nor publicized.

Even though girls may demonstrate higher achievement on standardized tests for most subjects than boys and receive higher grades from their teachers, they are caught in their own acceptance of a stereotyped role. Once high school is completed and they face the bias against their sex in higher education and the job market, many revert to a role which permits them to be attractive and intelligent, but not too intelligent; smart enough to realize that their "true" happiness can only be found as the devoted wife of a man who will provide for them and whenever necessary do the thinking for them. Counselors encouraging girls to get as much education as they are capable of absorbing, of developing their identity as a unique individual, separate and distinct from the men who will be their husbands, realize all too well the cruel reality which they will face. Yet passive acceptance of the "system" has not guaranteed happiness for women; denying one's intelligence and abilities can only cause confusion, guilt, wasted talent, and deep unhappiness, not only to the woman herself but to her husband and children. Counselors working with girls must help them recognize the inconsistencies of today's society and develop strategies for counteracting and coping with the obstacles they will face.

Teachers, men and women, should recognize their bias, at times in favor and at times against women. Teachers may favor girls in grading, yet they frequently discourage them in considering "masculine" studies: math, science, history. Caught, perhaps, in their own stereotype of "woman," they do not encourage girls to seek scholarships, run for school office, or assume direction for class activities. Although girls prove themselves as conscientious and good workers, "everyone knows that no one (meaning boys) likes to work for women and nobody (meaning boys) likes a 'pushy' girl." After all, "it's still a man's world."

despairingly for the first sign of chin stubble (which all his friends already boast) may be so distracted that going to school and facing his friends becomes a painful ordeal. The support and empathy of sympathetic teachers and counselors at this stage of a boy's development cannot be discounted.

Although it is known by most teachers and counselors that boys have a decided advantage in terms of strength and energy over girls, many forget, or never knew, that boys are about ten to sixteen months behind girls in the development and control of hand and body muscles. This lag in physical development, operant when the boy enters the first grade at age six, continues through adolescence. It doesn't take much imagination to see that inability to control the fine finger manipulations needed to learn how to write will handicap him as he struggles to master this skill, an ability strongly stressed by some teachers, at all grade levels. Is it any wonder that boys may dislike writing!

Sexton also notes that "left-handedness in males is also at least 50 percent greater than in girls. (While this is not a disability, left-handedness can make writing and academic learning more difficult.) Many reading and learning problems result from dyslexia. . . . This genetic disorder . . . is about five times more common among boys than girls."[7]

Bentzen,[8] who discovered that three out of every four retarded readers are boys, concluded that reading for them is a "trap." Furthermore, she stated that for every girl with a vision, hearing, or speech disorder, there were *four* boys. If a student were blind or crippled, every effort would be made to help him. Yet the boy who is already behind in the learning race by as much as a year when he enters school because his hand and body muscles are not as developed as those of the girls in his class may arbitrarily be labeled "lazy" when he tires of attempting the fine finger movement demanded in writing, or called "inattentive" due to some hidden physical defect. Teachers, both men and women, in their anxiety not to show preferential treatment toward boys or girls,

7. Sexon, *The Feminized Male,* p. 9.

8. Frances Bentzen, "Sex Ratios in Learning and Behavior Disorders," *The National Elementary Principal,* Vol. 46, No. 2 (1966), pp. 13-17.

are guilty of the cruelest bias when they fail to recognize such crucial differences as these. The counselor and school nurse, alerted by the teachers, can identify students with special physical problems which affect the students' ability to learn. And when pupils are referred for counseling because of "inattention," "daydreaming," or "lack of effort," the counselor should not rule out a physical basis for such behavior.

The disparity between tested aptitude and grades received by boys may be related directly to their *behavior* in class. Teachers have told me "well, conduct counts in my class. If the kid won't behave, I just lower his grade!" Just sit in the administrative office of any public school for an hour or so and you will quickly see that most students sent as "discipline problems" are boys. Although it is a difficult hypothesis to prove, there are indications that some teachers are rougher on boys they consider discipline problems and are more likely to fail them. Once antagonism exists between teacher and student, communication between them is greatly hampered. The teacher, repelled by the student's behavior, makes fewer efforts to discover the reasons for his academic difficulties, believing his disruptive behavior is the reason he has not learned. Often the reverse is true. Because he cannot understand the material, the student expresses his frustration in disruptive behavior, behavior he knows will result in punishment, perhaps in this way seeking through this retribution the teacher's recognition of his failure. Sometimes disruptive behavior is an effort to stop the teacher from teaching, a desperate attempt to hold back the flood of material which threatens to engulf him. Don't fall into the trap of accepting grades at their face value, of deducing that boys are not as smart as girls ("just look at their grades").

Boys do not always become disruptive in class because they are frustrated or feel a need to "prove" themselves; sometimes they are just plain bored. The majority of school activities are alien to the kinds of pursuits many boys enjoy. Boys from six to sixty acquire an almost fanatical passion for sports. As a participant, sports provide an outlet for their surplus energy, for building a sense of camaraderie and group loyalty highly valued by boys, and even a release for hostility and aggression. Boys will pour over books on sports, disproving the misconception that boys don't like to read, willingly committing to memory an impressive number of statistics. It is not surprising to hear an eight-year-old rattle off batting averages of dozens of players, dates when various teams won the championship or the pennant, or recount the time in which a record was set, down to the second. Boys like physical activity; they are good at it; witness their superior grades in physical education, an area where girls do not receive their highest grades. And yet what kinds of activities fill the seven and one-half hours of the school day? Reading, writing, answering questions (questions which to many students, boys and girls, have no relevance to their interests or future plans) and above all, sitting (quiet, preferably motionless) are the mainstays of the daily regimen in most schools. Teachers and counselors who hope to understand boys had better understand the things that interest them. Many women teachers and counselors know nothing about sports and games and could care less. Men teachers are also guilty of not recognizing and capitalizing on the most effective ways that boys learn. Walk into most classes taught by men and you will see them directing reading or writing activities or hear them talking (or hollering) at students. They should be more strongly censured than women teachers, for they should know from their own experience the most productive approaches to learning, approaches which appealed to them and which stress problem-solving, abstract reasoning, and working with things rather than words. Team teaching and simulation games, for example, which have proved so effective in training officers in the military (male) and executives in big business (also male) can easily be adapted to the classroom. Teachers should be aware that boys and girls have different learning styles and provide equal opportunities to learn in the manner most comfortable for each. Excessive concentration on reading, writing, memorizing–the verbal activities favored by girls–and ignoring methods stressing abstract reasoning, gaming, and the inquiry approach which fit boys' learning styles is a cruel and flagrant exercise of bias.

Counselors, whether men or women, who work with boys must realize that boys can be caught in stereotypes, too. The "ideal" male cannot walk into the counselor's office and reveal his feeling of personal inadequacy, doubts about his academic abilities, or total absence of plans for the future. The ideal male *knows* where he is going, how to get there, and no obstacles will keep him from his goal.

Dick Rockwell was in Mr. Harrington's office discussing his college major and career plans. "I'm going to be an engineer," he told the counselor.

"Oh, what kind, Dick—civil, chemical, electrical?" "Ah, well, I haven't decided that part, yet, but definitely engineering," answered Dick. Mr. Harrington had looked over Dick's record before the conference and knew he was repeating Algebra II, was barely holding a C in physics and had gotten a D in chemistry last year. He wasn't very hopeful about the boy's chance of succeeding in an engineering program. He felt that Dick actually disliked math, so he pressed him a little as to the reason behind his choice.

"Well, my parents think it would be a good field. There's good money in it, you know, and, of course, they expect me to go to college. I've wanted to be an engineer ever since I can remember."

Dick was very active in the school's photography club. He had won awards for some of his photos and he worked weekends in a camera shop. Mr. Harrington felt he had far more interest in that field than in engineering. Conferences with the boy's parents revealed only their pride in their son's career choice and their insistence that he have a college degree and a professional career. Talks with the math and science teachers did nothing to allay the counselor's concern. Teachers in both fields felt the boy would not survive the college-level math and science courses.

Sadly, this turned out to be true. The boy was unsuccessful and miserable in the engineering program at a local college. A switch to Business Administration and continued work experience in photography pointed to a brighter future for Dick.

If the counselor could have penetrated Dick's fear of being thought unmanly because he didn't know what he wanted to do with his life or being thought stupid by asking questions about various fields, much of his anxiety and frustration and that subsequently suffered by his parents could have been averted. About a year after Dick switched to Business Administration, he dropped by the school and told the counselor he never really wanted to be an engineer but he found that by telling his parents this was his choice "they were off my back; you know, no more nagging about what was I going to be."

Counselors and teachers sometimes forget how sensitive boys are. Boys fear being laughed at, and their feelings can be as easily hurt as any petite female by sarcastic digs hurled at them by faculty. Nor are boys permitted the luxury of a good cry (an indulgence exclusively exercised by women). The ideal male doesn't ever cry (instead he has ulcers and heart attacks and dies far earlier than his mate). Some boys have grave doubts about their social acceptability; they know they are supposed to be the aggressors, yet they are timid and uncertain in approaching girls, adults, even their peers, fearing rejection.

Counselors unaware of these anxieties, seeing a six-foot, 200-pounder wearing a varsity letter on his sweater, might mistakenly believe "that kid's got the world by the tail." Even younger and smaller boys are treated as if they were little adults; counselors and teachers urge them "to act like a man." Parents fondly refer to their sons as Mommy's (or Daddy's) "little man." But the qualities of manhood, self-reliance, compassion, courage, integrity, the ability to make decisions, to cope with personal problems, to handle one's emotions, and understand others are not fully developed at birth. Boys need help in all phases of their maturation. Counselors must recognize the problems and concerns of their male counselees and develop an atmosphere of acceptance which will encourage free and frank exchange of whatever issues they wish to discuss.

IS EVERYBODY (ELSE) HAPPY?

Having "disposed" of bias between the sexes, happily concluding "viva la difference," look now into the ugly face of prejudice and discrimination. Some people delude themselves that racism and discrimination against minority groups no longer exist. The "awkward problems" of the 1950's, triggered by the Supreme Court decision striking down segregation; advanced by marches, strikes, and protests; and rekindled by busing in the 1970's to some is a dead issue, "Solved, Case Closed."

As counselors and teachers, we recognize we should not merely pay "lip-service" to the concept of equality for all students. Every child–white, brown, black, yellow, from whatever ethnic group, whether Protestant, Catholic, Jew, or of no religious affiliation– deserves the same opportunities for personal fulfillment. Victim of our own stereotypes, we may hold in our minds an image of a "typical" American (totally nonexistent and quite unreal). The United States as a pluralistic society has been able to accommodate a wide variety of cultural patterns and life-styles, yet too many Americans continue to think of a "Mr. (or Mrs., Miss, or Ms.) Average American." This stereotype is based, say Sidney Dorros and John Browne,

> on a dominant cultural standard that is Western European (mainly English) in origin, and Protestant, middle-class and male-oriented. . . . This . . . is particularly unrepresentative of the roles and contributions of nonwhites to American society, but it is also unrepresentative of the great majority of other Americans. In terms of national origin, for example, there is no majority in the United States. No matter where your ancestors came from, you are in a minority group.[9]

Yet the school "world" is almost exclusively peopled by middle-class, affluent, suburban, white, Christian Americans. "Under pressure from the Civil Rights movement, several publishers have tried to create urban multi-ethnic readers . . . (but) study of several readers published in 1965 and 1966 concluded that most of them expressed a subtle racial bias and contained the same inappropriate cultural, developmental and learning models as earlier texts."[10] Such texts presenting a fantasy world having little appeal and no relationship to their own lives cause students to doubt the acceptability of their own culture. How can these students develop a positive sense of self-worth when they use textbooks containing damaging socioeconomic, racial, and sex-role stereotypes?

Their confusion is further compounded by the behavior of their

9. Sidney Dorros and John Browne, "What You Can Do Now to Improve the Treatment of Minorities and Women in Your Teaching," *Today's Education,* January (1973), p. 42.

10. Sara Goodman Zimet, "The Messages in Elementary Reading Texts," *Today's Education,* January (1973), p. 43.

teachers and counselors whose expectations of what disadvantaged and minority children can achieve academically and the levels (educational and vocational) to which they should aspire often tell a far different story of how "equal" a black- or brown-skinned child really is.

Mrs. Schultz, the junior member of a ninth grade language-arts/ typewriting team was bemoaning the ineffective lesson just concluded. "I really 'bombed' in there this morning, didn't I? They just didn't seem to understand how to write a business letter, did they? First period didn't seem to have so much trouble; I wonder what I did wrong?"

Mrs. Johnson, her teammate, comforted her with the comment, "Now, Irene, don't blame yourself, you know those black children in the third period just can't absorb what the others can. Just think of the homes they come from and you've already seen their IQ scores. We just shouldn't expect so much of them."

This attitude initiates a vicious circle in which the student comes to believe he is unable to achieve and in accordance with the self-fulfilling prophecy becomes a failure. In *Pygmalion in the Classroom,* Rosenthal and Jacobson's description of the first day of school is a graphic illustration of teacher expectations: "The black- and brown-skinned ones are lower-class and will have learning problems unless they look exceptionally clean. . . . If the teacher sees a preponderance of lower-class children, regardless of color, she knows her work will be difficult and unsatisfying."[11]

"The teacher wants her children to learn, all of them, but she knows that lower-class children do not do well in school, just as she knows that middle-class children do do well. All this she knows . . . measuring them for success or failure against the yardstick of middle-classness."[12]

Numerous studies indicate that students from homes classified as "lower socioeconomic" do not perform as well on IQ and achievement tests as middle-class youngsters. Truly disadvantaged when they enter school, they must engage in an often hopeless and

---

11. Robert Rosenthal and Lenore Jacobson, *Pygmalion in the Classroom* (New York, Holt, Rinehart and Winston, Inc., 1968), p. 47.
    12. Ibid., p. 47.

heartbreaking struggle to catch up with their middle-class counterparts. Their ignorance of formal speech patterns and the mores of school culture can add further to the teacher's antagonism toward them. Poor nutrition, crowded home conditions, lack of parental guidance, also mitigate against the child's success in school. Yet some teachers and counselors, by condemning the homes as inadequate, feel they have somehow corrected the problem. In a speech given at New York University, Dr. William Glasser, author of *Schools Without Failure,* who has worked so effectively in the Watts schools in Los Angeles, reminded teachers and counselors that school is school's business and urged them not to let poor homes be an excuse for their poor teaching. Although there has been criticism of some of the statistical procedures used in *Pygmalion in the Classroom,* this summary statement deserves consideration: "we may say that by what she said, by how and when she said it, by her facial expressions, postures and perhaps by her touch, the teacher may have communicated to the children of the experimental group that she expected improved intellectual performance. Such communications . . . may have helped the child learn by changing his self-concept, his expectations of his own behavior, and his motivation as well as his cognitive style and skills."[13] This behavior and attitude would certainly apply to counselors in their dealing with counselees.

How ignorant most of us are of any culture or religion but our own. The ethnic character of many neighborhoods is breaking down in most cities where in days past the East side might have been predominately Irish; the West, German; South, Polish; and North, Italian, with a sprinkling of other nationalities "thrown in." Most young people are completely unaware of the rich cultural heritage of the various ethnic groups (sadly, sometimes, even of their own nationality). Teachers can do much to encourage, to the mutual benefit of all students, an exchange of the mores and customs of the nationalities represented within the classroom. Each child should be proud of the country of his ancestors as well as of his new country. Being an American should not mean forgetting that your forebears came from Rumania, or Finland,

---

13. Ibid., p. 180.

Greece or France. Teachers can plan cooperatively with their students teaching programs to include materials of multicultural character. Providing opportunities for students to examine intergroup tensions and motivating them to examine their own attitudes toward other groups can provide a sound base on which to examine their duties and responsibilities as citizens in our pluralistic democracy.

Counselors must also search their own consciences and recognize whether they have been guilty of discrimination in the advice they have been giving to minority students.

Marsha was one of the few black students at Paine Junior-Senior High. Her academic record was not superior but she had followed the college entrance program. Routinely, all juniors were interviewed by the counselors to discuss college plans. Mr. Papagallo asked Marsha her plans, and she indicated she was intending to go to college but had not made up her mind which one or what she would major in.

"Well, of course, there is X College (predominately a Negro school); I'm sure you would be accepted there, Marsha," Mr. Papagallo told her.

"Oh, I was thinking of State University (southern and predominately white) or maybe Vassar," Marsha replied. "My parents don't want me to go to school any farther south than the University; they think I would get a better education in the North."

"But, Marsha, how could you hope to make it at those schools? I mean, you know your teachers here at Paine have been very understanding with grading and all, but with the competition at those schools, do you think you are being very realistic?"

"Well, what about XYZ College (small, predominately white, coed school in the middle-Atlantic states)," Marsha asked.

"Well, maybe academically you could make it, Marsha, but, well, ah, would you feel comfortable there? I mean with only about 5 percent of the students being black, you might feel out of place."

Counselors could be far more effective than they presently are if they would recognize that prejudice and discrimination are still very much alive within the faculty as well as the student body (and possibly within themselves). Organizing group counseling sessions on racial attitudes would be one means of attacking this problem.

Faculty sessions on the same issue could be fruitful and revealing. When students report prejudicial actions by teachers, counselors should have the courage to investigate them, to discuss the matter with the teacher, bringing the situation out in the open; possibly not a pleasant conference, but being the recipient of prejudice is not pleasant for the student either.

Gayle Bernstein dropped by the counselor's office to ask about an application for the forthcoming SAT examination. She looked so upset the counselor asked if something was bothering her. "Surely you aren't worried about the college board exam, Gayle, you'll do just fine."

"No, it isn't that, it's, oh, well, nothing, I guess."

"Nothing, or nothing that you want to talk about with me, Gayle," said Mrs. Grove, the counselor.

"Well, it's just that Mr. Mahler has scheduled a unit test and I won't be in school on that day."

"Why not, Gayle?"

"It's Yom Kippur."

"Oh, well, didn't you tell him?" asked the counselor.

"Yes, and he said that just because I was going to have some holiday, he couldn't reschedule the test just to accommodate a few people. And, Mrs. Grove, Yom Kippur isn't a holiday, it's a holy day; I must be at home with my family. Why can't he understand?"

SUMMARY

Bias, prejudice, and discrimination, although illegal, are still among the realities of the world, and they are still very much present in our schools. Counselors and teachers must recognize that such feelings can exist within themselves, other members of the faculty, and the students. From recognition can come strategies for eliminating these destructive forces and their corrosive effect on teaching and learning.

SUGGESTED READINGS

Bird, Caroline: *Born Female—The High Cost of Keeping Women Down.* New York, McKay, 1968.

    Highly readable account of the effects of sex bias and discrimination on women's ability to achieve their full potential.

Coles, Robert: *Children in Crisis.* Boston, Little, 1967.

Eight years in preparation, Coles describes observations and interviews with parents, pupils and teachers in the South and the effect of the stresses and pressures on whites and blacks as integration became a fact.

Cuban, Larry: *To Make a Difference: Teaching in the Inner City.* New York, Free Pr, 1970.

Practical suggestions for improving teacher attitudes and teaching performance based on the author's involvement with the Washington, D.C., inner-city project.

Janeway, Elizabeth: *Man's World, Woman's Place—A Study in Social Mythology.* New York, Morrow, 1971.

A provocative examination of the myth and reality of the "appropriate" role of women in the past and present and the psychological effects and difficulties resulting in changing role expectations.

Riessman, Frank: *The Culturally Deprived Child.* New York, Har-Row, 1962.

Approaches for understanding and assisting the culturally deprived child, including a positive involvement of the child's culture in the school setting.

Rossi, Alice S.: "Equality Between the Sexes: An Immodest Proposal," *Daedalus,* Vol. 93, No. 2 (Spring, 1964), pp. 6, 7, 52.

One of the most respected advocates for equality between the sexes presents a logical rationale for achieving such equality; highly readable.

Silberman, Charles: *Crisis in Black and White.* New York, Random, 1964.

Details with frightening clarity the corrosive effects of racism on blacks and whites; issues of black self-hatred and identity crisis explored. Proposals made for resolving these critical problems.

CHAPTER 3

CLUES TO UNDERSTANDING—THE STUDENT'S PERMANENT RECORD

WHERE DO YOU BEGIN your search to understanding your students? Considering that the average secondary teacher works with 150 to 200 students daily and the usual counselor-counselee ratio ranges from 250 to 600 per counselor, mere *recognition* of each student is often difficult. There are teachers and counselors who never even reach the recognition level with all their students. Admittedly, some students work hard to protect their anonymity. Quiet, unobtrusive, they sit in the back of the classroom, never volunteering an answer, causing no trouble—unreached and unreachable.

Yet even for these students, facts are available, information which provides clues to understanding them. Some schools refer to the data maintained on every student as the "Student Inventory," "Permanent Record," or "Cumulative File." A sample set of such record forms is shown in Figures 1 through 8.* These files sometimes contain

BIOGRAPHICAL DATA
full name of student
date and place of birth
present residence, phone number
parents' names, occupations, business addresses, level of education
whether parents are living or deceased
whether student is living with parent or guardian
religious preference of family
number of brothers and sisters and their ages

---

* These figures reprinted with permission of the Falls Church Public Schools, Falls Church, Virginia.

sometimes a picture is included at Grade 1, entrance into junior high, and at Grade 12

HEALTH INFORMATION
medical history
dates of physical examinations with findings and recommendations
record of childhood diseases
vaccinations and immunizations
physical handicaps, allergies, need for special medication
present physical condition, height, weight, evaluation of vision/hearing
dental record

ACADEMIC INFORMATION
names of courses taken
grades earned in each course
number of credits earned
tardiness and absences
rank in class
quality point average at graduation
date of graduation
name of next educational institution, if any, selected

STANDARDIZED TEST RESULTS AND PERSONALITY RATINGS
scores on all standardized tests taken
usually a mental ability test in Grade 1 or 2
reading readiness test in Grade 1
aptitude and achievement test results throughout all school years
interest inventories and vocational aptitude tests
college aptitude tests
teacher ratings of personality and citizenship
counselor ratings of personality and academic potential

INTERESTS, ACTIVITIES, WORK EXPERIENCE, FUTURE PLANS
students supply information on hobbies, participation and school activities, sports, clubs, the nature and extent of their

work experience, and plans for future education and career choices

OBSERVATIONS AND CONFERENCES

some schools include written reports by teachers of in-class and out-of-class (playground, cafeteria, study halls, etc.) observations of students as well as notations of conferences held with or about the student by counselors, teachers, and parents

Although most students realize the school maintains records on them, they and their parents are frequently unaware of the nature of the data and how the information is used. Over a three-year period, I polled 489 undergraduate and graduate students to see how many knew what was in their high school permanent files. Though more than 90 percent knew such a file existed, only 10 percent had ever seen the contents and less than 1 percent had reviewed them with a counselor. These students explained that they were volunteer aides in the Guidance Office and had surreptiously stolen a look at their folders. They corroborated from the examination of their own files that some information was out-of-date or incomplete and that critical or judgmental statements by teachers and counselors had been included sometimes without any substantiation.

Parents who come to school for a conference may be shown some of the folder's contents, but it has been common practice to refuse parents permission to see all the material in the file. A 1961 decision of the New York State Supreme Court (Johnson vs. Board of Education of City of New York, 220 N.Y.S. 2d 362) held that "a parent, as a matter of law, was entitled to information contained in school records under proper safeguards, and such inspection could not be denied on the theory that the records were confidential."[1]

An irate parent in the same state finally succeeded in viewing the child's IQ score after a ruling by the State Supreme Court in the parent's favor. Had this youngster lived in New Jersey, how-

---

1. Thomas W. George, "The Law and Pupil School Records: Issues and Views," *Bulletin of the National Association of Secondary School Principals,* Vol. 56, No. 365 (1972), p. 135.

PERSONAL DATA

NAME .... (LAST) .... (FIRST) .... (MIDDLE) .... SEX .... DATE OF ENTRANCE INTO FALLS CHURCH CITY SCHOOLS ....

PLACE OF BIRTH .... BIRTH DATE .... (MONTH) (DAY) (YEAR) (VALIDATION)

ADDRESS 1. .... HOME TEL. 1. ....
2. .... 2. ....
3. .... 3. ....
4. .... 4. ....

SIBLINGS	M	F	BIRTH YEAR
1.	☐	☐	....
2.	☐	☐	....
3.	☐	☐	....
4.	☐	☐	....
5.	☐	☐	....

(CHECK ONE) LIVING WITH PARENTS .... STEP-PARENTS .... GUARDIANS .... OTHERS ....

FATHER'S NAME ....
LIVING .... DECEASED .... (DATE)
BIRTHPLACE .... (TOWN) (STATE)
.... NATIONALITY .... CITIZENSHIP ....
OCCUPATION ....
CHURCH PREFERENCE ....
GRADE COMPLETED ....

MOTHER'S NAME ....
LIVING .... DECEASED .... (DATE)
BIRTHPLACE .... (TOWN) (STATE)
.... NATIONALITY .... CITIZENSHIP ....
OCCUPATION ....
CHURCH PREFERENCE ....
GRADE COMPLETED ....

COMMENTS (FAMILY BACKGROUND) ....

CAUSE AND DATE OF DROP-OUTS (CHECK)			
ECONOMIC REASONS			
FAILURE IN WORK			
PERSONAL ILLNESS			
MALADJUSTMENTS			
OTHER REASONS			
DATE			
AGE			
GRADE COMPLETED			

COMMENTS:

PHOTOGRAPH
(12TH GRADE)

SIGNIFICANT PERSONAL DATA (INTERVIEWS, ANECDOTAL RECORDS, DISCIPLINARY ACTION, FOLLOW-UP, ETC.) SIGN AND DATE ENTRIES.

CA-1 CITY OF FALLS CHURCH PUBLIC SCHOOLS – FALLS CHURCH, VA. (OVER)

Figure 1. Personal Data Form, Falls Church, Virginia, City Schools. (Reprinted with permission by the Falls Church Public Schools, Falls Church, Virginia.)

MARYLAND STATE DEPARTMENT OF EDUCATION

PHYSICAL HEALTH INFORMATION

PUPIL DATA SYSTEM
PDS 5 SIDE 1

Pupil Number ____ Legal Name: Last ____ First ____ Middle ____ Any Other Name ____ Mo. / Day / Yr. Birth Date ____ Sex M or F ____ Race Code ____

	Mo.	Yr.	Mo.	Yr.	Mo.	Yr.	Mo.	Yr.	Mo.	Yr.	Mo.	Yr.	Mo.	Yr.	Mo.	Yr.	Mo.	Yr.	Mo.	Yr.	Mo.	Yr.	Mo.	Yr.	Mo.	Yr.	Mo.	Yr.	Mo.	Yr.	Mo.	Yr.	Mo.	Yr.
Height																																		
Weight																																		

Routine Screening Examination

Vision

Mo.	Yr.	Kind	By	Correction Indicated	Correction Made

Hearing

Mo.	Yr.	Kind	By	Correction Indicated	Correction Made

Teeth

Mo.	Yr.	By	Correction Indicated	Correction Made

Physical Examinations

Date Mo.	Day	Yr.	Gr.	Reason for Examination	Follow-up Needed Yes	No

Observable ☐ Yes ☐ No
Diagnosed ☐ Yes ☐ No
(Refer to Manual of Instructions) Type ____

Exceptionalities or Impairments

Immunization

	Primary Yes	No	Booster Yes	No
Smallpox				
Rubella				
Mumps				
Polio				
Diphtheria				
Pertussis				
Tetanus				

Diagnostic Procedures

	Most Recent Yes	No
Tuberculin		
Tine Test		
Chest X-Rays		
Other		

Limitations on School Activities
____
____

BEBCO 260 - 70

Figure 2. Pupil Health Data Form, State of Maryland. (Reprinted with permission by Maryland State Department of Education, Baltimore, Maryland.)

Interpersonal Appraisal Techniques

MARYLAND
PUPIL DATA SYSTEM
PDS 5   SIDE 2

REFERRALS FOR PHYSICAL, BEHAVIORAL, OR PSYCHOLOGICAL REASONS

Pupil Number   Legal Name: Last   First   Middle   Any Other Name   Mo. Day Yr. Birth Date   Sex M or F   Race Code

Referrals for Physical Reasons

Date			Gr.	Local Unit No.	School No.	Referred		Report of Referrals			
Mo.	Day	Yr.				By Whom	To Whom	Date			Location	Recommendations
								Mo.	Day	Yr.		Yes	No

Comments:

Specific Medical Instructions

Referrals for Behavioral or Psychological Reasons

Date			Gr.	Local Unit No.	School No.	Referred		Report of Referrals			
Mo.	Day	Yr.				By Whom	To Whom	Date			Location	Recommendations
								Mo.	Day	Yr.		Yes	No

Comments:

BEBCO 260 - 70

Figure 3. Referrals for Physical, Behavioral, or Psychological Reasons, State of Maryland. (Reprinted with permission by Maryland State Department of Education, Baltimore, Maryland.)

ACADEMIC RECORD – GRADES 7 AND 8

NAME OF PUPIL................ LAST .... FIRST .... MIDDLE

BIRTH DATE................ MONTH ...... DAY ...... YEAR

DATE			
SCHOOL			
GRADE			
C. A.			

SUBJECT	19___ 1ST SEM.	2ND SEM.	FINAL	SUBJECT	19___ 1ST SEM.	2ND SEM.	FINAL	SUBJECT	19___ 1ST SEM.	2ND SEM.	FINAL
ENGLISH				ENGLISH				ENGLISH			
SOC. STUDIES				SOC. STUDIES				SOC. STUDIES			
MATHEMATICS				MATHEMATICS				MATHEMATICS			
SCIENCE				SCIENCE				SCIENCE			
PHYS. ED.				PHYS. ED.				PHYS. ED.			
HOME ECON.				HOME ECON.				HOME ECON.			
IND. ARTS				IND. ARTS				IND. ARTS			
ART				ART				ART			
MUSIC				MUSIC				MUSIC			
DAYS MEMBERSHIP				DAYS MEMBERSHIP				DAYS MEMBERSHIP			
DAYS ATTENDANCE				DAYS ATTENDANCE				DAYS ATTENDANCE			

COMMENTS:
PROMOTED........ ; RETAINED........

COMMENTS:
PROMOTED........ ; RETAINED........

COMMENTS:
PROMOTED........ ; RETAINED........

TRANSFERS

FROM................TO........DATE........

RECORD OF TRANSCRIPT/RECOMMENDATION

DATE	TO WHOM

Figure 4. Academic Record Form, Grades 7 through 8, Falls Church, Virginia, City Schools. (Reprinted with permission by the Falls Church Public Schools, Falls Church, Virginia.)

Interpersonal Appraisal Techniques

CITY OF FALLS CHURCH PUBLIC SCHOOLS—FALLS CHURCH, VA.

ACADEMIC RECORD — GRADES 9 TO 12

NAME OF PUPIL ....
LAST   FIRST   MIDDLE

BIRTH DATE ....
MONTH   DAY   YEAR

| DATE |
| SCHOOL |
| GRADE |
| C. A. |

SUBJECT	1ST SEM.	2ND SEM.	FINAL	UNIT	SUBJECT	1ST SEM.	2ND SEM.	FINAL	UNIT	SUBJECT	1ST SEM.	2ND SEM.	FINAL	UNIT	SUBJECT	1ST SEM.	2ND SEM.	FINAL	UNIT
ENGLISH					ENGLISH					ENGLISH					ENGLISH				
PHYS. ED.					AM. HIST.					AM. GOVT.					PHYS. ED.				
TOTAL UNITS EARNED					TOTAL UNITS EARNED					TOTAL UNITS EARNED					TOTAL UNITS EARNED				
DAYS MEMBERSHIP					DAYS MEMBERSHIP					DAYS MEMBERSHIP					DAYS MEMBERSHIP				
DAYS ATTENDANCE					DAYS ATTENDANCE					DAYS ATTENDANCE					DAYS ATTENDANCE				

COMMENTS:

RANK IN CLASS .... GRADE AVERAGE ....
NUMBER OF GRADUATES ....
DATE OF GRADUATION ....

EXPLANATION OF GRADING SYSTEM
A—94-100   D—70-77
B—86- 93   F—69 OR LESS (FAILING)
C—78- 85

Figure 5. Academic Record Form, Grades 9 through 12, Falls Church, Virginia, City Schools. (Reprinted with permission by the Falls Church Public Schools, Falls Church, Virginia.)

Figure 6. Test Results Form, Falls Church, Virginia, City Schools. (Reprinted with permission by the Falls Church Public Schools, Falls Church, Virginia.)

SUMMARY OF GROWTH – JUNIOR-SENIOR HIGH SCHOOL

CITY OF FALLS CHURCH PUBLIC SCHOOLS
FALLS CHURCH, VIRGINIA

NAME _____

(LAST)	(FIRST)	(MIDDLE)			

	7	8	9	10	11	12
GRADE						
YEAR						
EVALUATOR(S)						

PERMISSION TO REPRODUCE THE FOLLOWING PERSONALITY RECORD GRANTED BY THE NATIONAL ASSOCIATION OF SECONDARY SCHOOL PRINCIPALS   THE SCALES BELOW ARE CONTINUOUS.   COLORS INDICATE THE YEAR EACH SUMMARY IS MADE—I.E.   (1) RED—7TH GRADE   (2) GREEN—8TH GRADE   (3) BLUE—9TH GRADE   (4) ORANGE—10TH GRADE   (5) BROWN—11TH GRADE   (6) VIOLET—12TH GRADE

1. MOTIVATION	PURPOSELESS	VACILLATING	USUALLY PURPOSEFUL	EFFECTIVELY MOTIVATED	HIGHLY MOTIVATED
2. INDUSTRY	SELDOM WORKS EVEN UNDER PRESSURE	NEEDS CONSTANT PRESSURE	NEEDS OCCASIONAL PRODDING	PREPARES ASSIGNED WORK REGULARLY	SEEKS ADDITIONAL WORK
3. INITIATIVE	SELDOM INITIATES	CONFORMS	DOES ROUTINE ASSIGNMENTS	CONSISTENTLY SELF-RELIANT	ACTIVELY CREATIVE
4. INFLUENCE AND LEADERSHIP	NEGATIVE	CO-OPERATIVE BUT RETIRING	SOMETIMES IN MINOR AFFAIRS	CONTRIBUTING IN IMPORTANT AFFAIRS	JUDGEMENT RESPECTED-MAKES THINGS GO
5. CONCERN FOR OTHERS	INDIFFERENT	SELF-CENTERED	SOMEWHAT SOCIALLY CONCERNED	GENERALLY CONCERNED	DEEPLY AND ACTIVELY CONCERNED
6. RESPONSIBILITY	UNRELIABLE	SOMEWHAT DEPENDABLE	USUALLY DEPENDABLE	CONSCIENTIOUS	ASSUMES MUCH RESPONSIBILITY
7. INTEGRITY	NOT DEPENDABLE	QUESTIONABLE AT TIMES	GENERALLY HONEST	RELIABLE, DEPENDABLE	CONSISTENTLY TRUSTWORTHY
8. EMOTIONAL STABILITY	HYPEREMOTIONAL / APATHETIC	EXCITABLE / UNRESPONSIVE	USUALLY WELL-BALANCED	WELL-BALANCED	EXCEPTIONALLY STABLE

GRADE	7	8	9	10	11	12
INTERESTS AND ATTAINMENTS — IN SCHOOL						
OUT OF SCHOOL						
EDUCATIONAL AND VOCATIONAL PLANS						
WORK EXPERIENCE — DURING SCHOOL						
SUMMER						

Figure 7. Summary of Growth Form, Falls Church, Virginia, City Schools. (Reprinted with permission of Falls Church Public Schools, Falls Church, Virginia.)

Figure 8. School Activities, Offices, and Awards Form, Falls Church, Virginia, City Schools. (Reprinted with permission of the Falls Church Public Schools, Falls Church, Virginia.)

ever, the parent's request would have been denied! The Commissioner of Education ruled that since the testing program was not required by state law, the Board of Education retained the authority to withhold or release such information at its discretion.[2] The school's reluctance to share all the data stems from a fear that parents would be unable to understand standardized test scores and that confidential evaluations of teachers and counselors should not be revealed. Although the school's purpose in safeguarding records may be a worthy one, the danger posed by secret, inaccurate, or incomplete data cannot be minimized.

POLICIES FOR COLLECTING DATA

The Russell Sage Foundation's study on pupil records noted that "few schools have clearly defined and systematically implemented policies regarding uses of information about pupils, the conditions under which such information is collected, and who may have access to it. We do know, however, that important decisions affecting individual pupils are made, at least in part, on the basis of these school records."[3] The Foundation warned that deficiencies in record-keeping policies constituted a serious threat to individual privacy in the United States.[4] Specifically, they cited these areas of potential abuse:

1. Information about both pupils and their parents is often collected without the informed consent of either children or parents. . . .
2. Pupils and parents typically have little or, at best, incomplete knowledge of what information about them is contained in school records and what use is made of this information by the school. . . .
3. The secrecy with which school records usually are maintained makes difficult any systematic assessment of the accuracy of information contained therein. . . .

---

2. Ibid., p. 139.
3. *Guidelines for the Collection, Maintenance, and Dissemination of Pupil Records* (New York, New York, Russell Sage Foundation, 1970), p. 7.
4. Ibid., p. 15.

4. Procedures governing the periodic destruction of outdated or no longer useful information do not exist in most systems. . . .
5. . . . few provisions are made to protect school records from examination by unauthorized school personnel . . . nonschool personnel and representatives of outside agencies. . . .
6. Sensitive and intimate information collected in the course of teacher-pupil or counselor-pupil contacts is not protected from subpoena by formal authority in most states.[5]

When looking through a student's permanent file, you may find anecdotes written by teachers, counselors or administrators describing deviant or disruptive behavior. These should never be easily accessible in the permanent folder but should be kept in a "Confidential" file by the counselor or teacher who witnessed the incident and wrote the report. Read such anecdotes if you wish, but remember that such statements may reflect subjective opinion more than objective reporting; your perception about the student should not be affected.

In February, while Mrs. Horowitz was checking standardized test scores for her fourth period math class, she read the following summary of observations on one of her students, Ed Terry:

10-16-70—Bus driver of Bus 41 reported that Ed had used abusive language when told to stop roughhousing on the bus.

1-28-71—Mrs. Tyler reported Ed disrupted the class by showing off in front of the parents who were visiting during American Education week.

3-1-71—Mrs. Willard referred Ed to the office for grabbing a girl and slapping her in the face. He said she was his girl friend and was dating another boy, "two-timing me," Ed said.

5-18-71—Ed referred by music teacher for being disrespectful and refusing to remove the gum from his mouth while in class.

Ed has always been courteous to Mrs. Horowitz. He did the required work and had caused no problems in class. As she left the Guidance Office, Mrs. Horowitz remarked to the counselor, "I'm glad I read that Terry boy's record; I'll keep an eye on him from now on."

---

5. Ibid., pp. 13-15.

A discussion of the merits and limitations of such observational anecdotes will be found in Chapter 6.

The Sage Foundation Report[6] insisted that no information should be collected from any student without having received consent of the parents and the child (where he is competent to understand the nature and consequences of his decision) prior to securing the data. Depending upon the nature of the information to be collected, the consent may be given through the parent's legally appointed or elected representatives, such as the school board. For example, if the school were involved in a system-wide achievement testing program, the parents should be fully informed of the purpose of the tests and advised that such testing had been approved by the board. Since these test results would be useful in studying and evaluating the effectiveness of the total school program as well as aiding the individual student in analyzing his own progress, the consent of the parents' representatives is sufficient. However, if an ethical values survey or personal attitudes inventory were to be administered, each parent should have the opportunity to give or withhold approval for his child to participate. Such individual permission should be given in writing.[7]

In either situation, the school must recognize its obligation to inform the parents as to how the information will be used, the methods used to collect the data, how long the information will be kept on file, the persons to whom such data will be available, and under what conditions the data will be released.[8] A special PTA meeting devoted to the topic could be utilized, provided, of course, the school can inveigle the parents to attend. In communities of well-educated parents, written announcements may suffice, but how does the school reach parents who are illiterate or who do not speak English? Bridging the communications gap between home and school is a tough problem for which there is no easy answer. Recognition by the school of its duty to communicate is, however, a step in the right direction.

Limiting the individuals permitted access to the records may

---

6. Ibid., pp. 16-25.
7. Ibid., pp. 16-17.
8. Ibid., p. 17.

serve as a further protection of the individual student's privacy. Although the school releases permanent files to teachers and school officers who have a legitimate reason for using them, such information should not be divulged to any other persons except with written consent from the students' parents or in compliance with a judicial order or orders from agencies having subpoena power. Even in the latter situation, parents should be notified of such orders and the school's compliance.[9]

A confidentiality survey[10] of twenty-nine senior high schools in Maryland (representing twenty-two of the state's twenty-four school systems) conducted by mail questionnaire revealed that all students' records were maintained in either the Guidance Office or central office with open access to the materials allowed to counselors, administrators, and faculty. In 93 percent of the schools surveyed, parents were permitted access to their child's academic record, and 70 percent of the schools permitted the students to view their academic records. Information regarding teacher and counselor comments on academic performance, work habits, motivation, student strengths and weaknesses, conduct, and disciplinary action were open to 83 percent of the parents and 59 percent of the students. Permission for other individuals or institutions to see student records could be secured only from the schools' chief administrator in twenty-five of the twenty-nine schools responding and in only three schools were employers or civil authorities given free access to students' files. Although the overwhelming majority of students knew of the existence of the files, only 20 percent of the schools indicated that their students were aware of *how the records were used.*

In my years as a high school counselor, no written policy regarding the release of information about students was ever determined by the school or the school board. A flash of the badge from the FBI or an inquiry from the employment offices of our local businesses was sufficient to open our files for their inspection. Few counselors were aware that they might have been violat-

9. Ibid., p. 26.
10. Donald P. Dean, "Confidentiality of Student Records," unpublished research paper, Towson State College, Division of Education, Baltimore, May, 1973.

ing any student's civil rights. Certainly it was not their conscious intent to do so. Every effort was made to provide as much information as possible about the student so that the recruiter from "Basketball U" would seriously consider our student for their scholarship or the business or government investigator would get an accurate and complete picture of the individual student under consideration. From informal polling of some of the area counselors, the situation appears not to have changed markedly. Although "free" access to student files was granted in only three of the twenty-nine schools surveyed, the counselors with whom I discussed this issue indicated they were given wide discretionary authority by their principals regarding the granting of permission to see student records. I did detect, however, a growing concern by the counselors polled for protecting the students' rights to privacy and confidentiality.

USING THE PERMANENT RECORD

Creating an efficient and usable system is not easy. In designing the forms shown in Figures 1 through 8, input was received from teachers, administrators, and the counselors as well as planners at the State Department of Education and consultants from national associations (education and psychological) plus representatives of commercial firms producing school forms. Even after a year of drafting and redesigning forms, those ultimately selected proved less than perfect. Revisions were required almost immediately when previously unsuspected "bugs" developed. If a perfect pupil record-keeping system exists, I do not know of it. The more experiences counselors and teachers have with record systems, the more expert they become in determining those forms which best suit the needs of their particular student population. In the meantime, the faculty must "make do" with those forms available and try to utilize them to the fullest. Counselors could provide a "Guide" explaining to teachers and administrators how to use the files. A similar statement to parents and pupils fully explaining the contents and use of the materials in the student's permanent record file could go a long way toward alleviating the fear and distrust which silence and secrecy have caused.

Unfortunately, a student sometimes looks upon his permanent record as a modern Doomsday Book, especially when the counselor or teacher opens a conference with him by saying, "I've just checked over your folder, Phil," and then a pregnant pause. The teacher's or counselor's hand remains firmly on top of the folder so that the student has no chance to see, although he begins to suspect that highly incriminating accounts of his every misdeed are recorded inside the covers. Ironically, the counselor or teacher may be totally unaware that the presence of the folder and his reference to its contents are in any way threatening to the student. In fact, teachers and counselors usually consider reading the student's file a means of understanding the pupil better by possibly providing clues for establishing rapport more easily.

Specific Uses of Data in Permanent Folders

For the *guidance counselor,* the permanent cumulative record file can

1. *Provide the basis for more effective counseling with counselees.* By reviewing the cumulative file prior to a scheduled conference, the counselor can reacquaint himself with the student's personal background, noting interests, educational and vocational plans, as well as strengths and weaknesses or indications of inconsistencies as reflected in grades and standardized test results. Rapport may be more quickly established if the counselor uses every means to become more knowledgeable about each counselee.

2. *Reveal possible academic difficulties.* Periodic check of students' cumulative folders may alert the counselor to students whose potential, as measured by standardized tests, is not consistent with grades achieved in specific courses. Early recognition of a possible problem can enable the counselor to work with the student to overcome the difficulty and reduce the chance of academic failure with its accompanying frustration, which frequently forces students to drop out of school.

3. *Develop criteria to aid in the selection and placement of students.* Grades earned in previous courses, evaluation of

aptitude and achievement test results, added to the stated interests and goals of students, provide the basis for their placement in a variety of courses. Candidates for honors programs, for special interest classes in auto mechanics, typing, creative writing, drama, art, as well as remedial assistance, can be identified. Such data coupled with teachers' recommendations and cooperatively studied by teachers and counselors can result in greater accuracy in screening and selecting students.

4. *Furnish essential background data for student referrals and case studies.* Should it become necessary to refer a student to an outside agency for assistance which the school is unable to provide, the material about him contained in his permanent file would be of great help to the agency in understanding the present status of the student. In a later section, the use of the case study as an aid in analyzing students will be discussed.

5. *Suggest topics for research and follow-up studies.* Educational progress of graduates, evaluation of the curriculum, characteristics of dropouts and gifted pupils, are but a few areas which could be investigated from data available in the cumulative files.

Although some counselors find themselves unable to utilize the data in each student's permanent file to its fullest advantage, few would dispute the inherent value in such records. There are, however, some teachers who pride themselves on never looking at their students' cumulative folders. "I don't want to prejudice myself," they usually say when asked why they never look at the records. As a counselor, I often heard such comments and wondered what items in our files would be considered "prejudicial." Anecdotal records were not kept in the permanent folders. If such observational reports were written, they were filed in a "Confidential" file and reviewed for a teacher with the counselor present. Information available in the cumulative file included biographical data, academic standing, test results, activities, and the ratings of personality (similar to Fig. 7). Were teachers searching for "proof" of their own biases? Others avoided the permanent files because they said they were unable to translate the "hieroglyphics" in which test scores were reported. Yet I recall one math teacher who at the beginning of each semester scrupulously copied the IQ scores of each student opposite the student's name in his grade book. He later advised us that "no student with an IQ of 115 ever got more than a 'C' from me." An average IQ means a predetermined average grade? Self-fulfilling prophecy? Abuse of data? Admittedly, such things can and do happen, but don't overlook the positive aspects because some misuse information. Acknowledging that teachers and counselors have biases will not eliminate them. Perhaps the best that can be hoped is that these individuals will not use the cumulative files to buttress their prejudices. But for the teacher who approaches the student's file open-mindedly and uses the contents as an aid to understanding that student better, the reading of the folder can

1. *Present the student's achievement and aptitude as measured by standardized tests.* Periodic checks of students' cumulative files could alert the teacher to students whose classroom performance is well below their achievement test results. A teacher may have decided from a student's class work that the individual has no background in a particular subject, and yet examination of the standardized test scores indicates past achievement on a satisfactory or even above-average level.

2. *Indicate student's achievement as measured by students in his own school.* Many standardized test makers now report scores in percentile ranks for a specific city or county system as well as based on national norms. The teacher may discover that a student is placing at the median (50th percentile) when compared against national norms but in his school, perhaps a community where a high percentage of students go on to college, this same score falls below the median. Teachers can even determine the differences in achievement from class to class.

3. *Provide clues to students' interests, hobbies, future plans useful in designing class and individual activities.* Reading students' files may give the teacher a source of information about leisure-time activities and plans for future vocations which can be related to class work. A student who has ex-

pressed an interest in sailing might be encouraged to investigate local lake pollution as a science project. Boys who like
hunting may form the nucleus for a panel in social studies
on gun control laws. Girls whose presently expressed desire
is to be a housewife can be led to see the advantage of studying nutrition and genetics in biology. Such clues provide the
creative teacher with ways to relate the curriculum to the
reality of the student's world.

4. *Facilitate conducting parent conferences.* A teacher who has
taken the time to read the student's cumulative file prior to
a conference with his parents might find establishing rapport
far easier, or at least there could be a hint of possible difficulties! Knowing, for example, that the student is one of
seven; that the father is dead and the mother the sole sup-
porter of the family should make the teacher more understanding of the struggle which the mother is having in raising the family. Such empathy is usually reciprocated by the
parent, and a cooperative attitude to solve whatever problems face them is more easily developed.

For both pupil and parent, the cumulative record presents a
written picture of how the school sees the student. The parent may
thus develop greater insight about his own child, and the student
might deepen his self-understanding by recognizing his potential,
limitations, and achievements as reflected by his school record.
Such awareness could be of inestimable value when making educational and vocational plans. But to achieve these ends for teacher, counselor, parent, and pupil, certain cautions must be exercised, for as the late Ruth Strang, author of "landmark" works in
pupil personnel service, wrote, "reading records is to a considerable extent an art . . . the value of records depends largely on how
skillfully the information is interpreted and synthesized."[11] She
stressed the importance of looking for relationships, discrepancies,
trends, sudden or marked changes in health, achievement, social
status, and emotional behavior.[12]

---

11. Ruth Strang, *The Role of the Teacher in Personnel Work* (New York,
Columbia University Press, 1953), p. 399.
12. Ibid., p. 400.

The most common errors in interpreting records, she feels, are:
1. in making too sweeping generalizations and in drawing inferences not warranted by the data on the records
2. in failing to note important relationships
3. in being influenced by (one's) own prejudices or by previous impressions of the individual
4. giving too much weight and authority to test results.

Too seldom, she felt, is the distinction made between what the record *shows* and what it *suggests*.

To prevent such errors from occurring, individuals reading such records should keep in mind that:
1. The student is growing and changing. What was true of him last year is not necessarily true this year.
2. The record represents only a small sample of his behavior. There is much that is unknown about him.
3. The record often reflects the bias of the person recording. It may tell more about the person who made the record than it does about the student.[13]

CRITERIA FOR AN EFFICIENT RECORD-KEEPING SYSTEM

An effective cumulative record system should present data in a logical sequence, arranging similar categories together. The information recorded should be readily understandable and easy to interpret by counselors and teachers to students and parents. There should be adequate space to record information on the forms and additional space for interpretive or summary statements (a glaring omission with many systems). Heavy-duty card stock has proven most satisfactory for permanent record cards, and many school systems have also found that using a series of color-coded cards is a great aid for quick retrieval and refiling. In such a system, a different color is selected for each major division; for example, a blue card for recording biographical data, a green for test results, yellow for academic progress and grades. Since these records "travel" with the student (his elementary records are sent to the junior high school and the junior high then forwards them to

---

13. Ibid., p. 400.

Figure 9. Adapted from "Funky Winkerbean" comic strip. Copyright ©
1973 Publisher—Hall Syndicate. Reproduced with permission.

the senior high school, and they are permanently filed when the
student leaves school), durability is a prime concern.

SUMMARY

The permanent cumulative file houses data on the student's
home background, health information, academic progress, and estimates of potential and achievement. In some instances, the students themselves contribute information on their hobbies, activities, interests, and future educational and vocational plans.

The individual student and his parents must be aware of the
contents of the cumulative file and have access to this material.
The file should be a part of conferences between parents, pupils,
teachers, and counselors to assist the student in deepening his insight and self-understanding and in making realistic educational
and vocational choices.

SUGGESTED READINGS

Denton, David E.: Cumulative records—invalid and unethical. *The Educational Forum, 33 (No. 1)*:55-58, 1968.
A vigorous attack on the validity of assumption that counselors and teachers use cumulative records to understand or predict student behavior; hits hard on ethics of including student themes, etc., teacher and counselor comments, when data are not protected.

George, Thomas W.: The law and pupil schools records: Issues and views. *Bulletin of the National Association of Secondary School Principals, 56 (No. 365)*:13-39, 1972.
Extensive review of the latest court rulings regarding the use of students' cumulative record files.

Goslin, David A.: Ethical and legal aspects of school record-keeping. *Bulletin of the National Association of Secondary School Principals, 55 (No. 355)*:119-26, 1971.
Sociologist and chairman of the conference at the Russell Sage Foundation discuss reasons why the Foundation initiated its widescale study into school records.
Guidelines for the Collection, Maintenance and Dissemination of Pupil Records (New York, New York, Russell Sage Foundation, 1970).
Based on eight years of research, this report clearly defines the abuses presently existing in many student record systems throughout the United States and outlines steps for developing and maintaining efficient records while protecting students' rights. Must reading.

Mitzel, M. Adele: Why keep cumulative records? *The Elementary School Journal, 66 (No. 4)*:195-99, 1966.
Describes workshop approach for training teachers to use cumulative records, ideas applicable K-12.

Oelrich, Frederick: Must counselors tell all? *The Education Digest, 38 (No. 3)*:48-49, 1972.
Briefly discusses conditions which must be met under common law for student's records to be protected under concept of confidentiality.

Tenneyson, W. Wesley, Bocker, Donald H., and Johnson, Ralph H.: Student personnel records: A vital tool but a concern of the public. *The Personnel and Guidance Journal, 42 (No. 9)*:888-93, 1964.
Describes counselor responsibility in using students' records ethically.

Wares, Martha L. (Ed.): *Law of Guidance and Counseling.* Vol. 4 of *Legal Problems in Education Series.* Cincinnati, Anderson, 1964.
Comprehensive treatment of the law and student records; should be read by all counselors and teachers.

CHAPTER 4

THE STUDENT VIEWS HIMSELF—
AUTOBIOGRAPHIES

ASSUME YOU HAVE just finished reading the permanent folder of this student and have culled the following facts:

1. Name, Geralli, Angela   Grade 8
2. Living at 1582 Woodlawn Drive, City   (private home)
3. Born August 8, 1959
4. Entered City Junior High School, September 7, 1971, Grade 7 from City Elementary
5. Parents—Father, Anthony   Mother, Maria
6. Living with parents
7. Brothers and sisters—Anthony, born 1950; Theresa, born 1952; Harry, born 1953; Rita, born 1957; Maria, born 1963
8. Occupation of father—electrician
9. Occupation of mother—housewife
10. IQ—California Test of Mental Maturity (taken in Grade 2) 106
11. Summary of grades in elementary school—C
12. Best subjects in junior high school—music and home economics
13. Most difficult subjects in junior high school—mathematics, history
14. Future plans—undecided

From reading these facts, do you know whether Angela is outgoing or shy? Does she like school? Has she many friends? What are her worries, fears, aspirations? Beyond the bare statistics and the few relationships you can accurately make concerning them, there is still much about this student which remains hidden. Reading the student's permanent file gives the framework, the skeleton, upon which the counselor and teacher can build. Other approaches are needed to clothe the statistics with a human personality.

To the teacher and counselor interested in learning more about their students, particularly in discovering how students see themselves, the autobiography is one technique which holds promise. From St. Augustine's *Confessions* in 400 A.D. to James Baldwin's *The Fire Next Time,* the retelling of one's life story provides insights about an individual which can be revealed in no other way. Any event described by the autobiographer will be colored by his emotions, and his reactions will help to explain his relationships with others and his acceptance or rejection of his world and himself.

When a counselor suggests to a student that he write an autobiography, he is careful to have developed sufficient rapport and trust to reassure the student that any confidences divulged will be respected. The one-to-one relationship between counselor and counselee facilitates determining when preparing an autobiography would be a beneficial experience for the student, at the point of "psychological and academic readiness" and "at a significant stage in one's education"[1] as favored by Gibson and Higgins. Unhappily, many teachers who attempt this technique simply announce on the first day of the school term, "Class, I want each of you to write your autobiography and tell me all about yourself." All too often, the teachers fail to elaborate any further as to their need or intended use for such information, thus raising suspicion in the minds of some students as to the real reason behind the request. Rarely do these teachers reciprocate and tell the students anything about themselves.

Such a request is rarely greeted with cheers, smiles, or any evidence of enthusiasm by students. Silence is the most common reaction, followed by such unemotional and conventional questions as "How long does it have to be?" "When do we have to turn it in?" "Do we have to use pen?" Rarely, if ever, does a student ask

1. Robert L. Gibson and Robert E. Higgins, *Techniques of Guidance: An Approach to Pupil Analysis* (Chicago, Science Research Associates, Inc. 1966), pp. 161-62.

"Why should we write about ourselves?" Should anyone evidence sufficient interest (or temerity?) to pose such a question, some teachers would be completely nonplussed. Perhaps their initial surprise would stem from a student's challenging an assignment, but, more importantly, some teachers have never clearly scrutinized their motives in making this assignment. How will having the student write about himself help his teacher, or the student himself? What is the teacher hoping to learn from reading his autobiography? What will the teacher do with the information received? Some teachers who year after year use this technique fail to probe the considerations surrounding its use. If pressed on these points, some will admit that having students write an autobiography is an easy first-day assignment; easy for the teacher since no teaching is needed. It makes a good "ice-breaker" some will tell you. (Although the thought that an iciness is already forming between teacher and pupils on the first day of school is a bit discouraging.) Some feel it is a good way to get students back to the business of writing, and on a topic which would require no referencing on their part. And so, while the teacher has announced his reason for assigning an autobiography is to get to know his students better, in many instances it is simply a method for reinducting the youngster into the regimen of becoming a student again.

Yet the autobiography can benefit both teacher and student as surely as it can profit the student-counselee working individually with his counselor in a self-study. The teacher will see the student's world through the student's eyes. New data, not found in the school's permanent files, may be forthcoming. Certainly the stark statistics found in such records will take on new depth and meaning. And the student? How will writing about himself help him? Compiling his autobiography may provide his first chance to think systematically about himself as an individual who has already achieved and who hopes for future successes. By examining his present attitudes towards adults and his peers, he begins the process of developing his own personal philosophy of life. Increased self-awareness and sharper perception of his world and those about him could easily be the results of such self-reporting.

But to teachers who would use the autobiography as a device to evaluate composition skills; who will, in fact, circle every spelling error, deduct for each missing comma, and may even grade the work, the chances of acquiring a deeper insight and greater rapport with their students are highly questionable. If the teacher wishes to assess the group's verbal facility for her own purposes (devising remedial lessons or planning honors-level work, for example), another assignment with the purpose clearly and honestly stated should be substituted. Who can estimate the effect on a student's self-image when his autobiography is returned marked F? Is he to accept the teacher's implication that his life is a failure? Such an action betrays the announced purpose of the assignment, which was to get to know the students better, not to judge them. Evaluating the autobiographies is a flagrant abuse of the teacher's supposed intent. Students thus tricked will retreat behind a screen of wary resentment, thus minimizing considerably the chance of establishing warm and honest rapport between them and the teacher.

Miss Bennett was new to Jackson High School and on the first day of classes in September she told her ninth grade class that she would like them to write an autobiography for her so that she could get to know them better as individuals. Nancy considered Miss Bennett an interested and sympathetic person, and she revealed many of her inner feelings, doubts, and fears, even to writing about her unhappiness over having broken up with her boyfriend. Three days later, Nancy came into the classroom and looked unbelievingly at the bulletin board where her autobiography was on display, all errors circled and graded C—. Other students' "bios" were also on exhibit and there was a crowd at the board reading, laughing, and commenting about what had been written. Nancy went to her seat, feeling hurt and humiliated and vowing never to believe another teacher as long as she lived.

Assuming that the teacher who makes such an assignment *is* sincere in his desire to increase his understanding of his students; that he has no intention of grading or displaying them, either on a bulletin board, in the teachers' lounge, or the principal's office; and that he intends to maintain the bond of confidentiality imperative to such an assignment, is sincerity sufficient to make his use of the technique successful? Unfortunately, no. Too often students have been faced with teachers who were dishonest, and thus the trust needed to make this type of assignment effective is frequently missing. Telling about oneself is a highly personal act and requires the belief on the part of the writer that the reader will be sympathetic and receptive to what is written. Building the necessary rapport for successfully launching the writing of autobiographies is, admittedly, not an easy task, but it can be achieved if mutual respect and strict honesty are observed by the teacher in *all* his relationships with all his students.

Only after this rapport is established can the teacher ask his students to write a personal autobiography for him. For some students, "autobiography" is a somewhat frightening word, synonymous in their minds with a confession. Such students might be less apprehensive if they were asked to submit an *educational* autobiography, focusing only on that aspect of their lives. Although limited in scope, the student-autobiographer will usually express some feelings about himself. Having used this approach with graduate students in a course on the psychology of career choice, I invariably received greater insight into their motivations and attitudes after reading, and rereading, their educational/vocational autobiographies. Dr. Jean Grambs, noted author and educational sociologist of the University of Maryland, shared these additional approaches to "tailor" the writing of the autobiography so that it would be less of a chore, in fact, it might turn out to be fun! Rather than approaching the autobiography in the traditional way, ask students to write about

"The History of My Encounters with . . . (inserting the name of a subject–English, science, math, history, etc.)"

"What I Will Tell My Grandchildren About My Life in School"

"My Illnesses and How I Overcame Them" (or vice versa)

"The Five Most Awful Things That Happened to Me"

"The Five Most Important Things That Happened to Me"

"My Obituary"

Regardless of the approach, when the assignment is first announced, the teacher should explain why he feels it will be beneficial to him and how it might also be worthwhile and useful to the student. The teacher must excuse any student who feels this is an unwarranted invasion of his privacy or who sees any threat in writing about himself. Pressuring everyone to submit an autobiography may cause anxiety or frustration within some students. The teacher may advise the counselor of those students who appeared threatened by the assignment so that individual counseling could be considered as a means of coping with this apprehension. To achieve the greatest value from the autobiography, however, it must be written voluntarily by the student.

FORMS FOR WRITING THE AUTOBIOGRAPHY— UNSTRUCTURED AND STRUCTURED

Once the teacher has explained fully and honestly why he wishes the assignment done and what he hopes to gain from reading them and has guaranteed his students that their writings will be seen by his eyes only, he should provide plenty of time for students to ask questions. The counselor using this technique with an individual student should not merely suggest the writing of the autobiography and assume the counselee understands the purpose and procedures to follow. The teacher or counselor should be prepared to let the questions "fly" until the students are satisfied they know what to do. Nor should they be irritated by the triviality of some of the questions. Asking students to write their life stories is not an easy task and to further complicate the issue, students are conditioned to doing assignments which will please the teacher (or counselor). If students persist in asking "What do you want us to tell you?," the teacher or counselor might reply "Whatever you think I should know about you that will help me work with you better this coming year." If questions seem totally irrelevant to what the teacher or counselor hopes to gain from the assignment, blame should not rest solely on the shoulders of the students. Few adults would feel comfortable if given a similar assignment. They, too, would ask where to start, how much or how little is required, and would wonder whether to tell only what happened

ABOUT ME

Directions: Start your autobiography as far back as you can remember—your earliest childhood memories. Tell about those things that really made an impression on you, that stood out in your memory, whether happy or sad. Try to include those events which you feel have affected your life, such as moving to another city or entering junior high school.

As you write about the event, try to show how the event affected you and what people have truly influenced your life the most and how they affected the way you feel and act today. Mention your hopes and plans for the future; what you hope to be doing ten years from now, for example.

There's no limit to the length of your autobiography. Use as many pages as you feel you need to tell your story as fully as you can.

Figure 10. Directions for preparing an unstructured autobiography.

in one's life or how he felt about the incident. Added to these confusions is the fear that revealing one's true feelings might prejudice the reader against the student. The question persists about how honest to be and how much to tell. Thus the student who is writing such a personal narrative may seek guidelines which will provide safeguards for him.

Students can participate in class in developing an outline of the topics which they feel should be incorporated into such a paper. Some teachers and counselors who use this technique feel that a structured outline form should be distributed to all students, while still others believe that the writer should be perfectly free to include only those events which, in his opinion, are important in his life. Danielson and Rothney[2] found no significant differences between the structured and unstructured form of the autobiography in eliciting problems in the areas of finance; personal appearance and physical health; education; vocation; and social, emotional, personal, and family relationships. In the accompanying samples, Figures 10 and 11, forms for an unstructured autobiography are shown and also the more highly structured topic outline. The maturity of the students should provide clues for the teacher or counselor in deciding whether to use such an outline, providing one for those who wish it and allowing those who feel it limiting or unnecessary to omit its use.

---

2. Paul J. Danielson and John Rothney, "The Student Autobiography—Structured or Unstructured," *The Personnel and Guidance Journal,* Vol. 22 (1954), p. 30.

MY AUTOBIOGRAPHY

PART I   ME AND MY FAMILY
            when I was born and where
            my family
            illnesses
            my appearance, then and now
PART II   BEFORE I WENT TO SCHOOL
            early memories of parents, grandparents, relatives
            my friends and my familly's friends
            where we lived
            where we traveled
            my pets
            things I liked
            things I disliked
            things which bothered or frightened me
PART III THE SCHOOL YEARS
            nursery school
            elementary school
            junior high school
            senior high school
                my teachers
                my friends
                subjects—liked and disliked
                activities—liked and disliked
PART IV   OUTSIDE OF SCHOOL
            my friends—what kinds of friends I like to have
            places visited
            clubs, organizations, church memberships
            hobbies and pastimes
            work experience—jobs I've had; kinds of work I like to do
PART V   THE FUTURE
            how I feel about my future
            what kinds of things I would like to do in the future
            what kind of work I would like to do
            what things bother me about the future

Figure 11. Directions for preparing a structured autobiography.

READING THE AUTOBIOGRAPHY

Once the autobiographies have been submitted, the counselor or teacher is faced with the horrendous task of digesting their contents. Since 350 to 800 is a typical counselor-counselee ratio and 150 to 200 the typical student load for a secondary teacher, even a cursory reading will consume many wearying hours. Since far more than a superficial reading is essential, a careful and thorough perusal immediately compounds the number of hours needed. Yet one reading is rarely sufficient; two, even more, may be necessary. Since the teacher or counselor is not consciously reading for any specific information, the initial reading may not result in any strong impressions, whereas subsequent readings will reveal much significant and insightful data. The teacher or counselor must do more than merely read words. He must attempt to view each event described through the eyes of the student, a difficult task requiring time, sensitivity and empathy. The teacher facing 200 such papers may become overwhelmed by the thousands of words to be read and consequently overlook clues to understanding. Experienced teachers stagger this assignment over several months, requesting the autobiographies from one class each month over a five- or six-month period.

In checking with several counselor colleagues, I never found a counselor who requested all of his counselees to write their autobiographies. I must admit that I never asked my 650 to write theirs for me, either. Yet I can say without reservation that the autobiographies written for me by individuals and small groups of students were of enormous help to me in achieving greater insight about them and developing empathy toward them. Why more counselors do not use autobiographies might be attributable to a lack of recognition of the potential of this device; fear of never getting them all read and discussed with the counselees; poor rapport between counselor and counselees so that the autobiographies submitted would be of limited value.

Considerations in Reading—What Do You Look For?

Assuming a reasonable number of autobiographies to be studied at any given time, which aspects of these papers are likely, consciously or unconsciously, to affect the teacher or counselor while reading? Researchers of this technique have cited these points of importance: overall appearance, length, level of language used, quality or depth of expression, tonal variation, gloss, omissions, emphasis, organization, distortions, and lying.

Few teachers and counselors seem to make any permanent record of the autobiographies as they read. The usual procedures followed by most teachers and counselors I have polled is to return the autobiography to the student, with perhaps a few comments noted in the margin, rarely varying from the commonplace "How interesting"; "You've done a great deal of traveling" to reminders that certain sections had been omitted. Before long, the teacher's memory becomes hazy as to the content of the majority of the autobiographies, only the most vivid items will remain lodged in his memory and then perhaps not too accurately. Some teachers keep the autobiographies for the entire school year for occasional reference and then return them at the end of the term. Others use the autobiography as the beginning of a personal notebook or diary in which the student makes additional entries during the school year and which he resubmits at periodic intervals. The student has the right to have his personal document ultimately restored to him or should be assured that it will be destroyed after it has been read. In no case should the teacher give the autobiography to anyone else: principal, school psychologist, parent, or counselor.

Counselors, of course, have the advantage of being able to reread the autobiography *with* the student-counselee in a private conference and gain additional insight by having the student explain or clarify any points which seemed unclear when first read. Teachers, too, can arrange a conference for the purpose of clarification, but it is far more difficult for the teacher to find a mutually convenient time before, during, or after school for such meetings with students.

Counselors and teachers can also make notations on individual note cards or develop some type of reaction sheet to record significant incidents or make notes about things which impressed them as they read. Such a form is shown in Figure 12.

In reading the autobiography, the following considerations bear study.

Overall Appearance

The first impression received is the overall appearance of the autobiography. Typed, handwritten in pen or pencil, legible or illegible, neat, smudged, torn pages stained with chocolate, the

Autobiography written by_____ Date_____

I	SIGNIFICANT INCIDENTS

II	ORGANIZATION — length, language (choice of vocabulary, depth of expression)

III	OMISSIONS, GLOSSING OVER, INACCURACIES

IV	POINTS TO CHECK FURTHER

V	SUMMARY COMMENTS

Figure 12. Analyzing an autobiography.

autobiographies will probably be submitted in a variety of sizes and shapes unless the teacher has given explicit directions concerning the format. If no specific directions were given, does a messy paper indicate a careless or unconcerned writer? Does a neat paper indicate maturity and sound self-image of the writer? Generalizations on the significance of this aspect of the autobiography, like generalizations of any kind, are dangerous and often inaccurate. Of course a tattered, hard-to-read paper may affect the reader's attitude, but more importantly, it should raise the question "Why was this paper handed in like this?" Was the writer exhibiting a hostility toward the assignment, the teacher, or the counselor and meant a messy paper as a gesture of contempt? Or is such a paper mute testimony to the writer's low self-concept or an attempt to set up a smoke screen to cover his sense of threat or fear engendered by the assignment: the paper so scribbled as to be unreadable, for example. Unless the reader is sure that he has *the* answer, it is better to withhold judgment. Certainly if he is using a reaction sheet of some kind, he might indicate the unusual appearance, but be careful not to draw any conclusions about the character of the writer nor his motives, maturity, or sense of responsibility or possible personal problems.

Length

The next consideration is the length of the autobiography. Depending upon the age, sex, and maturity of the individual student, of course, the length of the autobiography could be quite significant. Perhaps the greatest danger here is to assume automatically that the length of the autobiography is *always* significant. An autobiography of a few paragraphs may not be an indication of poor self-image but perhaps reflects no interest in the assignment or lack of time in which to do it, or even distrust of the teacher or counselor and a reluctance to share his personal feelings, or even such a mundane yet crucial reason as a limited skill in putting one's thoughts on paper.

Froelich and Darley stated that high school students write autobiographies at least 500 words long; that one of 1,500 words would be considered relatively long while one exceeding 2,500

was reading See Spot Run, I was secretly hiding in my desk to read and think about later in recess **Time** magazine and **Life.** While everyone else played who's swiped teacher's gradebook, I wanted to play 3-D chess. . . .

My family is kind of big. It's kind of hard in a big family. I think I don't get as much in a big family as I would in a small family. But I am lucky because I have been able to find a job for exter (sic) money. Me and my father don't have the same opion (sic). It seem he don't want to listen to me. I try to understand his opion (sic) about things like hair, how late to stay out, etc. It seem to me my friends get more freedom then me. My family has been pretty good. . . .

Or these two written by senior high school students:

. . . I entered the tenth grade with flying colors. My life was all set for what I wanted to do with my career. I decided to be a cosmetologist. I got the idea to be a beautician because I loved to fix hair. . . . I also had met the most wonderful guy. He was a senior and I thought how great it was for a 10th grader to be going with a senior. I did not realize at that time that he would be graduating and I would never see him again. When I was a child, my speech, feelings, and thinking were all those of an ordinary child, now that I am a young woman, I have no more use for childish ways. What I see now is like the dim image in a mirror. What I know now is only partial. My life up to now is not complete. My life shall never be complete until the day I die.

. . . I am sixteen years old. I have a small family . . . my brother is five years old and my sister is 11 years old and at times they are big pests. I usually get yelled at for something my brother or sister does wrong! I was fat as a child but as you know I have thinned out a lot. I guess it's because I move around a lot. . . . I had a lot of fun in junior high but somehow senior high is very different. I get along with all of my teachers here and I always have. After I get out of the service and school, I want to become an art teacher if I can. I like to draw in my spare time and I like good music. . . . I somehow always manage to have bad luck. I am never lucky. But I guess I'm lucky to have such good friends.

The problem of semantics also cannot be ignored when reading an autobiography. Few words mean the same to everyone, and especially in today's youth culture words change their meanings with frightening rapidity. To read, for example, that a girl identified by the autobiographer as her best friend is considered as "really tough" might lead an unwary reader to assume the girl friend was uncouth or unladylike until the definition of "tough" as "great" or "terrific" is recalled. Even with words which are not coined or slang, confusion easily results. Trying to understand fully another's use of such words as "love" and "hate" quickly demonstrates the complexities of comprehending the feeling expressed by the student-autobiographer. The reader invariably and perhaps unavoidably puts his own perceptions into the words he reads. This may result in a distorted picture of what the student has intended, and the teacher or counselor should be cognizant that such inaccuracies are likely to occur, and read guardedly.

Quality and Depth of Expression

The maturity of the student-autobiographer will affect the level of expression he employs in writing his autobiography. Yet maturity is a most illusive factor to judge. The younger student will usually confine his account to what he *did* rather than how he *felt* about a specific incident.

As you read Charlotte's autobiography, written when she entered middle school at age eleven, note that all the descriptions deal with what occurred, what she did, rather than how she felt.

I was born on September 20. It was on a Wednesday. The nurse took me around to some of the people and said, "This is the little Smith girl!" I was the first one born in my family, I had black hair, brown eyes and a cute smile. I was a cute little devil! I lived at my grandma's.
Now I'm about 3 years old. I was in a pretty wedding, I was a flower girl. I always carry my Raggedy Ann doll. "Oh, no, I've got to get my hair washed" I hate to cause Mommy always gets soap in my eyes and I cry! (I'm about 5 now) Wow I didn't cry either! Bye again you guys! We're on our way to the lake. But before I left, Linda gave me a going-way party. It was just great! But my parents

didn't get along too well so they got a divorce. I'm living back on S. . . Road again.

Bobby (a friend of ours) and Mom took my cousin, my brother and I to the park in Pennsylvania. We got on the roller coaster 12 straight times. WE GOT SICK. But we got over it, and went again. My father gets me and my brother every weekend. We either go horseback riding or Dad takes me to an Italian restaurant. When we go I usually eat Veal Parmesean.

I'm 11 years old and doing great!

As the student develops a deeper and wider awareness of his world and the people and events which have shaped his life, he will probably include more subjective passages describing his response to events. Basic to a student's revealing these kinds of emotions is a willingness to write the autobiography. The student who feels compelled to write such an account or who is defensive, trying to hide problems or anxieties or feelings of inadequacy, may limit descriptions to factual and rather flat statements of the "who," "what," "when," "where," and "how" variety. Those who read Charlotte's autobiography felt she was not the carefree child she portrayed but rather one who was hiding a loneliness and insecurity which she could not bear to face, which happened to be a correct reading of the situation, corroborated by Charlotte's teacher who knew the home situation quite well.

Tone

As the counselor or teacher reads the autobiography, he becomes aware of emotional tone in the description of some events. The presence or absence of emotion in describing events significant to the writer may provide a deeper insight into his feelings and perceptions about himself and his world. Sex differences cannot be discounted when reading autobiographies for tone and depth of expression. Admitting fear, anxiety or pain could be construed by some boys as showing unmanly tendencies, and, therefore, such feelings, although actually experienced, are never acknowledged.

Of course it is much easier to be aware of tonal variation in spoken exchanges: the speaker changes his facial expressions, uses gestures further defining his feelings, alters the quality and volume of his voice to suit his meaning, and combines body language with his words to convey a variety of meaning to the alert and watchful listener. Culling this same type of reaction from the written word alone is more difficult, yet recognition of this quality can provide one of the most fruitful leads in the interpretation of autobiographies, according to Froelich and Darley.[4] Even though the writer is recalling an event in the past, his memory of the event will be colored by the response he actually made at the time. Thus when writing of the incident, pleasant or unpleasant associations of the experience will be reflected in his description. The reader's task then is to ascertain whether the autobiographer's response to a particular event is unusual, either more or less intense than would be anticipated. Rereading the autobiography can reveal where there is a variation in tone in describing certain events.

Gloss, Omissions and Emphasis

As reading discloses tonal variations, the counselor or teacher may also become aware of apparent attempts to gloss over certain events or to deemphasize them. For example, the student who wrote "I was the only child in our family until last May when my little brother was born. He cries a lot and needs a lot of attention," led his teacher to feel the student might be implying his parents were not spending as much time as they used to with him and that they might perhaps love this new baby more than they loved him. The teacher discreetly mentioned this to the parents during a routine conference on the boy's academic progress and learned that the parents, too, had observed signs of jealousy.

The reader must also be alert to things which are not discussed by the student. No mention of a father or mother when both parents are known to be alive and living in the home may suggest rejection or conflict between parent and child. The student who has suffered academic failure and does not acknowledge it is perhaps ignoring an event too painful for him to reveal. The reader may wonder at the implications of these omissions and should certainly realize that sometimes what is not told can be of greater importance than what is reported. Of course, there remains the obvious

---

4. Ibid., pp. 185-87.

question, "How is the reader to know what has been deliberately omitted?"

The teacher who has a seventeen-year-old boy in the ninth grade can safely assume that something has prevented his keeping up with his age group, but he cannot assume that an event or circumstance not mentioned is missing in the student's life. No mention of love and harmony in the home could be caused by the student's taking such affection for granted and concentrating on other experiences in his life. A simple oversight could also account for some events not being included. Sometimes a lack of patience or time, or both, causes the writer to "run out of steam" and end his account abruptly without relating a complete and accurate picture of his life. Omissions put additional unanswered questions into the reader's mind, points to ponder, and perhaps as he gets to know the student better, to discover some of the answers.

But what of overemphasis, of the student who writes at great length and in great detail about a seemingly trivial incident? A new dress for a party or making First Class Scout is recounted for several pages. This may be the situation of stressing one moment of success or happiness to blot out more frequent moments of despair and desperation. Or the event may have occurred so recently that every detail is still fresh in the mind of the student and his emphasis upon it is quite unconscious.

Distortions, Lies, and Unconscious Error

How and when does the reader "draw the line" between fantasy, creative writing (a little embellishment of the facts to make life seem more exciting and impress the reader a bit), and outright, deliberate lying? This is perhaps the most difficult area to evaluate accurately. What may appear to be distortion, even falsification, to one may be reality to another. The student whose real life is so painful, who finds it unbearable, impossible to describe objectively and accurately may readjust his description, creating a new dimension to reality. Yet even a distorted statement gives some insight into how the student views some segments of his world. As Allport noted in his classic study years ago, "it is often more important to study the belief that men betray than those that they parade."[5]

Yet how does one know which statements to suspect and which to accept at face value? The student who wrote, "I never get mad at my younger brothers and sisters no matter how dopey they act" or "all my friends say I really have the best personality of anybody they've ever known" is putting quite a strain on the credulity of the reader. Why would the student distort the facts? Poor rapport with the counselor or teacher, lack of interest in doing the assignment, fear: these are but a few possibilities. And what of unconscious error? Is this, too, caused by fear, poor rapport, or lack of motivation? More often unconscious error represents the perception of the writer in viewing the event. It is an indication of his self-image and may contain a truth beyond the literal meaning of the words themselves. The senior who wrote, "last year my English teacher really had it in for me. He hated my guts. No matter how hard I tried, nothing I did ever satisfied him. He wouldn't never give me a decent grade," may have believed he had given a truthful account of the situation. What was considered unimportant to him is the "other" truth. The student submitted few assignments, frequently cut class, was disruptive and rude. Of course, there are two sides to every story (the assignments may have been stupid; the class dull; the teacher a bigot). Or, the teacher may have been blameless. The reader should not jump to the conclusion that the student is displaying early manifestations of a persecution complex nor that he is an inveterate liar. Suspected inaccuracies may be noted on a reaction sheet or 3 x 5 card, but judgment as to the motive behind the statements cannot be made until some attempt is made to ascertain the whole truth of the matter, perhaps an impossible task.

Organization

Once the initial reading of the autobiography has been completed, the teacher or counselor will have an impression of its

---

5. Gordon W. Allport, *The Use of Personal Documents in Psychological Science*. Bulletin 49. (New York, Social Science Research Council, 1942), pp. 30-31.

overall organization. If an outline were given to the students, most papers will present a uniform pattern. Deviations from the prepared outline will be quickly discovered. The reasons for such action are not so easily resolved, but the reader may want to make a note of the fact. For the student not provided an outline, the teacher or counselor would question why the student chose to highlight the items he did. Did he start with his present life and work back to his early years? Or, if he used a chronological order, were there any noticeable gaps? Was there reasonable continuity throughout the autobiography or did it appear to be a fragmented and random review of selected events? Again no firm conclusions can be drawn from organizational structure, but it provides yet another lead to a better understanding of the individual student.

Read the following autobiographies of one boy and two girls, students from middle and junior high schools. See if you concur with the teachers' analyses. At the end of this chapter, you will find additional autobiographies for your analysis.

I am Linda, and I am a girl. I am healthy and strong, and sometimes brave, but not all the time. My hair is brown and my eyes are brown. I am a little tall for my age. I like to eat somethings, and somethings I do not like. I will be 12 on February 23. I live on a nice road on a farm. My family is nice and kind. My mother is kinda tall. My father is tall. My brother is 8, my sister is 4.

I like to ride my bike and play in the sand. I do not want to go to college, so I would like to be a housewife, or a nurse, or I would like to be a sewer like my very own mother, or a teacher if I could take a look at the children inside. Then I would think if they would be noisey or if they would be quiet, and if they would be noisey I would not take the job, and if they were quiet, I would take the job. And I would like to be a babysitter. I don't think I could sit very long, but I would like to earn some money, and then when I got older I would want to become a movie star and then earn a lot of money. And then I would be on television and everyone would get involved in watching me every time my show was on, and I sure do hope I look good and everyone would like the act.

Or, I would like to be a plain old housewife, and wash dishes and iron. But boy, would I be tired. But then if I don't want to go to college, then I guess I would have to be a housewife. Then if I was a housewife and got married and me and my husband had a baby, I would not know where to get the money to pay a baby sitter every day. And there wouldn't be anyone to fix dinner if I worked, and we just moved in, and then I would have to hunt and hunt for those darn canned goods, and you know how it is when you just move and you don't know where anything is. And that would make me mad hunting for stuff to cook for dinner or supper or what have ya. So I guess I would have to be a darn old housewife and sit around the house till it's time to cook supper, and until then I work and then get bored and tired, and then I would be so glad when the days over.

TEACHER'S COMMENTS

This is a frustrated little girl. She is quite practical, but yearns for many things. She has definite ideas about what "babysitting" is about, but she also knows the value of money, lots of it. She has little-girl ideas of being a movie star, TV actress, and wants everyone to look at her. Really this child doesn't get looked at too often, unless she does something startling.

Evidently, there has been a lot of moving around in this family, and frantically trying to find something for supper at the end of the day. She has evidently been told over and over that a "darn old housewife" doesn't have much excitement in life, and that it's a very boring life.

This little girl does very startling things in class sometimes. Most of the times she is quite passive and gets along very well with her classmates until she explodes in fury or startling behavior.

Well, I am 13 years old right now and my birthday is January 5. I have short brownish hair. My full name is Cynthia J. . . . I have light tan skin. I am pretty tall. I have green-blue eyes, small nose, I don't wear glasses. I love all sorts of pets and wild animals. I cannot swim, but I can do other things. I have 1 grandmother, 1 grandfather, 3 aunts, 2 uncles, and very, very, very many cousins. I have 1 sister, 1 brother, and 1 mother.

I live in a white-shingled house with black shutters. It is surrounded by lots of trees. It is very big and high. It has 3 bedrooms, 2 bathrooms, dining room, pantry, living room, kitchen, back porch and basement.

My family is very nice to me. Yesterday my mother gave me a pants-suit. My sister is very nice too and gives me games sometimes on my birthdays. My brother gives me money and loans me things. I think I sure am lucky to have a loveable family. My mother works the hardest to earn money for the family since my dad died of a heart attack. He had three, and died on his fourth one. Today is his birthday—he is 53.

My mother is 46. My sister is 11, my brother is 24. My family loves me and I love them. My dad did a lot to help me before and I still and always will love him. My whole family loves me and I love them. They are always good to me and I am thankful for such a good family.

I like to do art and gim (sic) and to play in school. I like Science, Social Studies, spelling and reading especially, but I don't like Math. Well, at first I would of liked to be a nurse, but I changed my mind. I would like to be a teacher, I think, or a plain housewife, I think. If I were a housewife I would try to live on a farm. And if I were a teacher, I would work till I had enough money to quit.

TEACHER'S COMMENTS

She has a very nice home, lots of pets. Her older brother is loved and appreciated, as well as her younger sister. Her mother works hard, since Dad died. But over and over, the refrain of "her family is always good to her, they love her very much, she is so thankful for such a good family, her family is very loveable." Evidently she is constantly reminded of how she should appreciate all this love. How succinctly she sums up her feelings of teaching in the last line!

(Jeff)

I ran away from school in first grade because I hated the teacher. It meant that when I ran away from first grade, I thought I was getting away from her. When I ran away one time, I ran out of classroom and the teacher caught me and took a chunk out of my neck. It meant that I never liked her any more. I hated her ever since and I still hate her.

I was stealing light bulbs and got caught. I got in trouble and they say I stole 15 of them. I only stole 2 and my friends got caught and the people said they stole 15 light bulbs, too. It meant that we had to give them more than we should have to give them.

I was catching for a baseball team and I got hit in the head with a bat by one of the players. I was out for a week. I was in the hospital for 3 days treated for concusion (sic). It meant that when I play catcher for a team I will make sure I am far enough from the batter.

I like to get my car and be a racecar driver for the kick of it and my real job I am going to be a mechanic for cars and other auto-mobiles. I predict I will be what I said I will be a car racer for kicks. I don't know about the other because I don't want to go to college.

TEACHER'S COMMENTS

Jeff is a student of average ability, but he has a reading problem. He has always been polite, a little slower than the other students, physically more developed than other boys his age. He is quite pop-ular. His grades fluctuate from year to year. There is no mention of the incident of running-away in the school records. He gets along well with the teachers here. He doesn't mention his family. Both parents are living; his mother is Oriental. Jeff depicts a rather poor picture of his life. His only recollections are being punished more severely than he thought was necessary and a painful accident.

(Mark)

I was born in Africa and then I moved to California and lived there for 3 years. Then I lived in Hawaii for 3 years. I fell out of our sail boat and got pinched by a crab. My sail boat turned over. I moved here and met Thad and that was a real bad scare. I want to beat up Thad someday. My most enjoyable time is when Thad went on a camping trip.

TEACHER'S COMMENTS

Mark found the mechanical task of writing difficult and has writ-ten the least information of all the autobiographies I've received. He seemed to say as little as possible; however he made an abrupt change from an ordinary experience to one of hatred and tension. He uses sarcasm in relating to his acquaintance, Thad. Mark omitted any reference to parents and family and did not develop several other topics which the students had agreed were to be in-cluded in the autobiography.

ADVANTAGES AND DISADVANTAGES OF THE AUTOBIOGRAPHY

After examining the many variables which affect the autobiog-raphy, do the limitations and dangers inherent in the device over-shadow the potential good which can result? It has already been noted that the *writer* may gain a greater awareness and insight about himself and those he knows by recording and clarifying his feelings. This may also provide release for pent-up emotions, a catharsis. Such information can make the counselor or teacher aware of those attitudes, experiences, and aspirations and thus facilitate the developing of a more effective climate in the classroom for learning and greater rapport in counseling sessions. Coupled with other information, such as the permanent file or anecdotal observations, the autobiography may throw new light on previously unknown, obscured, or unexplained data about the student. In his narrative, the student also has the freedom to emphasize those events in his life of greatest consequence to him, again providing clues to his responsiveness, emotional stability and self-image. But perhaps the most obvious advantage to the use of this device is that it is usable at most elementary grades, all high school levels, with all subjects, and can be secured with relative ease.

To counterbalance these advantages, critics have pointed out the serious disadvantages of assessing the validity and reliability of this instrument and the problems of accurate interpretation. Kowitz and Kowitz caution that

> narrative data such as . . . autobiographies demand a high level of professional skill if they are to be used. . . . Too often the flavor of the narrative is perceived . . . and is interpreted in terms of personal beliefs and limited experience. The illusion of potential profit from narrative data, which arises from its closeness to reality, often forces the inexperienced analyst to rely upon oversimplifications and stereotypes. These techniques help protect the analyst from the dazzling variety of possibilities but they also negate the potential of the narrative data.[6]

The reader is further faced with the problem of reconciling the picture which the student-autobiographer presents of himself with the reality which the teacher or counselor sees day after day. Which is the real student, the one described in the autobiography or the one who appears withdrawn or hostile in the classroom? There is also a serious danger of the reader's giving words an interpretation which the writer never intended. Lee and Pallone cite

---

6. Gerald T. Kowitz and Norma G. Kowitz, *Operating Guidance Services for the Modern School* (New York, Holt, Rinehart and Winston, Inc., 1968), p. 108.

"innumerable problems of interpretation rooted in poor or infelicitous choice of words by students."[7]

RECORDING THE AUTOBIOGRAPHY—THE
LIFE-HISTORY INTERVIEW

An experiment using written and tape-recorded autobiographies with ninth grade boys in a Baltimore County high school indicated that of ten questions asked, eight had totally different answers when written and taped responses were compared.[8] For example, one question in the outline provided asked "Describe your neighborhood." One student wrote, "my neighborhood is a small community near Baltimore. It is a fairly nice place. We have a baseball and a football team which are very successful." However, when the same question was answered by the student and recorded on tape, the answer was "It's O.K. We live near a high school. We have a couple of hoods, just enough so I don't like to walk home at night. It's about average, I guess." But perhaps the greatest discrepancy was one student's answer to the question, "What do you remember best in your early childhood?," where the written answer was simply "my dog," but the taped response was "My father; he died and my mother remarried. I just as soon have my father around. I was close to my father."

In tape-recording responses, the teacher-researcher interviewed each boy privately. He read the question to the student and then remained silent; the student was free to answer only those items he chose and was given all the time he wished for his responses. At no time did the teacher react to the answer or make any kind of judgmental or evaluating statements. He admitted that it was not always easy to evidence no reaction regardless of what was said, yet he felt that any overt response on his part might prove inhibiting to the students. He enjoyed good rapport with the boys who participated, yet he felt they were tense at the outset of the

7. James M. Lee and Nathaniel J. Pallone, *Guidance and Counseling in Schools: Foundations and Processes* (New York, McGraw-Hill Book Company, Inc., 1966), pp. 226-27.

8. Richard E. Sullivan, "Autobiographies of 9th Grade Boys," unpublished research paper, Towson State College, Division of Education, Baltimore, Md., 1970, pp. 3-5.

questioning, although they soon relaxed and seemed to respond without apparent strain. Once the taping session was completed, he asked each boy how he had felt during the interview and each one corroborated his impression.

In every case more, and sometimes conflicting, information was given orally than in writing, leading the researcher to question both the reliability and validity of the *written* autobiographies he had received from his students. Replaying the tapes, he was able to detect nuances in tone which added to the significance of the words and which a rereading of the written autobiographies could never reveal. He also reported that the students made a greater effort to clarify their statements, pausing as they thought through their answers and adding qualifying remarks. From experience with these boys, he knew that written assignments of any kind were not popular; they would complete written work but rarely would take time to go back and "polish" what had been written. The tape-recorded interviews, he discovered were, all in all, enjoyable for the boys. They felt being interviewed about their life histories was quite exciting. They told him they thought more about the questions before responding orally than when they were writing their answers and they "got more out of it" when the autobiography was recorded.

Although the tape-recording took far more time than writing the autobiographies, the researcher felt this approach resulted in a far more reliable and valid autobiography. He concluded that he had definitely strengthened his rapport and empathy with his students.

SUMMARY

Writing about oneself can prove enlightening to the writer as well as the reader. For the writer, the autobiography can provide an opportunity for self-analysis, release of pent-up emotions, even serve as a catharsis. Although time-consuming to analyze and limited by the danger of misinterpreting what is recounted or by omission or distortion of significant facts, the autobiography still has definite merits to the reader. Once the limitations are recognized, the counselor or teacher can use the device to develop deeper insight into the world of his students, and, as a consequence, strengthen the rapport and empathy between them.

FOR READER ANALYSIS—AUTOBIOGRAPHIES

You may wish to duplicate the reaction-analysis guidesheet, Figure 12, to help you organize your analysis of the following student autobiographies. After an initial reading, list those events which you believe were of particular importance to the writer under the section, "Significant Incidents." After two or more readings, comment briefly on organization, omissions, glossing over, inaccuracies, and any points you would like to check into further. Sum up your impressions in the last section.

(Jaymie)   (Female)

Nearly eighteen years ago, a little after five o'clock in the evening, I was born. This time factor alone tells a great deal about my character, I was just in time for dinner. Even today my mother (jokingly?) tells me that the two things I do best are eating and sleeping.

All my life, one thing I could not stand was people fighting. I have always hated to see two people who meant a great deal to me, have an argument. I have always disliked having arguments myself also. Whenever someone was angry with me, I felt guilty, as if it was half my fault.

Another thing that has always been important to me is having a few really close friends. I always sort of pitied those popular people who never seemed to have time to develop any meaningful friendships, but who had many acquaintances.

Elementary, junior high, and senior high schools all passed rather quickly and uneventfully. School has never been that important to me. I always learned more by just talking with people I enjoyed being around.

I have always disliked seeing living things hurt. One time when I was ten years old, there was an episode in the news, of ex-President Johnson picking his dogs up by the ears. I was so disgusted when I read about his dogs yelping in pain, that I wrote a letter to the President about the matter. His personal secretary must have gotten a good laugh, but nevertheless I received a reply.

Since I'm not writing in any logical order, I might as well skip to my senior year in high school. So many people tell me that this was the best year of their lives. If this is the way it's going to be for me, I think I'll commit suicide. No, I'm just kidding. It isn't all that bad except for the fact that it's so boring. I'm really looking forward to college and to finding a worthwhile career. I think the reason why I dislike the present school system is because of the subjects offered and the large classrooms. I would have seriously considered being a teacher except for the fact that I hate the traditional classroom atmosphere. True learning cannot usually take place here.

(Johnny) (14)
My family is kind of big. And it is kind of hard in a big family. I think I don't get as much in a big family as I would in a small family. But I am so lucky because I have been able to find a job for extra money. Me and my father don't have the same ideas. It seems he don't want to listen to me. To me it seems my friends get more freedom than me.

I like school in some ways. In my opinion it is not too bad. I do get in trouble sometimes but it is not that I want to. It's just that me and the teacher don't get along too good. I am not the smart kid in school and I am not the dumbest kid either. I know I could try harder.

I have a lot of friends and I've learned a lot from them. I have friends who want me to try dope and I have friends who want me to drink. I also have friends who do care about me. I tried grass with friends and drinking. I don't hate them for trying that but I don't think they should do it.

I don't have much time for activities now that I work but I do a lot of things on Saturday. Me and my friend Dave go bowling mostly.

My future won't amount to much if I don't start getting better grades. I would like to get a good job and then get married.

(Karen) (16)
My family is very close although we fight a lot. I wasn't supposed to be, the doctors said I was dead and they weren't going to let me come naturally but they did and here I am! I can't remember my preschool and early elementary school days. I had encephalitis when I was around 8 and can't remember before then. I was smart, at one time, but I'm not any more as you know I can't spell. Boys never liked me. Junior high was fun, and they were good years. When I came to senior high they had me take a business course and that messed up everything. Now I am taking Algebra and French when I could be taking better things. I guess I'm stuck with it now. I have

one best girl friend named Michelle and I don't like getting too close to people because they are always hurting you. My mom and dad own a restaurant that isn't doing too well but they always see that I have what I want. I like sports but aren't good in them. I've skiied from the time I was 6 and love it. I am also fond of animals mostly dogs and turtles. I want to go to college and work in Interior Design. I also hope to be married some day and to have children. I hope you don't think I'm a weird kind of person and not very friendly. I guess I am, but I'll get by.

(Phil)

I was born the day before Easter seventeen years ago. In my younger days I can't remember much. I did not have as much freedom as did the other kids. In the second grade I met up with some of my good friends of today. We used to get in a lot of fights. Nothing really serious just like all of the other kids used to do. Later on around the fifth grade my mother died. I think this really changed my life in great way. My father remarried and my new mother was against just about anything I wanted to do. I still don't get along with her good. When we were in seventh grade that was when I think my life really began. I started to meet a lot of new people. They were eighth graders ahead of us at the time. They always would start fights with us, and try to beat us up. But we usually got away. My one friend got in a fight with one of them and beat the guy up so they all tried to get him. Eventually it all died down and they left. We were the big shots of the school. My friends and I continually got in trouble. They were going to kick us out picking on other guys but they didn't. Then I left that school. I left a lot of friends. I enrolled at "X" High; I wanted to play football but I couldn't. My mother didn't let me. So from the beginning I hated the school. I just wanted to go there to play sports. I got through the ninth grade with pretty good marks. Then the tenth grade started. That's when I really changed. I had no desire to go to that school and I showed it in my school work. I flunked almost every subject. The last marking period whether you believe it or not I used to go to about 2 classes a day. I got caught and almost got kicked out but I told them I was going to transfer so they didn't. I got detention for the rest of the year. That was a lot of fun. Next year I transferred here. That's where I met my girl friend. She's a senior now. I'm not doing too good here but it's better than the other school. I started to work for my brother a while back. He owns a gas station. Well that brings me up to now and I have no plans for the future. I just want things to happen naturally.

SUGGESTED READINGS

Allport, Gordon W.: *The Use of Personal Documents in Psychology and Science, Bulletin No. 49.* New York, Soc Sci Res, 1942.

A landmark work; focuses on the uncritical and critical use of personal documents. Briefly traces psychologists' developing interest in personal narratives. Consideration of limitations and advantages of the autobiography.

Davis, Sammy (with Jane and Burt Boyer): *Yes, I Can! The Story of Sammy Davis.* New York, Farrar, Straus, 1965.

An autobiography written in collaboration; this successful black entertainer describes his fight to the top in the world of show business but also uses his recollections as a background to present his philosophy of life.

Frank, Anne: *Anne Frank: The Diary of a Young Girl.* New York, Doubleday, 1952.

This poignant and tender account of a young Jewish girl's hidden existence in Nazi-occupied Holland during World War II reveals intelligence, charm, warmth, humanity, and a deepening maturity—a classic.

Froelich, Clifford P., and Darley, John G.: *Studying Students, Guidance Methods of Individual Analysis.* Chicago, Sci Res Assoc, 1952.

Although written more than twenty years ago, these authors provide the most thorough treatment of points to consider when interpreting autobiographies plus providing examples of analysis of actual autobiographies with cautions about limitations of this technique.

Gibson, Robert, and Higgins, Robert: *Techniques of Guidance: An Approach to Pupil Analysis.* Chicago, Sci Res Assoc, 1966.

Discusses supervision of the writing of the autobiography and determining at what point student will derive greatest benefit from writing.

Hatch, Raymond N., Dressel, P. L., and Costar, J. W.: *Guidance Services in the Secondary School.* Dubuque, Iowa, William C. Brown Company, 1963.

Discusses values and limitations of autobiography as well as procedures for interpretation.

Johnson, Walter E., Stefflre, Buford, and Edelfelt, Roy A.: *Pupil Personnel and Guidance Services.* New York, McGraw, 1961.

The unstructured autobiography is examined critically, advantages and limitations probed.

Kowitz, Gerald T., and Kowitz, Norma G.: *Operating Guidance Services for the Modern School.* New York, HR&W, 1968.

Describes difficulties of interpreting autobiographies and the importance of training and skill by the interpreter.

Lee, James M., and Pallone, Nathaniel J.: *Guidance and Counseling in Schools: Foundations and Processes.* New York, McGraw, 1966.

Validity and reliability and confidentiality in relation to the autobiography are critically analyzed.

Padover, Saul K.: *Confessions and Self-Portraits.* New York, John Day, 1957.

A brief history of the autobiography is followed by samples of autobiographical excerpts of famous people; very readable and informative.

CHAPTER 5

THE STUDENT VIEWS HIMSELF— QUESTIONNAIRES

QUESTIONNAIRES OFTEN PROVIDE valuable insights. A carefully designed instrument, geared to the maturity and interest level of adolescents, can reveal their interests, present concerns, problems, assess future vocational and educational plans, and reflect the individual's feelings, his acceptance of himself, of his own self-worth. For the counselor such information can be an important tool in building the rapport with his counselees so necessary for effective counseling, while the teacher can use such information to develop a greater awareness of his students as individuals.

The ease with which a questionnaire can be administered and completed by groups or individuals makes its use unobjectionable to most students. Tabulating and evaluating the information is usually quicker and easier than interpreting the contents of many pages of a typical autobiography. Data from questionnaires can aid in validating already existing information about students, add supplementary facts, and support or contradict hypotheses about an individual by actually sampling his opinions.

STANDARDIZED QUESTIONNAIRES

Many of the questionnaires used in schools are designed by counselors or teachers for specific uses with their students. There are, however, more sophisticated standardized interest inventories and attitude scales available. Among these are

1. ATTITUDE AND SOCIAL MATURITY SCALES
   Survey of Personal Values. Publisher: Science Research Associates, Chicago, 1967. Respondent checks from a set of three statements which activity is *most* and *least* important to him.

Example   *M*   *L*

to have a hot meal at noon

to get a good night's sleep

to get plenty of fresh air

Each item is keyed to an appropriate scale describing the following traits: practicality, open-mindedness, achievement, variety, decisiveness, orderliness, and goal orientation. May be used with high school and college students.

Survey of Interpersonal Values. Publisher: Science Research Associates, Chicago, 1960. Triad approach in "measuring certain critical values involving an individual's relationships to other people or their relationships to him."[1] The six values measured are support, conformity, recognition, independence, benevolence, and leadership. May be used with high school and college students.

2. PERSONALITY INVENTORIES

The Edwards Personal Inventory. Publisher: Science Research Associates, Chicago, 1966. True-false choice as the respondent reacts to 300 statements in each of five booklets.

Example   *T*   *F*

He is good at explaining things to others

Depending upon the scales wanted, only one or more booklets may be administered. The first two scales deal with planning, organizing, intellectual orientation, persistence, self-confidence, cultural interests, conformity, and leadership; Booklet II, problem solving, anxiety, and feelings; Booklet III, motivation, recognition, competitiveness, cooperativeness; and Booklet IV, self-criticism, anger, understanding, and dependence. May be used with high school and college students and adults.

Omnibus Personality Inventory. Publisher: Psychological Corporation, New York, 1968. Respondent reads a series of statements similar to that shown in the example of the Edward's Personal Inventory and decides whether it is true or false as applied to him. Fourteen scales are derived:

---

1. *SRA Manual for Survey of Interpersonal Values* (Chicago, Science Research Associates Inc., 1960), p. 3.

thinking introversion, theoretical orientation, estheticism, complexity, religious orientation, social extroversion, impulse expression, personal integration, anxiety level, altruism, practical outlook, masculinity/femininity, and response bias. May be used with high school and college students and adults.

3. PERSONAL AND VOCATIONAL INTEREST INVENTORIES

What I Like To Do. Publisher: Science Research Associates, Chicago, 1954. Geared for pupils in Grades 4 through 7, responses are made on a "yes," "no" or "question mark–?" scale for a series of 294 items. Separate interest scales are derived for art, music, social studies, active play, quiet play, manual arts, home arts, and science.

Kuder Occupational Interest Survey. Publisher: Science Research Associates, Chicago, 1964. Designed for senior high school students, college students, and adults uses a forced-choice approach to a series of three statements; respondent must indicate which activity he would like to do *most* and which activity he wishes to do *least*.

Example   M   L
Visit an art gallery
Browse in a library
Visit a museum

Kuder Preference Record, Vocational, Form Ch, CM, 1966, uses the same procedures but reports results in ten scales: outdoor, computational, scientific, persuasive, artistic, literary, musical, social service, and clerical. This form may be used in junior and senior high school, colleges, and with adults.

Work Values Inventory. Publisher: Houghton-Mifflin Company, Boston, 1970. Designed for high school and college students and adults, uses a five-point scale, asking individual to indicate how he values certain aspects of work.

Example
5–very important   4–important   3–moderately im-

portant   2–of little importance   1–unimportant

                    1   2   3   4   5

Work in which you

    1. . . . have to keep solving new problems

The values indicate the degree of emphasis placed by the respondent in the following areas: altruism, aesthetics, creativity, intellectual stimulation, achievement, independence, prestige, management, economic returns, security, surroundings, supervisory relations, associates, way of life, and variety.

The Self-Directed Search, A Guide to Educational & Vocational Planning. Publisher: Consulting Psychologists Press, Palo Alto, California, 1970. May be used with high school and college students and adults to explore occupations. The inventory uses free response items, forced-choice (like/dislike) regarding activities, competencies, occupations, and a six-point scale to estimate abilities. Instructions for ranking choices and a guide for beginning the search for possible careers are included.

4. Sentence Completion Scales

    The Curtis Completion Form. Publisher: Western Psychological Services, Los Angeles, 1968. Consists of fifty incomplete sentences devised to evaluate emotional adjustment in schools and industry. Lower scores indicate better adjustment than high scores, with 24 considered normal. Items selected are intended to reveal antagonism, jealousy, self-pity, pessimism, insecurity, social inadequacy, severe conflict, and environmental deprivation.

5. Assessment of Attitudes Toward School

    Survey of Study Habits and Attitudes. Publisher: The Psychological Corporation, New York, 1967. Two forms, one for grades 7-12 and one for college students, uses 100 items to assess students' feelings and practices about schoolwork; four subscales–delay avoidance, work methods, teacher approval, and education acceptance.

    QUESTA, Parts I and II. Publisher: Educational Testing

Service, Princeton, New Jersey, 1972. Perhaps the most ambitious questionnaire commercially available which "focuses primarily on values, attitudes, levels of expectations and satisfactions" of students, teachers, and administrators

> to solicit more information about the attitude of students toward their educational experience, facilitate the study of student change between matriculation and graduation, provide information about the attitudes, values and perceptions of subgroups within the school, such as students, teachers, and administrators; provide information that leads to constructive change in programs, policies and practices; identify sources of satisfaction, dissatisfaction, and tension within the school; help define the school for itself and as desired aid the school in communicating with the public; enable schools to compare themselves with each other in ways that could identify important differences.[2]

Part I of the questionnaire is to be administered to students upon their entrance into high school, while Part II is given at the end of the sophomore, junior, or senior year. Part II is also administered to all teachers and administrators initially and every third year thereafter. Respondents react to statements on a three- or five-point scale depending upon the nature of the item.

Example

In general my experience in this school has been a good one

(a) strongly disagree
(b) disagree
(c) agree
(d) strongly agree
(e) no opinion

This list of attitude scales and interest inventories is in no way meant to be inclusive, but rather illustrative of the types of questionnaires currently available. A check of the catalogs of the publishers of standardized tests, the Buros' *Mental Measurement*

---

2. *The Secondary School Research Program, A Prospectus.* (Princeton, New Jersey, Educational Testing Service, 1972), pp. 6-7. Copyright © 1972 by Educational Testing Service. All rights reserved. Reprinted with permission.

Yearbook,[3] which also provides critical evaluations of each test listed, or a text in psychological tests will supply a far more complete inventory.

CONSTRUCTION AND FORM OF QUESTIONNAIRES

Preparing your own questionnaire appears easy. "Anyone can make up a few questions" is the usual attitude about its construction. Yet designing a good questionnaire, especially one intended to acquire insight and understanding of an individual, is far from easy. First, determine what you want to know about the student. Should the questionnaire try to learn how the pupil sees himself in his own world, or an assessment of his satisfaction or dissatisfaction with his present academic program, or perhaps his plans for the future? Once the objective has been clearly defined, the types of questions best suited to elicit this data can be prepared.

The use of the forced-choice option is extremely popular in questionnaire construction. The respondent *must* select either "yes" or "no" or from a field of three items, such as "sometimes," "always," "never." But he is still required to select one of the terms given. The yes/no option is easily understood, but few individuals find themselves in a yes/no position on issues involving feelings and beliefs. Thus they find themselves frustrated when they must select from such choices. Even the three-step categories do not satisfy. Just what is the questioner's definition of "sometimes"? Does it mean once a week, once a month, every other day? Even the categories "strongly agree," "agree," "partly agree," and "partly disagree," "disagree," "strongly disagree," although offering more choices, can merely compound the confusion by such imprecise terms. Some respondents may circle "agree" because they are not sure how strong one's feelings must be to classify them as "strongly" agreeing.

Sometimes the questionnaire will contain open-ended statements which give the respondents an opportunity to write in their own answers. Although this frees them from a preselected choice, it is frequently very difficult to classify or categorize the variety of responses received and even more difficult to make statistical com-

---

3. Oscar K. Buros, *Mental Measurements Yearbook,* 6th ed. (Highland Park, New Jersey, Gryphon Press, 1972).

parisons of such data, thus defeating one of the purposes of questionnaire results: the ease with which they can be compared. In one survey where individuals were to complete a series of statements, one respondent completed the sentence, "I don't like people who . . ." with the words "don't like me." Anticipated answers were descriptive words or phrases such as "are mean," "cheat," "fight," and those tabulating this response were presented a real dilemma! The questionnaire-maker is faced with accepting responses which may be less than an accurate evaluation of the respondent's feelings or of permitting answers which can defy categorizing for comparison purposes.

Limitations of the Questionnaire

The wording of the items may also cause problems, for misinterpretation by the respondent will affect the questionnaire's validity and reliability. Assurance that the vocabulary is appropriate and understandable to the maturity of the prospective respondents can be determined by a trial run of the instrument on a similarly aged sample before its use with a larger group. Words which seem commonplace to the adult who prepares the questionnaire may be quite foreign to the adolescent answering. In one attitude survey, a series of statements were given to high school students to be answered "yes" or "no." Included was this statement, "I usually have good rapport with most people." Those who collaborated on the questionnaire's construction were very familiar with this word, but many students had no idea of its meaning. Yet some had already answered the question before someone asked for a definition. After the word had been explained, several students remarked, "Oh, is *that* what it means!" Just how much faith could be placed in the replies of those students who answered without knowing what the word meant! And how many other words were unfamiliar and undetected?

Format—Ease of Scoring

The design of a questionnaire should reflect an effort to make it easy for the respondent to answer. Using a check mark, "X," or simply blackening the space provided for responses; allowing plenty of space for writing free-response comments; and arrang-

ing the items attractively with sufficient blank space between questions and easy-to-read type encourages replies. Even seemingly
trivial details can have a significant effect on the responses received. For instance, asking the respondent for information already available to the questioner elsewhere could cause enough
irritation to affect negatively his attitude toward the remaining
items. Warters[4] stresses that questions which suggest an obvious
answer should also be avoided. Regardless of how a student actually feels, he may respond with the acceptable answer rather than
risk prejudicing himself with the teacher or counselor administering the questionnaire. National pollsters during the Kennedy Presi-
dential campaign found that the question, "Do you think a Catholic has the right to run for President of the United States?" which
invariably received a strong affirmative reply, actually was a
faulty barometer of the true feelings of many about having a
Catholic in the White House. Similarly, the high school student
asked if he has ever smoked pot, been drunk, or had premarital
sex relations may be very wary about admitting behavior which
he knows is illegal or disapproved. Questions which could embar-
rass or incriminate the respondent or reflect upon others evoke
responses of dubious reliability, while too many questions on too
wide a range of topics result in boredom and fatigue. A fourteen-
page questionnaire requires a high degree of motivation just to
complete and almost unlimited dedication to answer with thought-
ful consideration of each item. Rather than permitting these factors to influence the accuracy of the responses, it would be far
better to design several short questionnaires dealing with a single
specific topic, rather than one overwhelmingly long one trying to
cover "everything." It should also be remembered that even a
short questionnaire of a few pages which contains seemingly
inane questions can sorely try the patience of the respondent.

As a case in point, students surveyed on their attitudes and values by their school newspaper recently found themselves chal-
lenged by 154 items probing into family economic status, religious

---

4. Jane Warters, *Techniques of Counseling* (New York, McGraw-Hill Book
Company, Inc., 1964), pp. 181-85.

preference, feelings toward parents, peers, alcohol, sex, drugs, and control of the news media. Of those who completed it, several admitted rushing through the items "just to be finished with the thing," and giving little thought to their responses. Others, when asked to suggest the intent behind some of the items, were unable to imagine why some of the items were included; a few thought it a "big put-on, a gag."

Typical of the questions asked were these two

10. How old were you when you FIRST did each of the following?

	Age
Smoked a cigarette	——
Drank an alcoholic beverage	——
Smoked marijuana	——
Had sexual intercourse	——
Traveled more than 100 mi from home on your own	——
Traveled ouside the U. S. and Canada	——

11. Do you feel comfortable talking with your mother and father about

	Mother		*Father*	
	Yes	*No*	*Yes*	*No*
Your career?	——	——	——	——
Drugs?	——	——	——	——
Politics?	——	——	——	——
Sex?	——	——	——	——
Religion?	——	——	——	——

At no time were the respondents told the purpose of the questionnaire nor how the results would be used. Although the questionnaires were unsigned, one still wonders how honestly the questions were answered or how the tabulated results could be construed as an accurate barometer of student attitudes.

Questionnaires such as those excerpted above which are designed for research or survey use are usually returned with no identification to provide security for the respondent, hoping to encourage honesty in the replies. Counselors and teachers asking students to evaluate the effectiveness of the counseling services, quality of information provided on colleges, employment, class procedures, methods of grading, course requirements, and teacher or counselor effectiveness would use the unsigned questionnaire. However, if individual follow-up were one of the basic purposes behind the questionnaire, then a signature would be needed. Questionnaires probing areas of individual student concern or conflict would fall in this category. Whether the questionnaire is anonymous or signed, the students should be told of the purpose of the instrument, how the results are to be used, and they should be assured that if they do not wish to participate, they need not do so. Even with a signed questionnaire, the student must be guaranteed that all his replies will be confidential and that no information revealed will be disclosed to anyone without his permission. He should also feel free to omit any items which he is unwilling to complete.

DANGERS IN INTERPRETING QUESTIONNAIRE RESULTS

It must be admitted that freedom to choose whether or not to participate may result in a distorted sample. Often the disgruntled individual will respond to a questionnaire if it gives him an opportunity to criticize or complain and to have his opinion counted and reported, as in national opinion polls. Conversely, the highly successful individual will frequently return questionnaires sent by his college or high school which give him an opportunity to brag a little, to inform the world at large how far he has inched up the ladder of success. The problem is getting Mr., Mrs., and Miss "Average Respondent" to reply.

In the school setting, if a student feels uncomfortable or threatened by being asked to complete a questionnaire, he should not be compelled or pressured to do so; such a feeling is quite likely to affect the reliability of his answers. By the time students reach high school, they are very cautious about revealing their true feelings. They hesitate, as would most adults, to reveal feelings which they believe others consider unacceptable. Frequently they answer in a manner which they feel the questioner is expecting. And this, perhaps, constitutes one of the greatest dangers in using the questionnaire: the nagging question of "how honest is the respondent?" The establishment of good rapport and trust between the questioner and the respondent can reduce the danger of dishonest responses. Too often students are merely told to "fill this in" and frequently see little or no reason for answering questions which appear obvious, ambiguous, too personal, or foolish. Thus the student may rush through the items, dutifully filling in each blank, but paying little attention to what is being recorded.

Andy was being enrolled at Dixon Junior High, and while his mother was completing the registration forms, the counselors' secretary handed him a sheet of paper and said, "Andy, fill this in, please."

He wasn't given the opportunity to ask why and plodded through three pages of questions about his likes, dislikes, and career plans and hobbies. As he was leaving, he told his mother, "I had to fill out some dumb form about what kind of courses I liked and all that. They even asked what I didn't like. You know I really didn't know what to put down for that, 'cause I really don't dislike any subject much, but since they had a blank down there, I wrote in Geography. I don't really hate it that much, but I sure didn't like old man Sisler who had me for geography last year. I hope that was O.K.; I wonder what the thing was for, anyway?

In Figures 13 through 16, four types of questionnaires prepared by counselors and teachers are shown. Figure 13 was developed by a counselor and used as the basis for the initial interview with counselees in Grades 7 through 12. The information was also shared with the subject teachers. Figure 14 focuses on future educational and vocational planning and was used by a ninth grade teacher who developed a unit on occupations, sharing the answers with the counselors. Both questionnaires employ a "free-response" approach where the respondent completes the statements in his own words.

STUDENT INVENTORY—GRADES 7-12

Please provide the information asked for below so that we can help you in planning your program and in making plans for your future. Answer those questions which you feel do not apply to you. You may omit any you do not wish to answer. Thank you.

*   *   *

Name .... Grade .... Date ....
What subject or subjects do you like best? Why? ....
....
....
....

What subject or subjects do you not like so much? Why? ....
....
....

Please list all of your school activities—sports, clubs, offices held—and indicate how long you have participated in each.
....
....
....
....
....

Please list your hobbies and leisure-time activities.
....
....
....
....

Do you like to read? Yes .... No .... If "yes," what kinds of books or magazines do you like to read?
....
....

Do you like to watch television? Yes .... No .... If "yes," what kinds of programs do you like to watch?
....
....

you liked about each.
Please list the types of jobs you have had, how long you had each job, and what

Kind of Job	Held How Long	What You Liked About It

What are your plans for the future (after you finish high school)?
....

What occupations, jobs, professions have you seriously considered? Why?
....
....

What schools or colleges have you seriously considered after high school?
....
....
....

How would you describe yourself? Do any of the words below usually apply to you? Circle those which do.
active, ambitious, hard-working, impatient, imaginative, calm, self-confident, creative, serious, easily discouraged, often lonely, timid, lazy, even-tempered, dependable, cheerful, sarcastic, absent-minded, shy, good-natured, easy-going, quick-tempered.
What other words describe you? List them ....

. . . .
Would you like to talk with your counselor about any of the topics listed below?
Please check those of interest to you.
courses for next year . . . . . .   job . . . . . .   college . . . . . .
other . . . . . .   (please indicate topic) . . . .

Figure 13. Sample questionnaire. Student Inventory Form, grades 7 through
12.

Unfortunately, the counselor who developed the questionnaire
in Figure 13 never asked his counselees to give him their reactions. However, teachers who saw it questioned the inclusion of
the questions on reading and television. They felt that students
knew the expected answer to the question, "Do you like to read?"
and wondered if omitting the first part of the question and asking
what they *did* read might elicit a more revealing and honest answer. Students had been told they could omit any questions they
chose, and the counselor felt those who did not like reading would
simply omit the question. Teachers also wondered what use was
to be made of the answers received on both questions relating to
reading. The counselor indicated the replies would serve as possible ways of establishing rapport with the student by discussing
books or programs of interest to him. The items on possible occupations and future school choice were questioned by some who
wondered why the word, "seriously," was added. Exactly what
was the counselor's intent in adding the word when asking "What
occupations, jobs, professions have you seriously considered?
Why?" and "What schools or colleges have you seriously considered after high school?" The counselor felt the inclusion of this
word would encourage the respondent to focus on those jobs and
schools which were realistic choices for him and would serve as
another area for future exploration and discussion. This questionnaire went through four revisions and was answered by three sample populations of students and teachers before the final form
shown, yet this form was still criticized by another group of students and teachers after it had been administered; proof of the difficulty of developing a satisfactory instrument free of possible misinterpretation, distortion, and threat.

The teacher who used the Ninth Grade Survey Form, Figure 14, reported that her students asked few questions, completed the questionnaire quickly, but she wondered whether they put much thought into their answers. Friendly critics suggested she might add the heading, "Other," in Item 2, "What do you plan to do immediately after graduation from high school?," and add a blank line for the student to add his answer. Some girls might be considering marriage immediately after graduation; others may intend to "bum around" the country with a knapsack on their backs, so opportunity for such responses should be provided. Some questioned the use of the word, "graduation," in this item and thought it might be better to rephrase the question, "What do you plan to do when you leave school?" and add a separate item to ascertain if the student was planning to remain in school until graduation. Others felt the word, "immediately," added nothing to the ques-

NINTH GRADE SURVEY

1. Name .... Homeroom Section ....
         (Last)   (First)   (Middle)
2. What do you plan to do immediately after graduation from high school?
      Attend a four-year college ......
      Secure a job (Indicate type of work wanted) ....
      Attend junior college ......
      Attend community college ......
      Attend business school ......
      Attend school of nursing ......
      Attend a specialized school (Indicate type) ....
      Enter military service (Indicate branch) ....
3. What are your special abilities and talents? Please list below
....
....
4. What are your out-of-school activities? Please list below
....
....
5. What are your major interests? Please list below
....
....
6. Check below the topics you would like to discuss with your counselor
      Educational information for high school ......
      Planning for after high school ......
      Job information ......

Figure 14. Sample questionnaire. Ninth grade survey.

tion, in fact it might confuse the respondent and should be omitted. Item 4, "What are your out-of-school activities?," would require more space for adequate answering some felt, while others criticized Item 5, "What are your major interests?" as too vague. Was the teacher's intent to probe intellectual interests, vocational pursuits, or social aspirations in this question? And, some wondered, just how many major interests can an individual have? Thus this instrument, too, revealed possible areas of misinterpretation by the student-respondent which could affect the validity of the completed instrument.

Figure 15, which used a forced-choice, five-point scale, was devised by a team of middle-school teachers and counselors to de-

SELF-CONCEPT

The following sentences are to help you describe yourself. Read each statement carefully. Then select the number that you feel best describes you and put that number in the blank space at the end of that sentence.

5—completely true
4—mostly true
3—partly true and partly false
2—mostly false
1—completely false (never true)

1. I like being with my classmates. ____
2. I would rather be alone to do homework. ____
3. I like to express my ideas in writing. ____
4. I like to give oral reports in class. ____
5. I enjoy finding answers to hard problems in mathematics. ____
6. I am as smart as I want to be. ____
7. I like to take part in active sports such as tennis, baseball, football. ____
8. I get tired easily when I run or play in active games. ____
9. I like to work with my hands, making things with wood, metal or cloth. ____
10. I like to draw and paint. ____
11. I need lots of sleep. ____
12. I put off things I should do. ____
13. I give up easily on school work. ____
14. I get along with my mother. ____
15. I get along with my father. ____
16. I look good in clothes. ____
17. I am satisfied with my looks. ____
18. I feel sorry for my classmates who have problems at home. ____
19. I belong to school committees and clubs. ____
20. I am satisfied to be just as I am. ____

Figure 15. Sample questionnaire. Self-concept scale.

velop an awareness by students of their feelings about themselves and their ability to succeed in the world of work. A series of three questionnaires was prepared, analyzed in a graduate guidance class, and tried on a sample population of students and teachers and revised several times before this final form was administered. Each item on the self-concept scale, which was the second questionnaire in the series (the first dealt with attitudes toward different kinds of work and the student's feelings about himself), was used to assess the student's interest in certain types of career families, not specific jobs. For example, Item 1, "I like being with my classmates," was considered indicative of an interest in being with (and working with) people. Item 18, "I put off things I should do," was considered a measure of perseverance, initiative and motivational strength, while Item 9, "I like to work with my hands . . . ," and Item 10, "I like to draw and paint," manifested an interest in manually oriented and art fields.

Tabulation of the responses resulted in grouping answers checked 4 (mostly true) and 5 (completely true) into one category, true, and answers of 1 (never true) and 2 (mostly false) were considered false. Category 3 (partly true and partly false) replies were ignored. Difficulties developed as the teacher-counselor tabulators found questionnaires with a majority of the items answered with the No. 3 response. Yet they felt such responses did not invalidate the questionnaire since there were few students who did answer a majority of the items in this way, and that such indecision was an indication of either lack of maturity or interest in the questionnaire on the part of the student. Critics argued about the inclusion of some of the items, particularly Items 14 and 15, "I get along with my mother," and "I get along with my father," as affecting attitudes needed for career choices. Yet the team felt that their efforts were overall successful when the responses from this questionnaire correlated positively with the other two questionnaires which sought the same information but in a different format. All members of the questionnaire team concurred that justifying the inclusion of any item was based on acceptance of the group's basic assumptions about work attitudes. Others evaluating the questionnaire found it difficult to accept some of these premises, and so criticisms of specific items in the questionnaire were never fully resolved.

A form of open-ended questionnaire, the sentence-completion form, is used by some teachers and counselors to discover students' attitudes about themselves, their aspirations, and their fears. Figure 16 is an example of this type, which is actually a variation of the word-association technique. Although there are standardized sentence completion tests available, frequently teachers and counselors devise and administer those specifically designed for their own students. The twenty-item Personal Data Blank (Fig. 16) prepared by a junior high teacher made no attempt to evaluate the personalities of the students who completed the items. The teacher read the responses and felt that some of the answers indicated possible areas of concern by the student-respondents.

PERSONAL DATA BLANK

Name .... Grade .... Date ....

Below are 20 partly completed sentences. Finish each one by writing the first things that come into your mind as you read. If you can't think of an ending for any group of words, move on to the next, and come back to the ones you didn't finish later. Try to complete them all.

1. My favorite school subjects ....
2. I dislike school subjects ....
3. After school is over, I ....
4. My schoolwork ....
5. After high school ....
6. The best part of school is ....
7. My secret ambition is ....
8. I like people who ....
9. My hobbies are ....
10. I am at my best when ....
11. My friends like to ....
12. My parents don't realize ....
13. I get embarrassed when ....
14. I don't like people who ....
15. My favorite pastime ....
16. When the odds are against me, I ....
17. My family treats me like ....
18. My greatest weakness is ....
19. I'm good at ....
20. I want ....

Figure 16. Sample questionnaire. Personal data blank.

Those who evaluated this form questioned the usefulness of Items 1 and 2, feeling they were slanted so that they would give minimal information. The teacher agreed that such statements were unlikely to focus on students' problems but were included to be easy and nonthreatening. Critics felt the answer received from Item 9 might be a repeat of Item 5. The teacher also admitted that she had no proof that her evaluation of responses received was accurate, which raises one of the great dangers inherent in using projective devices, that of individuals untrained in questionnaire construction and in the psychology of projective techniques blithely preparing sentence completion items and then analyzing the results, perhaps incorrectly. Projective techniques have long come under fire by critics; a check of Buros' *Mental Measurement Yearbook* will find some hard words fired in their general direction. So teachers and counselors who decide to develop their own projective questionnaire, be warned and be wary.

SUMMARY

A well-designed questionnaire, unlike the autobiography, requires little if any composition skill by the respondent and can provide valuable clues to understanding students' perceptions and feelings. Although its effectiveness is limited by the difficulty of phrasing the questions for inclusion in the instrument, by possible misinterpretation of the items by the respondent, and the individual's reluctance to be completely honest, it offers a quick and easy technique for sampling opinions and attitudes.

FOR READER ANALYSIS—QUESTIONNAIRES

The following questionnaires were developed by counselors, teachers, and students. Although they are in no way intended to serve as models, they were actually administered to junior and senior high school students, and decisions were made based on the results received. As you examine the questionnaires, ask yourself which questions are "good" ones (those which in your opinion will secure the information desired); if you feel some items are not well written, see what you can do to improve them. Don't forget to read the directions, too. Are they clear and easy-to-understand?

Are options offered *not* to answer if the respondent does not wish to do so? Could the "tone" of the directions or the items themselves be improved, perhaps less formal, more "encouraging" to the respondent?

Student Council Questionnaire for Teens

We would like your opinion about how you and your family get along. Answer each question "yes" or "no."

1. Do your parents wait until you are through talking before having their say? yes no
2. Does your family do things as a group? yes no
3. Does your family talk things over with each other? yes no
4. Do your parents seem to respect your opinion? yes no
5. Do your parents tend to lecture and preach too much? yes no
6. Do you discuss personal problems with either of your parents? yes no
7. Do your parents tend to talk to you as if you were much younger? yes no
8. Do your parents show an interest in your interests? yes no
9. Do you discuss matters of sex with either of your parents? yes no
10. Do your parents trust you? yes no
11. Do you find it hard to say what you feel at home? yes no
12. Do your parents have confidence in your abilities? yes no
13. Do your parents really try to see your side of things? yes no
14. Do you hesitate to disagree with either of your parents? yes no
15. Do you fail to ask your parents for things because you are afraid they will deny your request? yes no
16. Do your parents consider your opinion in making decisions which concern you? yes no
17. Do your parents try to make you feel better when you are down in the dumps? yes no
18. Do your parents explain their reasons for not letting you do some things? yes no

19. Do you ask your parents the reasons for the decisions
    they make concerning you?   yes   no
20. Do you help your parents to understand you by telling
    them how you feel and think?   yes no

A Sentence Completion Project

Please complete the sentences in a way that will express your real
feelings. There is no time limit but try to complete the sentences
with the thoughts that come to your mind when you first read the
beginning word or words. Do NOT sign your name. The statements are to be anonymous.

 1. Teachers
 2. School work
 3. My education
 4. Homework
 5. A class is most enjoyable when
 6. My school
 7. Life seems worthwhile when
 8. Recreation time
 9. Final exams
10. The grading system
11. In the future
12. My family
13. The teacher I respect most
14. The school counselor
15. Failing
16. My ambition
17. My best work
18. My clothes
19. My friends
20. Girls
21. Boys
22. One change I would like to make
23. I feel like quitting when
24. I worry about
25. I never

26. I always . . . .
27. I would like to . . . .
28. I think of myself as . . . .
29. I am happiest when . . . .
30. When I am angry . . . .

Drug Questionnaire

The results of this questionnaire survey will be part of our discussion in class on drug abuse, alcohol, and tobacco as social problems. These questionnaires will be destroyed after being tabulated.

Grade . . . . . . Age . . . . . . Sex: Male . . . . . . Female . . . . . .

Directions:
Place a check on the appropriate line for each statement.

	Yes	No	No Opinion or Don't Know
1. Do you smoke cigarettes?	——	——	——
2. Do you smoke less than ½ a pack a day?	——	——	——
3. Do you smoke a pack a day?	——	——	——
4. Do you smoke two packs a day?	——	——	——
5. Do you smoke more than two packs a day?	——	——	——
6. Do you drink alcoholic beverages?	——	——	——
7. Have you ever been in the presence of anyone under the influence of illegal drugs?	——	——	——
8. Are any of your friends users of illegal drugs?	——	——	——
9. Have you ever seen any of the following:	——	——	——
heroin	——	——	——
marijuana	——	——	——
hashish	——	——	——

cocaine	——	——	——
methadone	——	——	——
speed	——	——	——
Others	——	——	——

10. If you checked any of the above drugs, describe the situation during which you saw the drug.

. . . .

. . . .

11. Have you ever had the opportunity to take an illegal drug?   —— —— ——
12. Have you ever taken an illegal drug?   —— —— ——
13. Have you ever smoked marijuana?   —— —— ——
14. If you answered "yes" to No. 13, do you plan to continue to smoke marijuana?   —— —— ——
15. Do you feel that marijuana should be legalized?   —— —— ——
16. Have you ever used LSD?   —— —— ——
17. If you have used LSD, did you use it more than once?   —— —— ——
18. If you have used LSD, do you plan to continue taking it?   —— —— ——
19. Have you ever injected any drug into your veins?   —— —— ——
20. From what source did you obtain your information about drugs. Check all which apply:

friends . . . . . .

family . . . . . .

school . . . . . .

church . . . . . .

other (specify) . . . .

SUGGESTED READINGS

Conrad, Herbert S.: Clearance of questionnaires with respect to "invasion of privacy," public sensitivities, ethical standards, etc.: Principles and viewpoints by the Bureau of Research, U.S. Office of Education, *Sociology of Education, 40:*170-75, 1967.

The chairman of the government's internal clearance committee discusses qualifying factors which affect the application of criteria used to evaluate the acceptability of questionnaire items and the role of the U.S. Office of Education and social scientists in exercising professional discretion in the preparation and use of questionnaires.

Oppenheim, A. N.: *Questionnaire Design and Attitude Measurement.* New York, Basic, 1967.

Addressed to the beginning researcher, the author outlines step-by-step procedures for designing questionnaires and surveys and techniques for the measurement of attitudes.

Hatch, Raymond N., Dressel, Paul, and Costar, James: *Guidance Services in the Secondary School.* Dubuque, William C. Brown, 1961.

Uses, advantages, and limitations of the questionnaire presented with clarity and thoroughness.

Warters, Jane: *Techniques of Counseling.* New York, McGraw, 1964.

Useful suggestions for phrasing questions to secure honest responses as well as traps to avoid in developing the questionnaire.

CHAPTER **6**

WHAT DO YOU SEE?—OBSERVATIONS

A LL OF US MAKE JUDGMENTS about people on the basis of what we see them do, or what we think we see them do. Words, gestures, and body movements convey rich meaning, but problems occur when we fail to interpret the action properly or when we make an inaccurate observation and then make a judgment on what we thought we saw rather than what actually occurred. Consider for a moment the muddled recollections of witnesses at a trial or the amazing variety in the descriptions of eyewitnesses following a fight between students, and you will realize that complete, accurate observations do not come easily. Yet teachers and counselors who carefully observe their students, study their actions, and interpret their behavior can gather much useful and insightful data.

Doubtless some teachers would insist they watch their students constantly. "I've always got my eyes on them, every minute; they don't get by with a thing in my class!" Yet what does the teacher really see during the minutes and hours of his teaching day or the counselor in the short counseling sessions he is able to schedule with his counselees? A counselor with a student load of 300 to 500 or a teacher with 100 to 200 may feel that any attempt to observe all his students would be an impossibility, and it would. A new and perhaps insecure teacher also may see the thirty-five young faces before him as a potential threat, a small army vying for control of the classroom. Another teacher may describe his students as a "bunch of goof-offs, lazy, unmotivated, and up to no good," while his colleague may see them as enthusiastic, curious, and eager to explore the subject at hand. In every class there are as many unique personalities as there are faces forming the group, each with special needs, problems, and hopes, waiting for needed recognition, assistance, and support from the

111

teacher and counselor. When viewed this way, the school can no longer be restricted exclusively to transmitting factual subject matter and maintaining personal files on students. Continuous interaction, positive and negative, between teachers, counselors, and students, as well as between the learner and the material to be learned, inhibits or facilitates learning.

To the teacher who is as interested in Sally as a person as in Thomas Jefferson as a statesman, Euclid's contribution to mathematics, or Margaret Sanger's missionary zeal, observing and recording students' behavior can yield another clue to fuller understanding of each individual. Teachers and counselors could develop a team approach to such observing. Unfortunately both teachers and counselors sometimes make judgments about their students and counselees on very superficial evidence. Toni doesn't participate in class, so she isn't interested. Harry often yawns, a sure sign of boredom. Carrie's expression is sly, so she probably cheats. Karl always slouches, fidgets, and looks around the room during class, obviously trying to provoke the teacher. Are these accurate evaluations of these students' behaviors? Or could Toni be shy; Harry tired because he works 4 PM to midnight; Carrie nearsighted and straining to see; Karl, six feet tall and uncomfortable in a too-small chair? If the teacher reads the "signs" wrongly and reacts on incorrect observations, the rapport between them could be shattered. Nonverbal language, transmitted on silent terms but often exploding with meaning, is a vital component to effective communication. We all use body language, consciously and unconsciously, to convey meaning we hesitate to put into words, and we interpret the posture and gestures of others, rightly and wrongly. Failure to receive signals sent out by students and counselees, or misinterpreting them, can result in teacher or counselor behavior towards students guaranteed to evoke a hostile response, possibly causing a serious rift between them.

Perhaps the most powerful nonverbal cue is the smile. Teachers and counselors can encourage, show support, approval, and acceptance for their students and counselees by this very simple action (requiring, it is said, only fourteen muscles, while a frown needs more than fifty). But if a survey were possible of all the teachers and counselors in all our schools, I feel sure the frown would prove the winner as the most frequently used nonverbal cue. A quelling look can restore a class to order, silence a talker, discourage a potential cheater, show doubt or disbelief over a student-counselee's statement. In each instance, not a word may be said, but the message gets through loud and clear.

During conferences with parents and teachers, sympathetic glances from the parent or teacher to the counselor can convey a world of meaning. Often a slight raising of the eyebrows by the teacher and an expression which says without words "now that I've met this parent, I can understand why the student is the way he is" passes between teacher and counselor. (I must also admit I have exchanged similar glances with parents when I was a high school counselor, implying that having met the teacher, the parent understood his child's behavior in the classroom.) Signs of conflict and tension by parent, teacher, or counselees are often manifested by nonverbal language, a tapping of the foot, sniffling, crying, "wiggling" in the chair, twisting the hands together. When there is disagreement or refusal to accept a statement made by one participant in a conference, the individual who doesn't wish to accept the remark may show this reluctance by simply crossing his arms across his chest, signaling that he is mentally "withdrawing" from any further discussion, blocking out any more words by this physical act. Accurately "reading" nonverbal cues is difficult but crucial to accurate communication.

Every time the teacher or counselor looks at a student, it could be said that he is making an observation. But what is seen is usually no more than a blurred image: Amy reading the textbook, Joanna giving an oral report, Zack late for class, Teresa asking for the entrance requirements for State U, Phil wanting to drop Spanish. The teacher or counselor may have a fleeting reaction to what he sees, but the overt focus is too often on the material, the subject matter to be taught, or the information dispensed, yet one is also very much influenced by the covert body language. Certainly teachers make judgments about their students while teaching—their academic ability, span of concentration—yet observations of a less intellectual nature, within and outside the classroom, can add deeper dimension and perspective to understanding the students' personalities. Teachers are frequently amazed to see students who are shy, even withdrawn, in their classrooms noisely exhuberant in the cafeteria, outgoing and poised in the school play. The boy who can't "crack" geometry may be the top scorer on the varsity football team. The counselor who sees Fred in a private one-to-one setting where he is relaxed and outspoken should visit the boy's classes to note variations in behavior. He might discover Fred is tense, frustrated, even frightened in some learning situations. Peer relationships, the acceptance or rejection of the individual student by his peers, and his reaction to adults should be noted by the counselor if he hopes to be truly effective in discussing the students' feelings about themselves and in their dealings with others. Is the student who appears tongue-tied in the Guidance Office a highly articulate captain of the swimming team? Is the vivacious sophomore who drops by regularly to "talk about nothing" quite withdrawn and lonely as she sits in the cafeteria? These clues are essential to counselor effectiveness and can be gathered only through direct observation of the students in a variety of settings.

RECORDING OBSERVATIONS—THE ANECDOTAL RECORD

However, the more formal type of observation, the conscious studying of an individual's behavior and the writing of an account of observed behavior can greatly assist both teacher and counselor in deepening their understanding of their students. Such written accounts of observations of a student, usually covering a period of several days or weeks, are often used by administrators and counselors in conferences with parents. Careless or biased accounts could present a distorted picture prejudicial to the student.

A written account of an observed incident of behavior with or without interpretation or recommendations for action (provided in a separate section) is frequently called an *Anecdotal Record*. Making accurate observations and recording the observed behavior are not simple tasks; they require concentration, objectivity, and skill. Ask any two individuals involved in an auto collision to describe the accident and you wonder if they both are talking about the same event! Even eye-witnesses at the scene have widely divergent versions of the truth. Similarly the teacher and counselor, often unskilled in observational techniques, may make errors which render the account false, worthless, and even damaging to the student.

Frequently the novice observer will find himself paying almost exclusive attention to the irritating, noisy students, and his "unbiased" observations will quickly prove what he always believed, that Ed Marley is a "big mouth" or that "Eliza is impudent." On the other hand, the introverted girl or boy who isolates himself from the group or who is actually rejected by his peers may go completely unnoticed. Behaviors which the counselor or teacher may consider acceptable for the school, such as conformity and docility, may be written up as indications of good adjustment. Yet these qualities ill prepare the student for the competition and pressure of today's world, for thinking for himself, for establishing his own values and standards.

Froelich[1] recommends that those observing students should emphasize their strong points. Sometimes the good qualities about a student do not make an impact upon the teacher's or counselor's consciousness. Ah, but just let Emma try to pass a note to Gen in science class and the teacher will notice *that* immediately. The counselor who has had Rick referred half a dozen times by his teachers for being impudent, for skipping class, or for forging excuses for absences may find his view of the boy somewhat distorted. The counselor might easily begin to think "Rick is just a troublemaker; now that he's sixteen, maybe we should just let him drop out of school and give us all a little peace." Teachers and counselors who have a negative picture of their students are sometimes genuinely amazed to find that these students do possess good qualities. Looking for the good points when making observations does not imply that a student's weaknesses should be ignored or glossed over but rather that while the student's shortcomings are recorded, his strengths are also noted.

This raises the question of how many times an individual should

---

1. Clifford P. Froelich, and Kenneth B. Hoyt, *Guidance Testing and Other Student Appraisal Procedures for Teachers and Counselors.* (Chicago, Science Research Associates, Inc., 1959), p. 73.

be observed in order to be sure that a fair sampling of his behavior has been secured. An isolated incident may really be an example of atypical behavior. Such an anecdote presents a distorted, erroneous picture and should there be only one observation recorded during the school year, a faulty and prejudicial assessment of the student's behavior pattern emerges. Certainly, observations should never be limited to a single incident but should extend over a period of days or weeks, observing the student in a variety of settings and activities. Even if the teacher is limiting his observations of the student to his own classroom, opportunities still present themselves to see the individual under a variety of conditions. For example, the student's reaction in a testing situation or participation in a group, giving an oral report or sitting in an undirected reading period provides samples of different behaviors. Counselors should enlist the help of several teachers so that their observations of students will have as broad a base as possible, including, too, anecdotes of out-of-class activities.

Of course, final judgment as to the significance of the incidents (is this reaction typical of Abby's true behavior or is she just having a bad day?) and the amount of time available for doing the observations have significant effects. Unless the teacher or counselor feels he has secured sufficient samples to be truly representative, he should make no decisions as to the stability of the individual's behavior pattern.

Advantages of Observations

Before suggesting guidelines for making objective, accurate observations, it might be well to consider the benefits which good observations can yield.

Observing a student over a prolonged period of time should aid in determining the typical behavior pattern for that individual (at least in the settings observed); unusual reactions to specific events (an unannounced quiz, receiving his report card, going over results of a standardized test) could be noted as well as marked changes in behavior which might indicate possible problems. Observations collected over a period of time give a longitudinal view of the student's emotional growth; and, as Prescott noted in an early study, anecdotes lend support or discredit tentative hypotheses about a student already held by the teacher or counselor.[2]

Those who have used this technique agree that upon rereading their written anecdotal records, their own feelings toward the student were more clearly revealed. As one teacher remarked, "Frankly, it was unsettling; I saw that I really had a very negative attitude toward Carey. If anyone had accused me of 'having it in' for any of my students, I would have been furious, but the way I wrote up that incident, it showed that I was very prejudiced against him. No wonder he looks at me as if I pick on him. . . . I do."

By substituting reports of actual behavior instead of vague feelings about students, the counselor or teacher can recognize symptoms of frustration, unhappiness, rejection. Through perceptive analysis of observations, reasons for behavior may surface; and the teacher and counselor can then cooperatively determine a course of action to alleviate some of the pressure felt by these students. Such concern invariably results in greater empathy between teacher, counselor, and student which facilitates teaching and learning and the student's emotional growth.

Discussion of the anecdotes by the teacher or counselor could result in greater insight and self-understanding by the student.[3, 4] Furthermore, anecdotes provide useful and often significant information which cannot be gathered by any other technique and add another dimension to the objective data already available. Consciously striving to write objective and accurate observations, seeing the good as well as the not-so-good points about a student, enables teachers and counselors to develop a frame of reference, as Ruth Strang in one of the earliest discussions of this technique in-

2. Daniel A. Prescott, *The Child in the Educative Process* (New York, McGraw-Hill Book Company, Inc., 1957), p. 212.

3. Don C. Dinkmeyer and Charles E. Caldwell, *Developmental Counseling and Guidance: A Comprehensive School Approach* (New York, McGraw-Hill Book Company, Inc., 1970), p. 307.

4. Arthur E. Traxler and Robert D. North, *Techniques of Guidance* (New York, Harper and Row, Publishers, Inc., 1966), p. 133.

dicated, for judging significant behavior.[5] The counselor's or teacher's heightened awareness of his students' feelings and reactions in a variety of situations provides valuable mood cues to establishing an emotional climate in classroom or counseling session most conducive to learning and self-understanding.

PROCEDURES FOR WRITING ANECDOTAL RECORDS FROM OBSERVATIONS

Observations may be recorded informally on file cards or a specific form, such as that shown as Figure 17, can be used. Some teachers or counselors observe a few students each day; first at random, selecting names from a 3 x 5 or 4 x 6 file in which a card is kept for each student. After the cards have been selected, the counselor or teacher may decide in advance what situation will be observed or what trait will be evaluated; perhaps the student's cooperation in a group project or his reaction to the return of standardized test scores. Or the observer may simply watch the selected students with no specific behavior in mind and react to whatever attitude the student displays. Others prefer to record incidents which in their opinion offer insight into the students' behavior *whenever* they occur.

Regardless of the system used, the observation should contain the name and age of the student, date of the observation, length of time covered by the observation, description and setting in sufficient detail to give meaning to the incident recorded.

The observation should focus on one individual alone, recording what he did and said as accurately and objectively as possible. His reactions to those about him, if these are significant to understanding the incident and the attendant behavior, should also be included. The importance of concentrating upon the individual being observed and of conducting the observation from a good vantage point are stressed by Gibson and Higgins,[6] who warn that the observer cannot afford the handicaps of obstructed vision or wandering attention if he hopes to make an accurate record.

---

5. Ruth Strang, *The Role of the Teacher in Personnel Work* (New York, Teachers College, Columbia University, 1953), p. 331.

6. Gibson and Higgins, *Techniques of Guidance: An Approach to Pupil Analysis* (Chicago, Science Research Associates, 1966), p. 112.

ANECDOTAL RECORD FORM

Student's Name .... Age ...... Date..........

Length & Location of Observation ....

Name of Observer ....

Description of Observed Incident

Interpretation—Recommendations

Figure 17. Form for recording observations.

They also plead that the observation be strictly impartial, without bias, and that "data from observations . . . never be interpreted in isolation but should be integrated with all other information available for pupil analysis."[7] The observer must be extremely careful when describing facial expression, posture, and gestures not to evaluate or judge but rather to record objectively what occurred. Interpretation of the incident and recommendations for action, when appropriate, can be included but should be placed in a separate section and clearly marked as interpretative.

Weaving interpretations and judgment into the descriptive segment of anecdotal records affects and often distorts the facts as shown in the two anecdotes, both describing the same incident, shown as Figures 18 and 19.

7. Ibid., pp. 112-13.

ANECDOTAL RECORD

Student's Name	Tricia "X"	Date	10/12/7-
Age 13	Length of Observation		15 minutes
Name of Observer			

Description of Incident

Tricia came into the English class about five minutes after the bell had rung and dropped her books on her desk; two of them slipped to the floor. It took her a few minutes to get them back into order. Some of the class laughed when the books hit the floor. After picking them up, she stacked them in rows, over and over again at her desk. Each time it seemed to make more noise. When I told her to stop doing this, she said, "Yeah, O.K., you don't have to holler." A few minutes later, she put her head down on the desk. When I asked her to sit up, she said, "Ah, let me sleep. Your class is so boring, it would put anyone to sleep." Again there was some laughing. I told Tricia that she couldn't sleep in class, but I would give her a pass to go to the nurse's office for the rest of the period and that I would see her after class. She took her books and went to the nurse's office.

Interpretation

Tricia was making a bid for attention today, and she got it. I did not report her to the principal, but later in the nurse's office, I tried to talk to her. She would not discuss her behavior. I warned her that I would not allow any further activities of this kind; I don't know what caused her to act like this. She has never been any problem in class before; she may have been seeking attention or releasing some frustration which was already built up before she got to my class.

Figure 18. Sample of an anecdotal record, narrative.

ANECDOTAL RECORD

Student's Name	Tricia "X"	Date	10/12/7-
Age	13	Length of Observation	15 minutes

Description of Incident

Tricia came into the English class late as usual and deliberately dropped her books on her desk, another of her attention-getting tactics. They scattered and fell to the floor, disrupting the class. Students went off into gales of laughter. She wasted as much time as she could picking them up and getting into her seat. During class, she shuffled her books repeatedly and was very fidgety. I told her to stop and she made one of her smart remarks. Later she put her head down on the desk, which she knows is against the school rules, and I told her to sit up straight or to go to the nurse's office if she felt ill, though I knew she was faking. Again, she answered rudely and loudly. Naturally, I could not tolerate this kind of insolence, but after a few minutes, I gave her a note to go to the nurse's office.

Interpretation

Tricia needs discipline. If you don't stop her, she'll disrupt the class all period long.

Figure 19. Sample of an anecdotal record, narrative.

The first account attempts to give an almost factual presentation of what occurred with virtually no judgmental statements. Perhaps the words, "each time it seemed to make more noise," could be considered judgmental, yet it conveys to the reader the reason why the teacher felt it necessary to tell Tricia not to keep stacking the books over and over again. It would have been helpful if the teacher had added what she actually said to Tricia when she told her to stop; there are many ways of requesting someone to stop doing something. The tone of voice and the words can express concern, humor, irritation, or ridicule; and Tricia's response may have been a rebuttal to a sarcastic quip from the teacher. Granted, it is extremely difficult to remember one's exact words, but in the name of fairness and accuracy, comments made to Tricia may have had a marked effect on her subsequent answers and actions. The teacher's interpretation of the first recording of the incident implies a sympathetic attitude toward the student and the teacher's bewilderment as to what provoked the behavior.

Even a quick reading of the second version of the observation suggests the anger which the teacher apparently felt toward this student. The words, "as usual," "deliberately," and "another of her attention-getting tactics," placed in the first sentence clearly reveal the teacher's expectations of Tricia's behavior. Even the phrase "gales of laughter" is a loaded expression, conveying to the reader an excessive reaction to a trivial occurrence. Yet, precisely what is a "gale of laughter"? Did everyone burst into a loud guffaw, half the class giggle? Again the statement "wasted as much time as she could" is the teacher's evaluation that Tricia was purposely dallying. An expression such as "very fidgety" is certainly open to many interpretations; what would seem innocent activity typical of a particular age to one observer could be construed as malicious efforts to disrupt the entire class by another. In the interest of accuracy, Tricia's comment when she was told to stop rearranging the books should have been cited (as it was in the first writing of the observation) rather than consigning whatever was said to the vague category of "one of her smart remarks." In the following sentence, "later she put her head down on the desk, which she knows is against the school rules . . ." the teacher seems to imply a deliberate flaunting of authority by Tricia, and then adds the coup de grace with the phrase "though I knew she was faking" by striking down the possibility that Tricia might have truly been ill. Reading the anecdote further, Tricia's response to the teacher was made "very rudely and loudly," yet no specifics are included. It is perhaps the last line of this paragraph which reveals the teacher's own self-image, "naturally I could not tolerate this insolence." How eloquently these words tell us that this teacher's concern is for her position; any threat to her authority will not be countenanced. To this teacher, the possibility of mitigating circumstances seems unworthy of investigation.

Although many teachers favor the simple narrative shown in the two anecdotes to make a report of the observation, others use a timed approach, usually recording a fifteen- to twenty-minute segment, noting changes in behavior in that time period recounted in one- or two-minute intervals. A sample of such an observation is shown in Figure 20.

Mark had previously been an A student in geography, attentive and a strong contributor to the class discussions. The teacher had

TIMED OBSERVATION

Grade	10	Pupil	Mark
Teacher	Mr. Rafferty	Age	15 years 2 months
Class	Geography	Date	3/22/7-

Description of Observation

Time
1:00 Listens attentively to directions
1:02 Bends over, ties shoe
1:04 Sits up, listens to oral report on Greece by a student
1:06 Taps on desk with fingers
1:07 Chews on pencil
1:08 Puts head on desk, one leg is stretched out on chair, other leg on floor; arms stretched out on desk, head on desk
1:09 Talks to girl next to him
1:10 Raises hand, answers question with wrong answer about mountains of Greece
1:11 Tilts chair, sways slightly back and forth
1:12 Takes pencil from desk of girl next to him
1:13 Raises hand and gives totally unrelated answer to question
1:14 Looks around room
1:15 Covers eyes with hands
1:16 Stands up, goes to pencil sharpener and sharpens four pencils
1:20 Returns to desk and begins copying homework assignment

Interpretation

Mark seemed to find it difficult to concentrate today. It appeared that he had to force himself to listen and then, from the answers given, his attention still wandered. It did not appear that anything in class distracted him; perhaps something else is troubling him.

Figure 20. Sample of a timed anecdotal record.

become concerned that his interest seemed to be waning and wanted to verify this suspicion before discussing the situation with him. During the conference following the observations, Mark told the teacher that he had made the baseball team and was anxious to be out on the field practicing (the geography class was the last period of the day). This anecdote is a brief, yet descriptive, account of the behavior, with no judgmental or prejudicial phrases used in recording Mark's conduct. He acknowledged that he was "edgy" during class because of his desire to be out playing baseball and felt that the teacher had made an accurate evaluation. He was not upset that Mr. Rafferty had made the observation but rather seemed pleased by his concern. He "promised" to try to keep his attention on the topics discussed in the future.

Problems in Making Accurate Observations and Anecdotal Records

When will the counselor or teacher have time to do these observations? Obviously disruptive behavior forces itself upon the teacher's consciousness, but in order to secure a representative sampling of typical student behavior, other incidents must also be recorded. The teacher who wishes to make observations of all his students over a school year may find himself severely frustrated in his efforts. With an average secondary class load of 150+ students, the teacher who wishes to observe each student four or five times finds himself attempting 600 to 750 observations, a chore to daunt the hardiest spirit. The elementary teacher with fewer students may find it easier to schedule time for observing, but in the name of reality and sanity, it should be admitted that attempts to study every student may be doomed to failure. Counselors with 400 or more counselees readily accept the impossibility of observing each of their counselees. Nevertheless, studying a few students can prove of enormous benefit in developing teacher- or counselor-awareness and through careful planning, the needed opportunities can be found.

Even when time is set aside in which to make observations, usually only rough notes can be made at that moment. These must then be recopied into a more complete form. The interim period between the actual observation and the completed write-up may affect the accuracy of the recording. In the case of recording an unplanned incident, the counselor or teacher may be forced to "carry" the entire episode in his mind until such time as he is able to transfer his thoughts to paper. Several hours may elapse, and in those hours hundreds of additional student-teacher or student-counselor interactions will have occurred, further affecting the accuracy of the final memory of the observed incident.

Choosing the proper words to convey emotional tone surrounding the actual facts of the incident further complicates the task and lengthens the time needed to prepare accurate anecdotal records.

The counselor or teacher may also be affected (consciously or unconsciously) by such factors as the student's socioeconomic level; he may excuse some behavior if the student comes from a "good neighborhood" and condemn similar conduct from a student of lower socioeconomic level. The intelligent student's disruptive behavior may be written off as high spirits while a less able youngster's identical actions are recorded as malicious. I still remember as a new counselor the earnest advice of a colleague who cautioned, "Be sure to treat the kids from the Bellmonte area with special attention; remember, average income there is over $50,000."

Don't forget, too, that teachers and counselors rate students' behavior against their own set of values and frame of reference and experience. Middle-class teachers or counselors unaccustomed to obscenities and profanity in formal conversation (the school setting) who find a job in an innercity school may react with contempt and disgust (a poor application of nonverbal language) when they hear their students use such words. Other teachers, finding themselves in a more affluent setting than their incomes permit, may resent the spending money, trips taken during school time, and cars which their students accept as their "right." Some are too quick to condemn students whose personal appearance or behavior doesn't measure up to their own standards, forgetting that there isn't one standard to which everyone must conform.

The president of prestigious Haverford College during a recent sabbatical leave took a variety of jobs from ditchdigger to garbage collector encountering a "wealth" of life-styles and standards. He used his leave in this unorthodox way because he felt that "as a college president you begin to take yourself very seriously and think you have power you don't."[8] His perspectives were so broadened that when he returned to preside at a board meeting, he stated "when I looked at the other members of the board, I could not keep from feeling there was something unreal about them."[9] How often do our students think there is something unreal

8. *The Baltimore Sun,* June 14, 1973, Sec. B, p. 1.
9. Ibid., p. 1.

about their counselors and teachers, believing themselves all-powerful and all-knowing, and who would impose *their* standards on the students?

Since it is impossible to notice and record all circumstances and details causing any given act of behavior, each individual observer will focus on different points, those of special importance to him. Hence each observation is highly variable and open to misinterpretation and distortion unless observers consciously strive for objectivity in describing each occurrence. Also, few teachers and counselors have much training or experience in recording observations or in making them. Rarely is there another observer available to see the incident who could make his own record which would then be used for comparison. Teachers inexperienced in observational techniques might ask the counselor or a colleague to form an observational team for discussing and analyzing jointly viewed incidents. Two viewpoints may help each observer detect unconscious bias and sharpen the ability to convey the incident more accurately, as well as recognizing previously unnoticed distractions or obstructions. Even if another observer cannot be found, the counselor or teacher should reread anecdotes after some time has elapsed and consider whether greater objectivity, clarity, and conciseness could have been achieved. More accurate anecdotal records would yield greater understanding of the student and how his behavior has affected the teacher's or counselor's feelings toward him. Guides for coding student behavior have been developed which can facilitate teacher and counselor training in observational techniques, both the observation and recording phases. Gordon[10] suggests that once observations have been systematically categorized, inferences based on the coded behaviors will serve as hypotheses which can then be further tested by additional observations.

Ethics of Making Observations and Anecdotal Records

The student is usually unaware that his behavior is being recorded. Are such actions an invasion of his privacy? Is the counselor or teacher assuming the role of "big brother," all-seeing and

10. Ira J. Gordon, *Studying the Child in the School* (New York, John Wiley & Sons, Inc., 1966), pp. 67-70.

ever-watching? Should the student be told in advance that he will be observed? If so, will such knowledge affect his behavior? Should students be given the privilege of refusing to be observed? Should they have the right to see what has been written, particularly if this record is to be placed in a permanent file to be seen by other teachers and counselors rather than maintained in the teacher's or counselor's personal files? Should observations be destroyed after a certain designated period of time? Have teachers the right to share their observations with others–administrators, counselors, other teachers, parents–without the consent of the student?

Such considerations cannot be ignored. The highly subjective nature of this procedure provides fertile ground for unconscious bias and distortion to creep into the written anecdotes. The teacher or counselor may honestly endeavor to record an accurate picture of what he saw and what he believed the behavior meant, yet if others are to read such anecdotes, they must be fully aware of the possibilities of distortion, bias, or misinterpretation.

Usually teachers who write anecdotes for their personal use destroy them at the end of the school year. But those made for use by others, administrators and parents, may be filed in the student's permanent file and may never be removed through any systematic, periodic weeding-out process. I recall reviewing folders for incoming sophomores and coming across anecdotes describing one young man's talent at hair-pulling as a second grader; the anecdotes had remained in his permanent folder through eight years of elementary and junior high school! If counselors use anecdotes to understand their students better, such records should not become part of the individual's permanent record; they should be maintained in a separate confidential file and destroyed as soon as their usefulness is over. Persons permitted access to the permanent student files should not find such accounts when making a routine examination of the student's folder.

Dinkmeyer and Caldwell[11] encourage the discussion of anecdotal records with the students, feeling that the student will provide additional insight for the teacher or counselor into the record-

11. Dinkmeyer and Caldwell, *Developmental Counseling and Guidance: A Comprehensive School Approach,* p. 320.

ed behavior as they discuss the written account of a particular incident. The pupil may also gain some insight about himself from such reading, as he becomes aware of how his behavior is interpreted by others. Used in a positive manner and fully cognizant of the variety of errors which can occur, observations and anecdotal records can evidence sincere interest by the teacher and counselor to understand their students and counselees.

SUMMARY

By observing students and recording and interpreting the behavior seen, counselors and teachers direct their attention to the student as an individual. Information already on file is further supplemented and enriched by sampling real behavior in a variety of settings. The dynamics of group and individual behavior can thus be better understood. The subjectivity of the technique and the possibilities of errors in recording and interpreting the observed behaviors must be taken into account when assessing the effectiveness of the device.

FOR READER ANALYSIS—OBSERVATIONS

As you analyze these anecdotal records prepared by teachers or counselors observing in the classroom, look particularly for words and phrases in the section, "Description of Observed Incident," which you feel are judgmental or evaluative rather than descriptive. Is there sufficient background or detail for you as a reader who did not observe the incident to "see" what occurred? Is an actual segment of one individual's behavior described or rather the teacher's or counselor's impressions? Has the observer intruded his interpretation of what occurred into the description portion rather than reserve this for the interpretation section?

ANECDOTAL RECORD FORM

Student's Name _____ David _____ Age ___ 12 ___ Date ___ 12/7/7- ___

Length and Location of Observation Science Class, Middle School, 9:30-10:15 A.M.
Observer's Name _____ Miss Barbara Ellison ___ (teacher) _____

Description of Observed Incident

David was demonstrating an experiment of how a nail can be magnetized by using a dry cell battery and coils of wire. The experiment went well. I complimented him on his presentation and told him to put the equipment back in the cabinet. The rest of the class started discussing the experiment. I looked over to see why David wasn't back in his seat. David had the wires connected to the battery in the goldfish bowl and was trying to electrocute the fish.

"David, get those wires out of the water, putting electric wires in water, you're liable to get a shock."

"O.K., Miss Ellison," David said. He then took the wires out of the goldfish bowl and when I looked over at him again, he was throwing one of the goldfish on the floor.

"David, put that fish back in the bowl. What a cruel thing to do."

"I didn't think it was cruel, Miss Ellison," David said, "I thought it was funny."

"David, I'll see you after class."

"Yes, Miss Ellison," he said, and suddenly the whole bowl was on the floor, splashing water on several of the students.

Interpretation—Recommendations

David is a very intelligent boy. His parents are divorced. Once, when I asked him his parents' address, he said, "My father doesn't live with us any more. I don't think he likes us." The boy seems lonely; he is not accepted by the class and feels rejected. I think every time he has misbehaved, it has been an attention-getting device.

ANECDOTAL RECORD FORM

Student's Name _____ Ronnie _____ Age ___ 14 ___ Date ___ 11/29/7- _____

Length and Location of Observation ___ Geography class, Jr. High, 10:07-10:25

Observer's Name ___ Miss Nancy Yarborough ___ (counselor) _____

Description of Observed Incident

10:07 Came into room and sat down in his regular seat
10:08 Played with magic markers
10:09 Got out of his seat to look out the door; teacher said, "Ronnie, sit down." He did and opened his book.
10:10 Put his foot on the chair; marking his sneaker with the magic marker. When a girl laughed, he yelled out, "she's a hyena"; (looking at her) "you make me throw up."
10:12 Kept coloring sneaker, paying no attention to class work.
10:13 Put right sneaker on table, kept coloring it while other students read aloud.
10:16 Put markers away in his pocket. Stood up, took out his wallet, looked through it, put it away.
10:17 Had rubber band and paper wad. When teacher called his name aloud, he said, "I'm going to shoot it."
10:19 Examined paper wad, shot paper under table.
10:20 Teacher went down to him and showed him the place in the book where other students were reading silently.
10:21 Slumped down in chair.
10:24 Took out magic marker, started coloring other sneaker.

Interpretation—Recommendations

In geography, Ronnie is relatively isolated from the group. He sits at a front table, his back to the class. Ronnie did not do any work; he did not attempt to follow the reading. During the whole time, he amused himself.

ANECDOTAL RECORD FORM

Student's Name   Carol Hill*   Age   15   Date   2/17/7-

Length and Location of Observation   History class, Jr. High, 45 min.

Observer's Name   Mr. Jim Zimmerman   (counselor)

Description of Observed Incident

Carol Hill entered the room and took her seat immediately. She started to do the drill from the board when the teacher approached her and said in a harsh voice, "Hill, get rid of that gum." Carol disposed of her gum but she was visibly embarrassed. She did not speak to the teacher at all. During the drill, Carol was called on for an answer. She did not know the answer, though from where I was sitting, I could see she had something written out in front of her. The teacher passed her by and called on someone else. Carol was staring at something when the teacher called on her again. "Hill, you're the only person in the class not paying attention." Carol did not reply. She turned red and lowered her head. During a directed reading assignment, Carol was one of the first to finish, but she did not participate in the discussion. When the dismissal bell rang, Carol almost ran out of the room.

Interpretation—Recommendations

Carol does not seem to get along with her history teacher at all. She knew she was not to chew gum in class (school rule), but I think the teacher could have used a little more tact in telling her to remove her gum. The teacher also has a habit of calling most students by their first names, but he never calls Carol by her first name (she has mentioned this in counseling sessions). There seems to be a definite feeling of hostility between them. Upon inquiry, discovered that a week earlier Carol was really "put down" by the teacher in front of the whole class. It seems that the entire eighth grade was to attend a class dance the last two periods of the day. Carol's class happened to have history that period. Carol was to have stayed after one afternoon for chewing gum in class. Carol did not show up (I don't know why). The history teacher told everyone to get ready to go to the dance, except Carol. She spent her time sitting in an empty room. She seems to have been very hurt from that experience. She has become very quiet and unresponsive in class after this incident.

---

* Pseudonym.

ANECDOTAL RECORD FORM

Student's Name _____ Kim _____ Age __ 16 __ Date __ 9/24/7- __

Length and Locations of Observation _____ Math, Sr. High, 2:08-2:40 PM

Observer's Name _____ Mr. David Prescott _____ (teacher) _____

Description of Observed Incident

2:08   Sits down, taps desk and then taps person in front of her in order to get their attention and talk to them.
2:11   Told to clear desk; get out a pen; quiz papers handed out.
2:25   Finishes quiz; looks over paper and changes an answer.
2:27   While waiting for others, looks through handbag for something to clean glasses.
2:29   Instructed to hand quiz in and exchange papers.
2:37   Raises her hand to ask question but lowers it again and walks to my desk to ask about her paper, just returned by another student.
2:40   Class is now going over all the problems together when PA system announcement of results of Student Council elections; Kim clapped her hands on three of them.

Interpretation—Recommendations

Kim is usually very quiet in class. Today she seemed more relaxed and outgoing.

SUGGESTED READINGS

Fast, Julius: *Body Language.* New York, Evans, 1970.
    Written for the layman, this easy-to-understand book discusses the science of kinesics, makes important points about the way people use their bodies to communicate their feelings and needs.

Galloway, Charles M.: *Teaching Is Communicating—Nonverbal Language in the Classroom.* Bulletin 29. Washington, D.C., The Association for Student Teaching, 1970.
    This brief monograph describes the influence of nonverbal language, cues for interpreting nonverbal language and using it to improve communication between teachers, counselors, and students.

Gordon, Ira J.: *Studying the Child in the School.* New York, Wiley, 1966.
    Excellent discussion and illustrations of techniques for coding student behavior, assessing personality, and studying peer relationships. Presents some useful forms which counselors and teachers can adapt.

Hall, Edward T.: *Silent Language.* New York, Doubleday, 1959.
    Nonverbal communication viewed by an anthropologist. Below-the-surface meaning of some commonplace forms of behavior and the cultural dynamics of communication. Though more than a decade since its publication, there are still some very provocative ideas here.

TABLE I

GUIDE TO PRINCIPALS' AND SUPERVISORS' APPRAISAL

Performance Factors	Far Exceeds Job Requirements	Exceeds Job Requirements	Meets Job Requirements	Needs Some Improvement	Does Not Meet Minimum Requirements
Communication	Talks with God	Talks with the angels	Talks with himself	Argues with himself	Loses those arguments
Timeliness	Is faster than a speeding bullet	Is as fast as a speeding bullet	Not quite as fast as a speeding bullet	Would you believe a slow bullet?	Wounds self with gun while attempting to shoot gun

Reprinted with permission from Dean Kelly, "Guide to Principals' and Supervisors' Appraisal," *Phi Delta Kappan*, Vol. 5 (Jan., 1969), cover 4 (back).

TABLE II

Trait	0	1	2	3	4	5
Initiative						

TABLE III

Trait	Poor	*Below Average*	*Average*	*Above Average*	*Excellent*
Cooperation					

TABLE IV

Trait	*Seldom Works Even Under Pressure*	*Needs Constant Pressure*	*Needs Occasional Pressure*	*Prepares Assigned Work*	*Seeks Additional Work*
Industry					

the quality and "5" showing the highest degree attainable. A sample of this scale is shown in Table II.

A single- or multiple-word designation may also be used by the rater, as shown in Table III.

More complete descriptive phrases may also be used as shown in Table IV in an excerpt from the National Association of Secondary School Principals transcript form.[1]

Space should be provided after each rating should the evaluator wish to support or explain his choice, yet in my experience few forms have such a provision.

Often teachers and counselors use rating scales in reporting a student's progress to his parents. Besides the information about current academic standing, there is frequently a checklist on attitudes and qualities, including such categories as Motivation, Dependability, Concern for Others, Initiative, Concern for Property, Cooperation. Parents often consider the development of these

---

1. "National Association of Secondary School Principals Transcript Form," (Washington, D. C., National Education Association, n.d.).

qualities of great importance to the child's success in school and will show as much concern if Mike is judged lacking in cooperation in his government class as if he received a D in the course.

Yet in conversations with counselors and teachers and from personal experience with completing hundreds of rating scales, some dissatisfaction exists by those who use this device. Complaints that a checklist or rating scale can't really show a true picture of an individual is perhaps paramount among these; the reluctance to reduce a person to a few check marks on a piece of paper.

Most who use the rating scale do not suggest that it will give a complete picture of an individual but contend that such scales attempt to measure aspects of an individual's development which cannot be adequately measured by tests or other instruments. Completed rating scales can be used to assist students in recognizing areas of possible weakness. Teachers have reported that a discussion of the rating scale with students of superior ability whose grades had started to "slip" showed the student where improvement (in the opinion of the teacher) was needed. If given an opportunity to read and discuss their evaluations, students would have a chance to see how their teachers and counselors "see" them, thus using the scale to promote student self-awareness. A study of the ratings may indicate to a teacher areas causing academic and personal difficulties for the student. The counselor, too, by studying teacher ratings on students can be alerted to possible problems and could initiate counseling before the problems become crises. A frank discussion by teacher or counselor with the student can further clarify the reasons behind the ratings. The student may admit that he hasn't been too cooperative lately; he has withdrawn from class participation and shown no initiative. Realization on his part that the teacher and counselor are concerned with his behavior and its possibly damaging effects to him may provide the catalyst for self-examination and change. Unfortunately such conversations do not always occur. In fact, some students are unaware that such evaluations of their character and attitudes are made by teachers and counselors or that such ratings are kept as part of their permanent file.

ADVANTAGES OF RATING SCALES

Rating scales have the advantage of being simple and fast to complete. They require less training for the teacher- or counselor-rater and provide an opportunity to compare the student after he has been evaluated by a number of faculty members. After several ratings have been gathered on one student, the counselor may see a pattern developing indicating a need for counseling; both teachers and counselors should carefully note wide variations in ratings given by different teachers to the same student. This examination is facilitated if the ratings are done year after year on the same card or sheet, using a different color to show a change in the rater. As teachers rate their students, usually once a year, they have an opportunity to see how they have been evaluated by other faculty. Too wide a divergence in ratings between those previously recorded and the current ranking of the teacher or counselor should cause consideration of the reason for the change, particularly if the change is downward.

Jerry received top ratings from his English, social studies, and Spanish teachers, but he was ranked below average by Mr. Risler, his physical education teacher, and Mr. Essex, his science instructor, in every category on the rating scale. A conference between Jerry and the counselor revealed that Jerry's parents had gotten a divorce at the beginning of the school year and that Jerry blamed his father for walking out on the family. His feelings of frustration and unhappiness were expressed by antagonistic behavior toward both his male teachers but were not revealed clearly to the counselor until he saw the ratings on the personality evaluation submitted in the spring.

A teacher or counselor about to mark low ratings for a student who finds that everyone has marked him on the upper ranges should examine his own feelings toward that student. Is there any unconscious bias toward the pupil which the teacher or counselor has not recognized or had some recent altercation or misunderstanding between them resulted in negative feelings which are being reflected in lower rankings on the scale?

STEPS TO GOOD RATINGS

Strang[2] cautions that good observations are essential to valid ratings. She suggests the following steps to aid in accurate observation.

1. Limit the number of characteristics to be rated.
2. Describe the behavior to be rated as nearly as possible in the form in which the teacher will be likely to observe it.
3. Provide space in which explanations and illustrations may be made to support the rating.
4. Allow sufficient time for observing before the rating is made and insist that no rating be made if there is not an adequate basis for doing so.
5. Give clear directions for using the rating scale; offer instruction and practice in improving observations.
6. Arrange to have the rating scale filled out by different persons who will observe the student under different conditions.

Additional points essential to securing accurate ratings are:

1. *Clear definition of the trait to be evaluated must be provided each rater.* To achieve accurate observation and fairly evaluate an individual student on a specific quality, the rater must have a clear definition of the trait he is to observe. What exactly is "motivation" or "initiative"? Unless there is common agreement among the raters as to the meaning of each trait, the validity of the ratings will be affected.
2. *Opportunity to observe EACH trait must be provided.* The characteristic to be evaluated must be *readily observable.* This presents many problems when traits such as "integrity" are to be scored. Teachers and counselors must be very careful not to make judgments in these areas unless they have had sufficient opportunity to make an honest rating.
3. *Differences in degrees of the trait must be clearly understood by the raters.* Regardless of whether a numerical or verbal scale is used, the raters must agree on the meaning of each step of the scale. For example, on a scale ranging

---

2. Ruth Strang, *The Role of the Teacher in Personnel Work* (New York, Teachers College, Columbia University, 1953), p. 331.

from "0" to "5," "0" would imply the individual possessed none of the quality, but what is the difference between a 1 and a 2 rating, or between a 4 and a 5? If it is agreed that 3, the midpoint on the scale, is "average," the rater has some guideline, though he may begin to wonder what precisely is "average," when applied to "integrity," for instance. Even the descriptive single-word scale which uses a range of "poor" to "excellent" in five "word-steps" causes difficulties for raters unless they have fully discussed the shades of meaning and agreed upon the distinctions which separate each category.

Dissatisfactions with these two types of ratings (0 to 5 and "poor" to "excellent") resulted in the longer descriptive phrases found on graphic scales. Even these phrases must be thoroughly discussed with the raters so that possible misinterpretation can be avoided. In Table IV, the category "needs occasional pressure" in relation to the trait, industry, caused some raters to seek a definition of "occasional." Some insisted weekly "reminders" to students would be considered "occasional"; others contended monthly prodding; while some thought that on the few occasions where a student had not met his responsibilities, "occasional" pressure would be needed. Yet a rater who held to the stricter interpretation of the word, "occasional," would rate his students or counselees much lower on the scale than those who defined "occasional" with more latitude.

LIMITATIONS OF RATING SCALES

Errors can occur despite careful attention to the points already noted; chief among these are personal bias, logical error, central tendency, and the halo effect.

Personal bias may be unconscious on the part of the rater. Each teacher or counselor rating a student has different personal standards, a different frame of reference and background of experience which may intrude itself into the evaluation. Students and counselees may find themselves being "measured" against teacher and counselor expectations based on their attitudes toward societal class. Teachers and counselors may also have negative feelings toward some students as a result of academic failure, disruptive

behavior, or simply poor rapport between them. Feelings of prejudice and sex discrimination against students could find easy expression in low ratings. Certainly no counselor or teacher should
rate any student immediately after an unpleasant confrontation,
nor should the counselor or teacher permit himself to be unduly
influenced by a recent favorable encounter with a student. The
evaluation to be valid must be based on many observations. Sometimes raters will be biased favorably toward students from affluent
homes and will accordingly consistently rate them on the high
side of the scale on every item. Or, if the teacher or counselor
knows the rating is to be used for admission purposes for college
or for employment, he may "overrate" the student. Conversely,
teachers or counselors repressing hostility toward minority groups
or pupils of low socioeconomic backgrounds might reveal such
feelings in lower ratings for these students. Perhaps the only defense against such bias is an appeal to the integrity of counselors
and teachers, combined with a conscious effort whenever ratings
are done to be fair, honest, and objective.

Logical Error results when the rater does not have a clear concept and definition of the trait to be rated. As stated earlier, it is
essential that all evaluators agree upon the meaning of the trait to
be rated. Explanation of each trait found on the rating scale as
well as discussion of the descriptive phrases or numerical values
of the scales must be provided prior to the actual ratings. Such discussions could be a most valuable in-service activity for any
faculty.

The error of *central tendency* occurs when the rater seems to
"bunch" all his markings toward the center of the scale (on the 0
to 5 scale, all traits are marked around the 3). When questioned
about this, some reply, "well, most of us are really only average,
aren't we; so that's how I show it." Raters who use this approach
may do so because they do not feel secure enough to make a more
precise judgment, particularly if they believe they have insufficient
observations of the trait. Teachers working with 150 to 200 students and counselors responsible for 300 to 500 counselees could
honestly feel they lack enough evidence to make a sound judgment. Others say, "I hate to mark a kid low, but really, very few

of us are on the top of the ladder, either" as a defense for hugging the middle point on the rating scale. Some teachers do not approve of rating students and feel a middle-of-the-road ranking is the safest way to fulfill their responsibility without really committing themselves. Raters who complete the forms hurriedly find that a center-step response speeds the job immeasurably and eliminates the need for any lengthy consideration of each trait. The insecure rater may find the task of specifying a point on the scale so threatening that he sticks to the center to avoid any pressure which might result if he were asked to defend his choice on the extreme ends. There is no quick and easy cure for raters who hover at the center point. Discussions between counselors and teachers might prove helpful, though the inclination to adopt this pattern of rating may be indicative of a lack of understanding of students as individuals, personal insecurity, or rigidity in the rater's personality. None of these is easily overcome, but perhaps awareness that the problem exists may encourage the rater to reexamine his attitudes.

The *halo effect* is said to occur when the rater is so favorably or unfavorably impressed with one trait that his rating on that one characteristic influences his responses to all subsequent traits. Thus the teacher or counselor will rate Tom at the upper end of the scale for "integrity," "motivation," "initiative," "industry," "leadership," and "cooperation" because Tom has been one of the best class presidents of Grade 7. If the teacher or counselor thought a little more deeply, he might remember that Tom had received two "deficiency warnings" last term for failing to do his homework; that he never sought additional assignments or volunteered for projects; had carved his initials into several desks, yet his effectiveness as class president was so impressive the rater was "carried away" and consequently Tom's ratings improved across the board.

Ratings done by others can influence a rater. Listening to comments made by teacher-raters while they completed rating scales in the Guidance Office, such statements as "You know, I never thought Janice Amberman was anything but average, but as I look at these ratings from the sixth and seventh grades, all 'above average,' maybe I've been wrong." or "Phil Herrick has really been a pleasure in my course this year, yet do you see how his other teachers have rated him? I wonder if that boy has just been 'putting me on'?" were heard time and time again. One easy way to avoid the halo effect is to judge all students on one trait at a time; then cover the rating on the previous characteristics when rating the next trait. A clear understanding of the meaning of each trait and careful thought when evaluating each quality will also enable the rater to realize that the differences between traits logically preclude giving identical ratings throughout the scale.

These rater errors which admittedly could affect the reliability of the rating scale are not the only disadvantages surrounding the use of scales. Critics attack the very "heart" of the rating scale with the assertion that there is no evidence to support a theory of generalized traits, but rather that specific habits and attitudes are learned in specific situations. So, they contend, how can a counselor or teacher rate a student on "industry" when he might be industrious enough in science (his favorite subject) but lazy in history (which he loathes)? If valid personality traits cannot be adequately defined, how can they be measured? Thus the wrangle continues. It should warn the prospective user to avoid making a final decision about a student's competence or potential on this *one* piece of evidence.

SAMPLE RATING SCALES

The "Summary of Growth" form of the Falls Church, Virginia, Public Schools (Fig. 7, p. 42) is characteristic of the ratings scales used by school systems and kept as part of the student's permanent record. Although only the ratings for Grades 7 through 12 are shown here, identical information is duplicated on the reverse of the form (which is printed on hard card stock to insure permanence) for Grades 1 through 6. This form is forwarded from the elementary school to the high school and acts as a summary of the student's personal growth, as evaluated by several of his teachers, throughout his entire school career.

Teachers received assistance during in-service meetings in understanding the descriptive phrases of the scale. Some questioned the first step under Item 8, "Emotional Stability," feeling they did not have sufficient training to judge a student "hyperemotional." Both teachers and counselors felt the use of color coding for the different years (red, Gr. 7; green, Gr. 8; Blue, Gr. 9; orange, Gr. 10; brown, Gr. 11; and violet, Gr. 12) was very helpful in determining patterns of behavior. During the junior and senior high school years, teachers of several disciplines rated the students so that the ratings would be based on observations made in a variety of settings. The addition of the teacher's name (and subject for grades 7 through 12) was thought useful in understanding ratings, also aiding the counselor who could arrange consultations with specific teachers to discuss ratings.

Most of us fall easy victim to the rating scales found in Sunday supplements and popular magazines. By checking just a few items, we are assured our "real" attitudes will emerge on an amazing variety of issues ranging from "What's Your True Personality?" to "Are You Raising Your Kids Right?" or "Are You a Conservative or a Liberal?" Although the validity of these scales may be open to question, a well-constructed rating scale can be used profitably by an individual for self-analysis. The "Study Habits Checklist," Figure 21, is such a self-reporting device. Teachers and counselors might use this analysis form with students as a basis for a discussion of work habits and attitudes, or the student may use it exclusively for his own consideration. Although students will quickly realize they *should* be answering "Always" to the majority of the items, if the checklist is for their eyes alone or will be used in conversation with a sympathetic counselor or teacher, they might be honest in responding. If they see they are not following many of the procedures and discussion with teacher or counselor implies these procedures would make studying easier and/or more effective, they might make an effort to change their ways.

If there is good rapport with the teacher or counselor, the student may discuss his completed checklist freely. Perhaps the student doesn't see the necessity to "look over a chapter before reading it in detail," Item 8 of the Checklist. The advantages of this procedure could be explained to him, perhaps even demonstrating the procedures for skimming.

STUDY HABITS CHECKLIST

	Always	Sometimes	Never
1. Do you keep your assignments up to date?	......	......	......
2. Do you keep a written study schedule showing the time you plan to set aside each day for studying?	......	......	......
3. Do you divide your study time among the different subjects to be studied?	......	......	......
4. Do you study by yourself rather than with others?	......	......	......
5. Do you have a table or desk large enough to work on?	......	......	......
6. When you sit down to study, do you have the equipment and materials you need at hand?	......	......	......
7. When you sit down to study, do you get settled quickly?	......	......	......
8. Do you look over a chapter before reading it in detail?	......	......	......
9. Before reading an astignment in detail, do you make use of any of the clues in the book such as headings, heavy print, pictures, etc.?	......	......	......
10. Can you find the main ideas in what you read?	......	......	......
11. As you read, do you make notes?	......	......	......
12. Do you take notes in class?	......	......	......
13. Do you review class notes as soon as possible after class?	......	......	......
14. Do you distribute the study of a lengthy assignment over several study sessions?	......	......	......
15. Do you try to relate what you are learning in one subject to what you are learning in other subjects?	......	......	......
16. When you have questions about your work, do you talk them over with your teacher?	......	......	......
17. When studying material to be remembered, do you summarize it to yourself?	......	......	......
18. Do you make specific preparations for examinations?	......	......	......
19. In preparing for an exam, do you review the important facts and principles?	......	......	......
20. Do you set purposes and goals for yourself in your studies?	......	......	......

Figure 21. Sample rating scale. Study habits checklist.

Teachers, too, like to know "where they stand" and a rating scale could check their "acceptance quotient" with their class. Figure 22 could be used by students to report the teacher's strengths and weaknesses as they see them.

MY TEACHER

Pretend that you could have your teacher *change* in some way. Please mark the way you would like to have your teacher in this class act by checking the circle (o) on each line that *best tells how you would like him/her to be.*

	Much More Than Now	A Little More Than Now	The Same as Now	A Little Less Than Now	Much Less Than Now
1. Help with work	o	o	o	o	o
2. Make sure work is done	o	o	o	o	o
3. Make us work hard	o	o	o	o	o
4. Make us behave	o	o	o	o	o
5. Ask us to decide	o	o	o	o	o
6. Trust us on our own	o	o	o	o	o
7. Get angry	o	o	o	o	o
8. Act friendly	o	o	o	o	o
9. Show that he/she understands how we feel	o	o	o	o	o
10. Help us understand each other	o	o	o	o	o

Figure 22. Sample rating scale: My Teacher. From Robert Fox, Margaret B. Luszki, and Richard Schmuck, *Diagnosing Classroom Learning Environments* (Chicago, Science Research Associates, 1966), p. 14. (Reprinted by permission of the publisher.)

SUMMARY

The rating scale is a quick and convenient method for evaluating students' personal qualities. Whether a numerical or descriptive-phrase scale is used, the rater must be cautious to avoid allowing personal bias or the errors of central tendency, the halo effect, or logical error to affect his evaluations. Discussion of the ratings with teachers or counselors provide the student with another avenue for better understanding, greater awareness of how others see him, and may highlight areas of possible future difficulty.

FOR READER ANALYSIS—RATING SCALES

These rating scales were designed by teachers, counselors, and students. As you examine each one, look particularly at the terms used to express the differences between the steps. Are they differentiating and clearly understandable to the rater? Are the behaviors being rated clearly defined? Are they observable? What changes would you make to improve each rating scale?

STUDENT REPORT ON CLASSROOM TEACHING

Directions: Select the one descriptive phrase under each item which best describes your feelings about your teacher and circle the corresponding letter. Do NOT sign your name.

General Rating

1. How would you rate your teacher in general, all-around teaching ability?
   A. An outstanding and stimulating teacher
   B. A very good teacher
   C. A good teacher
   D. An adequate teacher
   E. A poor and inadequate teacher
2. How well does the teacher adapt the course to your level of understanding?
   A. Nearly always adjusts to my level
   B. Usually adjusts to my level
   C. Adjusts to my level more often than not
   D. Adjusts to my level about half of the time
   E. Seldom adjusts to my level
   F. Is lower than my level
3. What is the feeling between him and the students?
   A. One of the best in developing feelings of good will
   B. Better feeling than in most classes
   C. About average
   D. Not as good as in most classes
   E. One of the poorest in developing good feelings
4. How interesting (or stimulating) does he make the material?
   A. One of the most interesting teachers I have had
   B. Above average in creating interest
   C. Just about average
   D. Less interesting than most teachers
   E. Presentation is dull
5. How well does he seem to know the subject?
   A. Thorough and profound scholarship
   B. Knowledge broad and accurate
   C. Well-rounded knowledge of the subject
   D. Adequate knowledge in most areas

E. Inadequate knowledge
6. What kind of interest does he show in students and student opinions?
    A. Actively seeks student opinions and helps students arrive at satisfying solutions
    B. Permits students to express opinions and raise problems which are of concern to them
    C. Tolerates student opinions but has an attitude which discourages frankness and openness from students
    D. Displays little interest in student problems or opinions; hard to talk with
    E. Appears to be antagonistic to students and student problems
7. How efficient is he in the use of time?
    A. Classes show evidence of very efficient use of time
    B. He is above average in efficient use of class time
    C. This is about an average class in efficient use of time
    D. We have a feeling that we are often wasting time
    E. The teacher wastes much time and makes poor use of the rest
8. How clear are the goals in this class?
    A. I have known from the beginning what we were expected to get from the course and I can see the relation of what we are doing to these goals
    B. The goals are clear but sometimes it is hard to see now what we are doing contributes toward these goals
    C. The goals of the course are about as clear as in the average course
    D. I am beginning to see what our goals are but I was confused for a long time
    E. I don't know what we are supposed to achieve in this class
9. How clearly are responsibilities in this course defined?
    A. I always know what is expected of me
    B. I usually know what is expected of me
    C. I usually have a general idea of what is expected of me
    D. I often am in doubt about what is expected of me
    E. I seldom know what is expected of me
10. How clearly does he present his subject matter?
    A. Among the best of instructors in clarity of presentation
    B. Clearer than most instructors
    C. About average in clarity of presentation
    D. Less clear than most instructors
    E. Among the poorest of instructors in clarity of presentation
11. To what extent are practical applications to the course mentioned?
    A. Practical applications continually given
    B. Practical applications stressed
    C. Practical applications often mentioned
    D. Few practical applications given
    E. No practical applications given
12. Do you feel that you are able to get personal help in this course if you need it? I feel that, if necessary, I could
    A. Get a great deal of personal help from the instructor
    B. Get quite a bit of personal help

    C. Get a moderate amount of help
    D. Get a small amount of help
    E. Get no personal help from the instructor
13. Are the course grading policies fair?
    A. Unusually or exceptionally fair
    B. Fairer than most
    C. As fair as the average instructor's policies
    D. Unfair to some
    E. Unfair to many
    F. Don't know what they are
14. How are exams constructed?
    A. One of the best
    B. Better than most
    C. About average
    D. Not as good as most
    E. One of the poorest

XYZ JUNIOR HIGH SCHOOL

Mathematics Progress Report*

Date . . . .

Dear . . . .

The following report is to inform you of . . . . 's progress in mathematics at this time. If you wish to discuss this report personally, I will be glad to arrange a personal conference, or, if it is more convenient for you to talk by phone, please call at 123-4567.

The evaluations noted below are based on evidence available to me as I have been teaching and observing your child.

The scale I am using for rating is 5—excellent; 4—very good; 3—good;
           2—weak, needs improvement; 1—failing;
           0—inadequate basis for judgment

SOCIAL AND PERSONAL HABITS
—— directs his individual activities effectively
—— responds quickly and willingly to directions from teacher
—— is dependable
—— takes proper care of school property
—— practices good manners

WORK AND GENERAL STUDY HABITS
—— brings materials to class (paper, pencil, etc.)
—— uses time to good advantage
—— tries to improve work
—— prepares assignments and submits work on time
—— participates in class discussions

* Adapted from a rating scale supplied through the courtesy of Mr. William Beck, mathematics instructor, Baltimore County Public Schools, Maryland.

The ratings below of mathematical skills are based on what is expected of a student in this class in this school and in relation to what will be expected in the next course in this subject.

MATHEMATICAL SKILLS
—— an accuracy in the use of numbers
—— an understanding of mathematical terms and concepts
—— a facility in the use of numbers
—— achievement on tests
—— correctness of homework

SPECIFIC STRENGTHS

SPECIFIC WEAKNESSES

COMMENTS

> Respectfully yours,
> (Signature of mathematics teacher)

THE SELF-CONCEPT AS A LEARNER SCALE*

Name ....
Section ....
Date ....

Instructions: These statements are to help you describe yourself. Please answer them as if you were describing *yourself to yourself. Do not omit* any items. Read each statement carefully; then select one of the following answers; and next record the number that represents that particular answer in the blank space at the end of that statement.

Responses:	Completely True	Mostly True	Partly True and Partly False	Mostly False	Completely False
Number:	5	4	3	2	1

Remember, you are not trying to describe yourself as others see you, but *only as you see yourself.*

1. I am usually eager to go to class. ——
2. I never ask teachers to explain something again. ——
3. I try to change when I know I'm doing things wrong. ——
4. I wish I didn't give up as easily as I do. ——
5. I get my work done, but I don't overdo it. ——
6. I would rather do well than poorly in school. ——
7. Once in a while, I put off until tomorrow what I should do today. ——

* Courtesy of Dr. Jean D. Grambs, School of Education, University of Maryland, College Park, Maryland.

8. I become discouraged easily in school. ——
9. I give up easily in schoolwork. ——
10. I do things without being told several times. ——
11. I am satisfied to be just what I am. ——
12. I like school jobs which give me responsibility. ——
13. I like to start work on new things. ——
14. I cannot remember directions for doing things. ——
15. I do well when I work alone. ——
16. I am satisfied with my ability to speak before a class. ——
17. I am able to get my work done on time. ——
18. I have difficulty deciding what to study. ——
19. I sometimes use unfair means to do my schoolwork. ——
20. I do my share of schoolwork. ——
21. I give up if I don't understand something. ——
22. I try to be careful about my work. ——
23. I get tense when I'm called on in class. ——
24. I make mistakes because I don't listen. ——
25. I do things without thinking. ——
26. I have trouble deciding what is right. ——
27. I find it hard to remember things. ——
28. I think clearly about schoolwork. ——
29. I can't express my ideas in writing very well. ——
30. I can tell the difference between important and unimportant
things in a lesson. ——
31. I do poorly in tests and homework. ——
32. I change my mind a lot. ——
33. I feel good about my schoolwork. ——
34. I don't always understand what is going on in class. ——
35. I am as smart as I want to be. ——
36. I solve problems quite easily. ——
37. I can figure things out for myself. ——
38. Good grades come easily to me. ——
39. I know the answer before the rest of the class. ——
40. I can usually see the sense in others' suggestions. ——
41. I find it easy to get along with classmates. ——
42. I enjoy being part of the class without taking the lead. ——
43. I take an active part in group projects and activities. ——
44. I try to play fair with my classmates. ——
45. I try to understand the other fellow's point of view. ——
46. I am an important person to my classmates. ——
47. My classmates have no confidence in me. ——
48. I am not interested in what my classmates do. ——
49. I find it hard to talk with classmates. ——
50. I feel left out of things in class. ——

SUGGESTED READINGS

Bernard, Harold W.: *Psychology of Learning and Teaching.* New York, McGraw, 1965.

Explanation of the "guess-who" rating scales; how teachers and counselors can use this technique most effectively.

Bonney, Merl E.: *Personal-Social Evaluation Techniques.* Washington, D.C., The Center for Applied Research in Education, Inc., 1962.

Types of rating scales commonly used, values, purposes, limitations concisely presented; suggestions for construction and use of scales and cautions to be exercised by raters.

Brigham, John C., and Cook, Stuart W.: The influence of attitude on judgments of plausibility: A replication and extension. *Educational and Psychological Measurement, 30:*283-92, 1970.

Initial research of the 1950's indicating individuals' ratings of social statement are predictable with their own attitudes verified in this updated research that plausibility rating scales prove to be an effective method of direct attitude assessments of the raters.

Cronbach, Lee J.: *Educational Psychology.* New York, Har-Brace, 1963.

Discusses inconsistency between self-ratings and observed personality, useful to counselors and teachers in understanding students.

Dinkmeyer, Don C., and Caldwell, Charles: *Developmental Counseling and Guidance: A Comprehensive School Approach.* New York, McGraw, 1970.

Examines self-rating scales, also suggests items to include in rating scales.

Finn, R. N.: Effects of some variations in rating scales characteristics of the means and reliability of ratings. *Educational and Psychological Measurement, 32:*255-65, 1972.

Research determined that changing the number of levels on rating scales affected the reliability of the rating.

Thorndike, Robert L., and Hagen, Elizabeth: *Measurement and Evaluation in Psychology and Education.* New York, Wiley, 1961.

Extensive evaluation of uses and limitations of ratings, types of scales, difficulties in achieving accurate ratings, factors affecting raters' ability to rate accurately, types of errors, and techniques for improving rating effectiveness.

CHAPTER 8

TELL ME THE TRUTH—
FACT-FINDING CONFERENCES

> "Words, words, words
> I'm so sick of words
> I get words all day through
> First from him, now from you
> Is that all you blighters can do?"
> "Show Me!" from *My Fair Lady*[1]

WORDS COME SO EASILY to the faculty—students are bombarded with facts, advice, directions, and corrections, all expressed in words. Yet another use for the spoken word, one which teachers frequently fail to utilize, is conducting fact-finding conferences or interviews with their students. Counselors recognize the individual student conference as the heart of the counseling relationship; many counseling sessions are primarily fact-finding in nature.

PURPOSES OF FACT-FINDING STUDENT CONFERENCES

Although a thorough discussion of the many techniques of counseling is beyond the scope of this book, counselors and teachers might profitably reassess the way they conduct fact-finding conferences. Teachers may not even realize they conduct fact-finding interviews. But, if an after-school meeting with a student is to determine the reasons, the facts, behind the student's behavior then it deserves to be called a "fact-finding" conference.

Take the case of Carl, for instance. One fact is clear. He has been consistently late for homeroom for the past two weeks. In an after-school conference with his teacher, he explains that he now

---

1. Alan Jay Lerner and Frederick Loewe, *My Fair Lady,* "Show Me!," recorded for Columbia Records, No. OL 5090, 1956. Copyright © 1956 by Alan Jay Lerner and Frederick Loewe. Used by permission of Chappell & Co., Inc.

works 4 PM to midnight to augment the family income, as his dad has just been laid off at the automobile plant. This fact-finding interview *amplified known information and added new data,* while it gave the student a hearing, a fair chance to tell his "side" of the situation.

Counselors and teachers use the fact-finding interview not only *to get* information but also *to give information to students.* There are many questions of an educational, vocational, and personal nature that students feel free to ask in the privacy of a one-to-one session which they might be reluctant to voice in a class.

Becoming better acquainted with students through such conferences, teachers and counselors *understand the student's concept of himself as they provide him an opportunity to express his opinions and his feelings.* In a class of thirty-five or with a counselee load of 400, the teacher or counselor might easily fail to realize many important facts about their students and counselees. For example, Tim, who appears reticent during class discussions, is an excellent conversationalist in a more informal setting; and Gayle, who seems so outgoing, nervously chews her nails much of the time during classes. Signs of maturity and confidence or tension and unhappiness are easier to detect when the focus is on the single individual.

Personal conferences between a teacher or counselor and a student *can develop an atmosphere of mutual respect, a relationship which could result in motivating the student to solve problems* of personal adjustment, academic failure, or vocational choice, for such interaction by a faculty member with a student says "I care about you; you are important."

To establish such a relationship, however, requires much more than mere talking together. A poorly conducted interview can cause hostility and misunderstanding between teacher or counselor and student.

Read the following brief conversation between Jane and her algebra teacher. What was the teacher's purpose? Did she accomplish it? How about the student, did she tell her side of the story? Were the facts fully revealed? Was the situation solved to both parties' satisfaction?

Teacher: Jane, I called you in after school today to talk about your work in algebra. Well, Jane?

Jane: I'm not sure just what you mean, Mrs. Alexander.

Teacher: Jane, your work has been going down steadily for the past three weeks. Now, what's the matter?

Jane: I . . . I don't know.

Teacher: What do you mean you don't know? Don't you understand what we cover in class?

Jane: Yes, I guess I do.

Teacher: You guess you do? You do or you don't, Jane. Of course, you might understand better if you and Sandy weren't talking so much. You can't be listening if you are talking with her, now, can you?

Jane: No, Mrs. Alexander.

Teacher: And, of course, you would do better if you'd turn in your homework every day. Do you know that you haven't handed in your homework seven times so far this quarter? And you know what failing to do your homework will do to your grade, don't you?

Jane: Seven times? I know I missed a few times, but . . .

Teacher: You know that you have to do your homework if you are to really understand the class work, don't you, Jane?

Jane: Yes, Mrs. Alexander.

Teacher: Well, then, I think we've discussed what's troubling you in algebra, haven't we? I'm glad we've had this little talk. We understand each other now, don't we?

Jane: Yes, Mrs. Alexander.

This short sequence illustrates many of the faults of bad interviews; from not putting the student at ease to failing to accomplish the goal of the conference, discovering the cause of the poor academic performance.

Why did this interview go wrong? Perhaps the key reason was that at least one of the participants failed to assume the appropriate role in the conference. We all play many parts during the course of a day; most of us switch from one role to another with little difficulty. But there are times when we must consciously shift gears and remember who we are supposed to be; the fact-finding interview between teacher and student frequently proves to be one of these situations. It is not easy to throw off the mantle of authority, and some teachers find they are reprimanding the student (as Mrs. Alexander did) rather than listening to him or her during the conference. Counselors, too, may fall into the trap of telling students what they ought to do rather than allowing the student to work out his own solution to the problem.

In such a setting, the diffidence the student (whether age six or sixteen) feels before an adult, especially one who has considerable power over him (never forget who puts that final grade on the report grade or who writes the college and employment recommendations); a feeling of defensiveness if the student feels guilty; a natural desire to be seen in a favorable light; a reluctance to be scolded or nagged, combine to inhibit free and honest communication between the two parties.

GAMES WE ALL PLAY

Other blocks to effective communication are the verbal and nonverbal "games" in which we all occasionally indulge. Students, teachers, counselors, and parents revert to some of the ploys described in such popular books as *Games People Play*[2] and *I'm OK, You're OK*[3] whenever they feel their positions threatened. For instance, female students learn very quickly which male teachers are susceptible to a few appealing tears to extricate themselves from punishment for a late term paper or similar academic "crime" (they rarely waste tears on women teachers). Boys are just as fast to identify teachers who favor athletes or those who insist on good posture and respectful replies. All students "psych" out teachers, counselors, and even their parents with frightening acuity; the faculty (and parents) are not always so perceptive. Considering linguist Mario Pei's estimate that there are 700,000 distinct gestures used in human communication,[4] perhaps there is some excuse for poor "gamesmanship" by us all! Yet teachers and counselors and parents play games, too, and students are wise to them. For example, teachers who profess deep concern for their

---

2. Eric Berne, *Games People Play: The Psychology of Human Relationships* (New York, Grove Press, Inc., 1966).

3. Thomas A. Harris, *I'm OK, You're OK, A Practical Guide to Transactional Analysis* (New York, Harper and Row Publishers, Inc., 1970).

4. Joost Meerloo, *Unobtrusive Communication, Essays in Psycholinguistics* (Assen, The Netherlands, Van Gorcum, Ltd., 1964), p. 142.

students before parents and counselor, yet use ridicule and sarcasm in the classroom, don't fool their pupils. One of the sharpest
criticisms by disenchanted counselees against their counselors is
their verbal hypocrisy. "Sure," they say, "counselors listen *so* sym-
pathetically to everything we say; even give us the impression they
believe us, and then they go back to the teachers or our parents
and tell them everything we said." Some counselors play games
between parents and teachers by seeming to agree with each of
them in separate conferences while criticizing the absent teacher
or parent.

Although sometimes these games are consciously, even ma-
liciously, played by the participants, individuals may in certain
situations use a particular ploy as a defense, unaware they are em-
ploying such a strategy. In other cases, the truth might be too difficult for the student, counselor, teacher, or parent to hear, much
less accept, so he retreats behind nonverbal and verbal barricades.
Breaking down these barriers is not an easy job; sensitivity to the
individual's feelings (and your own) during the conference
through careful listening to what is said and noting any outward
manifestations of anxiety can reduce the threat which results in
such strategies.

GUIDELINES FOR CONDUCTING FACT-FINDING INTERVIEWS

The obvious injunction to speak to others with the same concern and courtesy you expect to receive is not sufficient to guarantee successful conferences. But it is important advice nevertheless.
The teacher or counselor talking with a student or his parent must
strive to make the student or parent feel at ease as the conversation begins; the conference is meant to be a dialogue not an in-
quisition.

Every counselor remembers during counseling training hearing
his professors stress the necessity for developing good rapport between himself and his counselees; without such an accepting relationship between them counselor effectiveness is negligible. Show
concern for the physical comfort of the student (don't you sit in
a comfortable swivel chair while he or she sits bolt upright in a
straight-backed chair). Be sure the light is not shining straight into

his/her eyes. And should tears pour forth during the session, always have a box of tissues quickly at hand. One counselee had so many "crying jags" in my office that when she finally graduated, she presented me with a replacement box of tissues.

Concern for details is the beginning step in building rapport. The physical environment affects the mood and reaction of the individuals in the setting. It was amazing to see how much more enthusiastic a group of counselors became about their offices when the rooms were repainted from a dull green to a soft, warm yellow. The students, too, remarked it seemed a more congenial place. Elementary counselors find that having stuffed animals and attractive pictures in the office give a child an opportunity to walk in and make some harmless comment about an animal or a doll or something "going on" in the picture to mask any feeling of tension or fear. Before the child realizes it, he is safely in the office; he and the counselor are talking about some very nonthreatening object, and if the counselor is patient, the youngster may relax sufficiently to talk about what is really bothering him.

Providing a nonthreatening physical environment for conferences is useful for building good rapport, but, unfortunately, teachers rarely have a brightly painted, curtained office, for talks with students. The setting for their conversations will usually be the same classroom in which the teaching takes place. But even this environment can be changed for best effect. The teacher doesn't have to stay behind the desk, does he, while talking to a student after school? That desk between the two might be too high a barrier for the student to bridge, and communication between them will consequently suffer. Creating an area in the back of the classroom by arranging bookcases and filing cabinets could provide space for conferences, even choosing two chairs at the back of the room, beyond immediate view, can improve conversation. A caution, however, if you are a male teacher talking with a female student, be wary of seclusion which might be misinterpreted as a deliberate attempt to get the student off in an isolated corner. Some adolescent girls have particularly fertile and romantic imaginations and your innocent conversation with Marybelle might be misconstrued by her as an indication of your "love." Should

Marybelle enlarge upon the situation to friends or family, you may find yourself faced with an accusation that would be difficult to disprove.

Alertness to nonverbal clues is also essential to success in conferences, regardless of where the meeting occurs.

Fred, a sophomore, dropped by Mr. Thornton's office in the gym and asked whether physical education was required for juniors.

"If it's not, I don't think I'll sign up for next year. It's nothing to do with you, Mr. Thornton; I think you're a great teacher, it's just, well, I could use the time on my other classes. My dad wants me to go to college, you see."

As Mr. Thornton watched Fred, he noticed that the boy was constantly twisting his fingers and hands as he spoke. Fred was short, not very husky, and Mr. Thornton had noted that he was often the subject of jokes by his classmates. In the course of the conversation, Fred said the boys in his gym class didn't like him, made fun of him, and he felt that students in other classes really didn't like him either. The two discussed the issue at length, but Mr. Thornton offered no solution, letting Fred do most of the talking. As Fred elaborated on his feelings of being rejected by his peers, his hand-twisting stopped. Having gotten his feelings out in the open to a sympathetic listener seemed to relieve his tension. The conference concluded with no definite decision about dropping the P.E. course next year, but Fred agreed to come back for another talk.

Often students come to a teacher or counselor ostensibly for some innocent bit of information while withholding the real problem troubling them. Sensitivity to signs of inner tension—clasping and unclasping the hands and arms, crossing legs, tensing of facial muscles, even tears—should alert the teacher or counselor that the topic being discussed may not be the issue of real concern. Recognizing the possibility that there may be other fears behind the words expressed and helping the student face the problems will occur only if the teacher or counselor is willing to accept the pupil's feelings without ridicule or laughter. If Mr. Thornton dismissed Fred's feelings of rejection by saying, "Oh, that's just a phase, Fred, you'll get over it," communication between the two would probably have ended there. Permitting Fred to express self-pity without pitying him was also the correct approach. Fred needs help in working out his own solution to his problem. Sympathy alone at this point will serve little purpose; recognition of Fred's strengths would be far more constructive. Regardless of the revelations, the counselor or teacher must remain unshockable and continually responsive and sensitive to what is said. A student's explanation that his poor classroom behavior is triggered by pressure from a homosexual buddy to try the gay world cannot be met by outrage from the teacher or counselor; the student already feels enough tension about the situation.

During a conference, let the student start the conversation where he wishes. At times it may be difficult to know whether apparent digressions are real explanations perhaps phrased badly because of uncertainty or guilt by the student or counselee, or if seemingly unrelated topics are more important than the topic the teacher or counselor expected to have discussed.

Most fact-finding conferences try to focus on a single issue, and in a twenty- or thirty-minute session, there may be several significant points to be noted for future meetings. Brief notes are useful memory aids. These should be maintained in strictest confidence and destroyed by the teacher or counselor when their usefulness is over. The student who has to repeat what was discussed at the last meeting might question the sincerity of the counselor or teacher who fails to remember what he has said (forgetting how many other conversations the teacher or counselor may have had in the interim).

Some interviewers tape record conferences; counselors, too, use this procedures but teachers, in my experience, rarely do so. Replaying the tape will pick up nuances missed in the initial conversation; emphasis missed at the initial hearing; the rising and falling inflection of the voice indicating hesitancy, repressed anger, insecurity, as well as providing a recall of the topics discussed. Should this procedure be adopted, the student or counselee must be advised that the conversation is being recorded and also what disposition will be made of the tape. Will the presence of a tape recorder inhibit conversation? Informal polling of 489 students and teachers indicated to me that those polled would not object to having conversations recorded, although none of them had ever experienced such a procedure. Some of these same students, when participating in a group-counseling role-playing demonstration admitted that the tape recorder made them rather self-conscious and careful of what they said. One student during the demonstration let out a "Goddamn" as part of his role but quickly said, "Heh!, I want that erased." Later 121 of these same individuals conducted some fact-finding conferences of their own. Those who taped their interviews reported reluctance by the respondents to having some of their views recorded and felt that many comments made "off-the-cuff" were significant to understanding the interview.

Verbal Pitfalls

Even if the setting is a pleasant one and a thoroughly "unflappable" counselor or teacher remains alert to nonverbal clues, there is no guarantee that all the facts will be forthcoming. There are several verbal traps which can ensnare teachers and counselors.

Abrupt comments, such as, "tell me, Joannie, why are you always causing trouble?" which may so intimidate the student that he or she retreats behind silence or one-word answers.

Pat expressions, like "I thought we needed to have a little chat," or "Would you like to tell me about it?" which are intended to open the conversation may seem trite and insincere to the student.

Overuse of "yes" and "no" questions which won't allow the student an opportunity to amplify or clarify his remarks. When a teacher or counselor resorts to these kinds of questions, he rarely learns much more than he knew before the conference began.

Miss Harrison was talking with all students who had received an academic warning (deficiency notice) for the first quarter. Gwen had received three: English, math, and science. The girl was new to Cross High and this was the first meeting Miss Harrison had with this counselee:

Miss H.: I called you down here Gwen to talk about your deficiencies.

(**Called you down** implies a scolding or a reprimand)

Gwen: I thought that might be the reason.

(Obvious answer, no new information gained)

Miss H.: You received three, you know.

Gwen: Yes.

Miss H.: One in English, math, and science.

Gwen: Yes.

(Repeating known information, but adding nothing new, making counselee ill at ease)

Miss H.: Gwen, why do you think you received them?

(Too abrupt)

Gwen: (remains silent)

Miss H.: Do you do your homework, Gwen?

Gwen: Yes.

Miss H.: Every day?

Gwen: Yes.

(First new information applicable to problem)

Miss H.: Yet you got three deficiencies.

Gwen: Yes.

(Regressing, no new information)

Miss H.: Do you pay attention in these classes?

Gwen: Yes.

(Applicable information)

Miss H.: And still you received three warnings?

Gwen: Yes.

(Regressing, nothing new)

Miss H.: Gwen, I know you aren't dumb. Your grades at Hillier Elementary were excellent; you know that.

Gwen: Well . . .

And it was at this point, after much wasted time and needless anxiety for Gwen, that the conference finally began to develop some of the reasons why Gwen was having academic problems. She was lonely; she had not made new friends as yet; she was afraid of the teachers; the classes were so large; changing classes every hour was confusing; she felt lost, rejected, and so she was withdrawing. Fortunately Miss Harrison had prepared for the conference by studying Gwen's record and was able to show confidence in her ability, although after far too many trivial questions. The more information the teacher or counselor has about the student, the easier it should be to facilitate the conference. But no conference can be successfully initiated without first establishing good rapport. If Miss Harrison had mentioned Gwen's record at her other school and expressed confidence in her ability at the outset, the conversation might not have been so daunting for Gwen. In defense of Miss Harrison, she probably had twenty or more such interviews scheduled for that day and for several following days, even weeks thereafter, until the whole procedure became a grim game of "20 Questions." In a rush to talk with each student, the counselor fell into the trap of *forcing the student to begin the conversation where the counselor wanted to focus,* another serious pitfall.

It is more effective and efficient (and comfortable) for the student or counselee if he is permitted to tell his story where he wishes to begin. Whether he starts with a short tirade against school in general, rules in particular, or those in a specific class in detail, the real issue, as defined by the student, will soon be identified. Then the teacher or counselor can help the student face the problem and determine his solution. Although the teacher or counselor may see the problem clearly, his telling the student what is wrong will not be acceptable to the student; each individual should work through to the solution on his own.

Talking too much is a universal failing of counselors and teachers during conferences. One learns a great deal with the mouth closed and the ears open. Good interviewers develop the ability to be good listeners. They also are willing to accept the student's viewpoint and feelings. This is not to say that the counselor or teacher should feel bound to *approve* or *agree* with everything that is said. The student who tells his teacher "there's nothing wrong with cheating, everyone does it. I know that others will be cheating during tests, so if I don't cheat, my grade will be lower than some kids who aren't as smart as I am but who *are* cheating" can't be expected to heartily endorse this sentiment. (He could tighten his test security, though.) Yet to judiciously reprove the student will not change his reasoning until he sees that cheating is not being rewarded by higher grades. The student suspected of smoking pot or using amphetamines or barbiturates, who comments, "Smoking grass is no more dangerous than booze. Doctors prescribe amphetamines and barbiturates; why, my mom even takes them" will hardly change his opinions if indignation is the only response the counselor makes. Accurate information about

the legal penalities concerning marijuana use, its possible psychological dependence, and the lethal effects of misuse of amphetamines and barbiturates might at least get the student to review his
attitudes.

Failing to use silence constructively greatly weakens the possibility of a successful conference. The student must have time to
react, mentally and emotionally, to what is said. If he is overwhelmed by an uninterrupted stream of words, the chance of any
inner response to the conversation is sharply diminished. Unfortunately those inexperienced in fact-finding interviews fail to realize that there must be time for thought between the points made,
the feelings revealed, or the conversation becomes a meaningless
dialogue, a "rap-session," with both parties talking and neither one
listening.

Poor timing of the questions creates another barrier to discovering facts in a conference. If a trusting relationship has been established, asking the question, "Eric, what's the *real* reason you cut
English on Tuesday?" might elicit a truthful answer. Introducing
this question too soon may result in stoney silence or a flip, useless
reply. No interview can be successful if the student is not honest,
cooperative, and responsive.

Additional Problems

One of the greatest limitations of fact-finding conferences is the
lack of time to schedule sessions. Thus, those whose problems are
most apparent to the teacher or counselor will be served while
those whose unhappiness or frustration is hidden, repressed, may
never receive the attention they need and deserve. Counselors
and teachers trying to see too many students in too few hours may
draw conclusions, erroneous ones, from a single, brief interview
or indicate to the student they understand the problems as stated
and stop the student from providing additional pertinent information. The quick generalization, the pat solution, come too easily
when all the facts are not in evidence. The counselor or teacher
cannot permit himself to listen only to those facts which bolster
his hypothesis or his bias. Those untrained in conference techniques may fail to see their own bias or they are unable to detect

the reasons behind a student's evasiveness or outright lying. Teachers more than counselors may not realize that their talking *at* students accomplishes little. Too often students condemn conferences with teachers and counselors as a waste of time, a monologue with advice. Despite these formidable problems, most counselors and teachers concur that time spent in talking with students, in providing an opportunity to hear their views and interpretation of the facts of a situation, is time well spent.

SUMMARY

The fact-finding conference provides a forum for honest exchange between the student and counselor or teacher. Building greater rapport and deeper student self-awareness through information acquired and amplified in these sessions are the primary advantages and overshadow the verbal pitfalls and difficulties arising from limited time, individuals untrained in interviewing techniques, and other problems cited in the chapter.

SUGGESTED READINGS

Benjamin, Alfred: *The Helping Interview*. Boston, H-M, 1969.
 Invaluable handbook; deals with internal and external factors surrounding the interview; questioning techniques; approaches for opening and closing interview; defenses and obstacles to free communication; techniques to facilitate communication.

Berne, Eric: *Games People Play: The Psychology of Human Relationships*. New York, Grove, 1966.
 Explores games as a form of social contact regulated by social sanctions; yet games must cease before real communication can begin; encourages self-searching by reader.

Communications, Bulletin of Kaiser Aluminum News, Vol. 23, No. 3, 1965.
 Words and pictures illustrate how much confusion results when verbal signs are misinterpreted. Highly informative and readable.

Dexter, Lewis A.: *Elite and Specialized Interviewing*. Evanston, Northwestern Pr, 1972.
 Stresses methodology of specialized interviewing; although focus is primarily on political interviewing, many types of cases are included.

Analysis. New York, Har-Row, 1970.

Harris, Thomas A.: *I'm OK, You're OK, A Practical Guide to Transactional*
 Distinguishes three elements in all people, and this communications system is applied to problems ranging from child reading to violence, prejudice, and student revolts.

Meerloo, Joost A.: *Unobtrusive Communications, Essays in Psycholinguistics*. Assen, The Netherlands, Van Gorcum Ltd., 1964.
Significant considerations of verbal and nonverbal communication; stimuli affecting communication; barriers to communication. Thought-provoking.
Richardson, Stephen A., Dohrenwend, Barbara S., and Klein, David: *Interviewing—Its Form and Function*. New York, Basic, 1965.
Focus on personality characteristics of interviewers, methods of training interviewers, effects of various question types on response quality and respondent participation.
Also see "Suggested Readings" in Chapter 6, "Observations."

CHAPTER **9**

GETTING IT ALL TOGETHER—
THE CASE CONFERENCE

T HE *case study* technique of gathering new data and updating known information about a student is used by counselors and teachers to gain additional insights and new perspectives about their pupils. Properly used, Allport believes ". . . it provides a framework within which the counselor can place all his observations gathered by other methods; it is his final affirmation of the individuality and uniqueness of every personality. It is a completely synthetic method, the only one that is spacious enough to embrace all assembled facts. . . ."[1]

When a student's behavior causes several of his teachers concern, group study of the problem is warranted. The *case conference* method provides joint consideration of a student's personal or academic problems by his counselor, teachers, parents, the administration, and specialists such as the school psychologist, nurse, and reading teacher. The group first analyzes the data which has been assembled and then moves from analysis to synthesis to diagnosis. A course of action or "treatment" is then determined to relieve the pressure or solve the problem.

CONDUCTING THE CASE CONFERENCE—COUNSELOR'S ROLE—ANTICIPATED OUTCOMES

Prior to the first meeting of all participants, the counselor reviews the student's permanent file to check biographical data, test results, academic record, interests, hobbies, extracurricular activities, notations about work experience, and plans for the future. Additional data secured prior to the conference is shared during

---

1. Gordon W. Allport, *Personality, A Psychological Interpretation* (New York, Henry Holt and Company, Inc., 1938), p. 390.

the meeting. For example, teachers who have kept anecdotal records on the student, noting his reactions in a variety of settings, may briefly summarize these for the benefit of those present. The student's current academic standing in each subject is supplied by each of his teachers. The psychologist discusses result of any tests recently administered to the student and the gist of any counseling sessions with him. Significant changes in the student's present physical condition are reported by the nurse. If the parents are not present, the counselor might comment on the student's neighborhood and home conditions as noted during a home visit as well as summarizing interviews held in school with the student and his parents. Although information from all these sources supplies clues to explain puzzling behavior, rarely does one single cause emerge. A combination of causes is more likely to be uncovered. Changes in the home (pending divorce, illness of a parent, a new baby), new responsibility for the student (additional home duties, too many extracurricular activities, a job), illnesses or accident to the student, change in peer relationships (first love or break-up with a steady) may have temporarily overwhelmed the student, causing erratic or disruptive behavior.

If too much material has been collected to be presented during the conference, the counselor may summarize the data in a format similar to Figure 23, distributing it at the conference, asking for additional comments by the participants at the outset of the meeting. Or he may suggest that the participants examine the materials personally before the conference. All such data gathered constitute a *case history* on the student.

At the beginning of the conference, the counselor usually restates the reason for the concentrated study of the individual student. One counselor opened a session by saying, "We're here today to see if we can help Rob O'Dwyer get through the eighth grade this year. He failed last year as some of you know, and he also failed in summer school. His mother called me and said the school isn't doing anything to help him. So, let's see what we can come up with."

At this point, the counselor usually asks each participant for his opinion of the student. Such comments may suggest causes for the

OUTLINE OF DATA FOR PRESENTATION AT A CASE CONFERENCE

1. Written statement of the purpose of the conference
2. Summary of data already on file
    biographical information
    health information
    academic record (grades, test scores, credits earned, summer school attendance, if any)
    record of absences and tardiness
    social behavior (past)
    summary of previous counseling sessions
3. New data
    record of interviews with students, specialists, parents, teachers
    observations of student by counselor, teachers, specialists
    new test results
    evaluation of present physical condition
    present academic progress
    present record of absences, tardiness
4. Statement by counselor as to possible reason for problem
5. Opinions of other conference participants as to possible reasons for problem
6. Recommendations (This section might not be prepared until several conference sessions had occurred.)

Figure 23. Outline for case conference.

failure or poor behavior, but sometimes the causes remain hidden. During this initial meeting, the participants may decide it is more profitable to outline a plan of action to alleviate the pressure or problem rather than continue to search for reasons behind the actions. Perhaps for the first time, the student and his problems receive the undivided attention of all his teachers and a variety of specialists, in a manner analogous to an emergency medical team working to save the patient.

In Rob's case, the counselor first called upon the reading specialist to report on the tutoring which she had been giving him. "Daisy, you tested Rob in reading, didn't you? What did you find?"

Reading Teacher: Well, in the first place, the test I gave Rob is not to test his capacity to comprehend but basically to see whether he can read the words from the book. He made simple errors. . . . He corrected himself . . . and that's a very hopeful sign in the kind of people I teach. On the fifth grade level he breaks down totally . . . basically he cannot function above the fourth grade level in reading. . . . This boy is really a character; he is the strongest "pull-to-the-left" person I've ever tutored. . . . He wants to go from right to left instead of from left to right. However he is showing some improvement. After I work with him, you will see great improvement. I see no reason why he can't improve. The kid is very, very diligent; absolutely, that kid is working every minute and when you get him back from me, he is going to be fatigued. . . .

As the counselor listens to the opinions and comments, he begins to "see" the student through the eyes of each participant. Sometimes he may wonder if the same student is being described, so varied are the reactions. For example, here are some actual comments from Rob's teachers.

Mathematics, Mrs. Wilston: Well, I think you should socially promote him; he is a disturbing influence in the class. . . . I've got him in the back of the room; he wants to do as he pleases. . . . He is really a disturbing influence and with a group that low to have a kid in the room who puts on a show or talks out when he feels like it or pulls some of the things Rob does, well, he steps out of line as far as an eighth grader is concerned. . . . I don't see how anyone can put up with him for a whole year. . . .

English and Social Studies, Mr. Vallon: I have no problem with him on discipline. The thing that bothers me more than anything is the decided lack of effort. He will sit there with his head down. This burns me. I don't mind if a kid is slow if he will try. . . . The class he's in and the level I'm teaching on, I think he ought to begin to catch something because all of these kids are losers; they're all slow. . . .

Industrial Arts, Mr. Albert: This year he's doing good work. . . . The whole class, and everyone knows, are way below the average level and all I have are D's and F's. I've C's for him. He is no discipline problem for me; he will do anything I ask him to do. He should be in the fifth period because they are not as slow as the sixth period. He hasn't turned in a notebook. I didn't get one from him last year. You can't push the issue too far if he's going to do partially what you ask him, so I'm going to let that slide by. So I have no complaints about him.

Physical Education, Mr. Allen: My observation of Rob is that he will get away with anything he possibly can get away with whenever possible. And as to whether he is forgetful or lazy, it is a toss-up; I'm really not sure what it is. But he gets in a rut partway through the year (you all know I had Rob last year), and starts to forget his uniform as he says or just doesn't bother to dress. Otherwise he isn't creating any disturbance in class. . . .

Although the *words* convey meaning, the *tone* in which the words quoted above were said had equally important significance. Hostility toward the student reveals itself in the "give and take" of a case conference. The alert counselor learns as much about the teachers' feelings toward the student as he learns about the student's difficulties. The counselor who listened to Rob's teachers remarked later, "How could a boy be expected to be cooperative and enthusiastic in the face of such negativism and antagonism?" The impact of a teacher's acceptance or rejection can profoundly affect the student's reactions and response.

As teachers discuss a student's behavior with their colleagues, they should become more aware of their own feelings and question their attitudes toward the student as well as developing greater understanding of the feelings of others who teach the student. As one teacher listened during a case conference, her five colleagues roundly condemned Andrea as impudent and unmotivated. She realized that the girl would have spent almost five hours every day with these teachers before arriving, the last period of the school day, at *her* class, truculent and angry, easily frustrated, inattentive, and quick to become disruptive. With five adults reiterating in words and actions their active dislike for Andrea, was it any wonder that Andrea became quite unlikeable?

Teacher's Responsibility in a Case Conference

The teacher's responsibility in a case conference should include an honest self-examination of his own motives in dealing with the student; some probing as to the extent of assistance he offered to the student (or was he quick to jump on the bandwagon to write-off the student as beyond redemption?). The teacher's role in a case conference cannot be a passive one, a listener-observer, who quickly defends the righteousness of his position, brandishing the grade book with its damning list of F's and stating categorically "the student is no trouble in MY class; I don't even know why I was asked to come to this meeting anyway," then lapsing into complete silence. If pressed by the counselor for additional information, such teachers will admit that the student *is* failing, but they note he is doing it quietly. And that's that. They recognize no obligation to seek either cause or solution to the student's problem. If he is failing, it is doubtlessly due to his own stubborn obstinancy; the teacher is blameless and unconcerned. Other teachers come to a conference unwilling to discuss their difficulties with the student, afraid that such an admission is an indication that they are poor teachers.

As the conference discloses symptoms and their interrelationships, what appears to be a simple case of laziness could be revealed as a far more serious situation stemming from nonschool causes, perhaps trouble in the home or with peers. The student no longer is a one-dimensional being, refusing to learn "X" amount of each subject, but a complex individual whose behavior is triggered by events outside the classroom, outside the school. Learning does not take place in a vacuum; students cannot leave their troubles on the doorstep and march into the classroom with minds totally free of worry or fear, able to concentrate on teacher-selected tasks.

LIMITATIONS OF THE CASE CONFERENCE

Recognition of the scope of the problem can be the beginning of a solution; acceptance of responsibility to participate in the solution is the next step. No pupil problem can be solved by the counselor, school psychologist, or the assistant principal or the parents; teachers must also become actively involved. As the issues are presented in the conference, the teacher may see that he has not fully understood the entire situation and may have been treating the student unfairly or too harshly. As the counselor sums up the findings resulting from the discussion, teachers and *all* present must be willing to cooperate in determining what steps should be taken to help the student and who should instigate each action. Procedures for follow-up must also be determined at this initial meeting, for one of the biggest criticisms of the case conference method is that after all the talking no solution is found.

Vickie was sixteen, "boy crazy," and had informed every one of her teachers that she hated school, wanted to drop out to get a job as a waitress where she would make big tips, but her mother insisted she stay in school and graduate. After a lengthy conference with her teachers, the counselor, the vice-principal for discipline, school nurse, psychologist, and Vickie's mother, no one could suggest any magic to make Vickie want to remain in school and begin to study. It was finally suggested that perhaps some individual counseling would help, and the counselor agreed to arrange a session immediately.

"You see," commented Mr. Iverson, Vickie's English teacher, as they left the conference, "after all that talk, I still don't know how to get Vickie to shut up long enough to teach her anything. I suppose Jenkins (the counselor) feels he has done all that he could to satisfy the mother. We've all sat around and wrung our hands and that will be the end of it. I doubt if we'll hear another word about Vickie unless she drops out of school."

"Well, I can assure you, I'm not sitting around until five o'clock again getting nowhere," added Mrs. Watson, the physical education teacher.

"I couldn't help but feel sorry for Vickie's mother though," commented Miss Marks, the typing teacher. "Vickie really has run her ragged. She looked as if she were at her wits' end."

Trying to find a time within the school day to arrange the conference when five or six teachers are free to meet is also a difficult task for the counselor. Asking teachers to remain after school poses many problems, too. Those who do not have coaching or club sponsorships often attend graduate classes or have personal obligations requiring their attention. Follow-up conferences may never take place simply because it is so difficult to schedule them to accommodate all interested parties. A little administrative assistance plus a great deal of administrative support for conducting such conferences can be of tremendous help in utilizing this technique successfully. Rarely is a problem about a student solved in a single conference. Any suggested course of action usually requires months before results are noticeable. After the initial session, some counselors see each teacher individually, reporting changes in the student's situation and getting the teacher's assessment of the student's in-class performance and behavior.

The enormous amounts of time required, from the initial session through the follow-up meetings, frequently prevent utilizing this technique for all who could profit from such concentrated study.

At the conclusion of the case conference, some action is expected. After a half-dozen or more educators and specialists have put their collective heads together to solve a problem, something had better happen! Yet participants may fail to realize that they do not have all the facts needed to make a decision. Some data is virtually impossible to obtain. Marital discord in the home, for instance, is difficult to confirm, yet it could certainly have a corrosive effect upon a student's mental health and in-school behavior. Too often opinions are accepted as facts. A description of a student's behavior by his teacher may be biased, inaccurate, or incomplete. Bad points are frequently overemphasized during a conference. Data concerning areas such as environmental factors or relationships with parents or siblings may be lacking, but their influence could be highly significant. It is difficult if not impossible to interview everyone who might be involved or concerned with the student, so important facts may be overlooked and judgments made on insufficient data. There is also a tendency to oversimplify the data, to generalize, to make the facts fit into a neat pattern.

Another frustrating aspect of the case conference method results when the problem revealed cannot be solved by the school.

B. J., a junior, had already been suspended three times in the current school year, and it was only November. He was insolent and rude to his teachers and his work in practically every class was at the near-failure point, although he was quite intelligent. At the conference with the counselor, his teachers, and the vice-principal for discipline, B. J.'s mother described his deteriorating relationship with his father. Her husband, she said, a Marine colonel, insisted on absolute and unquestioned obedience. The boy and his father were continually quarreling to the point that one night the boy, brandishing a butcher knife, had chased his father around the kitchen. There had been a growing estrangement as B. J. grew older and now there was practically no communication between them.

"The Colonel is worried that B. J. will get in with the wrong crowd and that's why he is so strict. I really think he is too hard on the boy, though. B. J. must be in by 11 on weekends when all other boys stay out later. He can't have a car even though he has a job and had saved up for a second-hand one. The Colonel really loves B. J., and he does so want him to go to college and do well."

B. J.'s teachers had commented that he seemed more difficult in classes where he had a male teacher; and in his government class, taught by an ex-naval commander, his behavior was the most disruptive. The counselor asked if the colonel would come to school to discuss the boy's problem but was told by B. J.'s mother, "The colonel feels the schools are too permissive today. He says he knows the right way to raise a boy and doesn't need any advice from outsiders."

This conference revealed the crux of the problem, yet the school was helpless to change the father's attitudes about raising a teenager. Unless the counselor and his teachers could reach B. J. and help him to develop strategies to understand and cope with his father, B. J.'s school problems could not be solved.

PARENT PARTICIPATION IN CASE CONFERENCES

Sometimes neither parent is willing to come to the school to discuss the student's problem. Facing a roomful of teachers and administrators is quite an ordeal. The bravest parent will feel apprehensive, defensive, and possibly just plain scared when "invited" to a case conference. Having summoned the courage to attend, the parent is further daunted when the counselor in his introductory remarks of "why we are here today" recounts all the troubles caused by Harry or Brenda. Dismay may turn to panic when the parent is asked for his thoughts on the reason for his child's unsatisfactory behavior. The parent may throw himself on the mercy of the "court," admitting he is a total failure as a parent and beg advice on what to do. Or he may insist the child is suffering from the "Jekyl and Hyde" syndrome, since he is a perfect delight at home, and demand to know what the school is doing to cause the frightening change of personality in his offspring.

In either case, little useful information can result. No blame should be leveled against the parent or his methods of child rearing, nor should the teachers or counselor feel threatened by the parent's questions. Each participant should feel "safe" enough to express his opinions and react to the comments of others; the counselor is responsible for facilitating this atmosphere; admittedly not an easy assignment in many conference situations.

STUDENT INVOLVEMENT IN CASE CONFERENCES

Surprisingly, the subject of the conference, the student, is frequently absent from the discussions. Usually the counselor or psychologist, through individual counseling sessions, determines the student's views of the problem which is then discussed during the conference. Too often when a student becomes an active participant in his own case conference, he finds himself in such a defensive position that his contribution amounts to little more than rebuttal to accusations from the faculty. Teachers are reluctant to express negative feelings or speculations before the student, and thus his presence may inhibit a full and free disclosure of significant information. Yet, without his viewpoint, how can a complete picture be developed? His participation can have tremendous value to him and to the others present. The student will see that the faculty is sincerely interested in helping him. He will also be able to explain the reasons for his behavior and his feelings about the issues discussed. Was Rob, mentioned earlier, really lazy and unwilling to try or was he so defeated and frustrated by his inability to read that he did not try, knowing he could not succeed? The teacher's and counselor's perception (as well as his parent's view) of the motives behind a student's behavior can be sharply revised after listening to the student's explanation. An atmosphere of mutual acceptance by all participants; a willingness to listen and to understand, and a commitment to arrive at a workable solution are basic assumptions to the success of any conference but are particularly crucial components in a discussion where the student is present.

Despite the limitations of the case conference already cited, most counselors and teachers feel the method is worthwhile. Not every problem can or will be solved. Yet identifying the parameters and scope of the problem may result in greater sensitivity by the faculty toward the student which may facilitate his developing coping mechanisms or in solving the problem successfully.

SUMMARY

The case conference method utilizes joint analysis and diagnosis of a student's academic or personal problems by his counselor, teachers, school specialists, parents, and the student himself. Although limitations of time and incompleteness of data upon which to make a decision must be recognized, those who have participated in such conferences feel that the benefits to the student, in greater self-understanding, and to the faculty, in deepening sensitivity to others, overshadow the disadvantages.

SUGGESTED READINGS

Frey, David H.: Group process teaching and the live case study approach. *Counselor Education and Supervision, 12 (No. 1)*:73-75, 1972.
Describes training for participants in case conferences with focus on difficulties inherent in developing data and hypotheses.

Lifton, Walter M.: *Groups: Facilitating Individual Growth and Societal Change*. New York, Wiley, 1972.
Valuable insights into the dynamics of the group and practical suggestions for conducting group sessions which the counselor responsible for case conferences could adapt.

Rothney, John W. M.: *Adaptive Counseling in Schools*. Englewood Cliffs, P-H, 1972.
Practical suggestions for counselor to use the case conference and the techniques of adaptive counseling. Examples of case study for practice analysis by teachers and counselors.

Willey, Roy DeVerl: *Guidance in the Elementary School*. New York, Har-Row, 1970.
Specific steps for conducting case study and conferences; examples of how curricular problems can be diagnosed through team effort of counselor and teachers. Applicable at both elementary and secondary levels.

Zelko, Harold P.: *Successful Conference and Discussion Techniques*. New York, McGraw, 1957.
A handbook for conducting effective discussions with focus on the role of the leader and participants.

CHAPTER 10

THE CHOOSING GAME–
SOCIOMETRIC DEVICES

T AKE A CLASSROOM full of unique individuals (students), add one adult authority figure (teacher or counselor), mix liberally and you set in motion a series of social interactions which will have a marked effect on each person present. Individual behavior changes when an individual becomes a member of a group. Sometimes the results are highly pleasant, as occurs when the tired businessman quaffs a few with his friends at the local bar before heading homeward, or stimulating, as happens when a quiet housewife gets excited as she participates in a "Great Books" discussion at the local library, or even frightening, when honest citizens form themselves into a senseless mob, looting and burning. The dynamics of a group cannot be ignored when counseling students who spend much of their school lives in group settings or in planning teaching strategies for those class groups.

Students will be reluctant to express opinions or even ask questions in a classroom atmosphere where ridicule or contempt is the reaction of their peers (or their teachers). As mentioned in previous chapters, a student who feels rejected by his classmates may feel so defeated and isolated that his academic progress (and social growth) can be adversely affected. It is often difficult to get an accurate picture of how students feel about each other in a class. Teachers' behaviors change from class to class as they react to different groups of students. Consciously or unconsciously, the teacher responds to how the group operates in working with them. Similarly, students quickly "psych out" their teachers to find what kind of behavior is acceptable and what will bring instant censure. Teachers admit to "keeping an eye" on particular students, recognizing that some exert a powerful influence over the behavior of their peers.

Counselors trying to help students develop a healthy self-concept must be aware of the degree of acceptance or rejection the counselee generates from his classmates and teachers. Sometimes teachers and counselors viewing the class through their adult eyes fail to realize that the student must feel secure with his peers, that teacher- or counselor-acceptance is not sufficient.

Mr. Markowitz called on Pam to put problem No. 5 from the Algebra II homework on the board. Pam had an A average in algebra and he felt she would have no difficulty with the problem, though it was tricky. He doubted most of the class had been able to solve it successfully. To his surprise, Pam said, "Gee, Mr. Markowitz, I, I'd rather not; I didn't get that one." There were a few smirks but no comments from the class. As Pam was leaving at the end of the period, he stopped and asked her if she really had not gotten the answer to the problem.

"Well, yes, I had it worked out alright, just the way you did it on the board, but the kids think I'm an egghead as it is. If I always get the answers, they'll never have anything to do with me. I'm sorry if I let you down, but . . ." and she walked away, looking very much alone.

Mr. Markowitz knew that all Pam's teachers liked her; felt she was very intelligent, stable, and cooperative, but he speculated how many of them mistakenly believed that she was happy and popular.

THE SOCIOMETRIC TEST AND THE SOCIOGRAM

Measuring the social atmosphere in a classroom can be attempted by means of a sociometric test which seeks to determine the degree of acceptance or rejection of students by their classmates. The "test" consists simply of either (1) a question asked by the teacher in which the student chooses students he would prefer to be with in a social or study activity, (2) students write the name of some other student in the class in response to a "guess-who?" question posed by the teacher (Who's the most cooperative boy in our class?), or (3) by asking students who they would like to be if they could be some other student in the room. The responses are then tabulated and graphically represented in a *sociogram*.

Examination of the sociogram will disclose those individuals most chosen, rejected, and the existence of cliques or sub-groups.

The question method is perhaps the simplest approach. For example, the teacher may tell the class that a field trip or a project requiring several students to work together is being planned. She asks each student to indicate those persons with whom he would like to sit on the bus or work with on the project. A variety of situations or activities can be used. Usually three choices are requested, but as many as five can be made. Kathleen Evans[1] and her associates cited Borgatta's criticism of requiring a specific number of choices because asking for a certain number might compel some students to make more than they would really make, and the fact that some might make no choices at all from the group would be obscured.

Questions can also be phrased in a negative way, such as, "List three students with whom you do not wish to work on this project." In my opinion, this procedure, which hopes to identify students needing help to gain some measure of social acceptance, appears to sanction or even encourage rejection of students by their peers.

Administering the sociometric test should be as informal as possible. The teacher explains the purpose of the activity or situation, asks students to indicate their choices in writing (making sure that the names of absent students are mentioned or written on the board), and advises students they are free to select anyone they wish. Students must be assured that their choices will remain confidential. They must also realize that it may not be possible for them to have their first choice when the activity groups are actually formed or the field trip occurs.

It is extremely important that students know each other well enough to have formed some group relationships. Two senior high teachers tried to use sociometric tests with their eleventh and twelfth grade vocational students. They were appalled to discover that these students, who had been in shorthand and/or retailing class for over four months (and perhaps had been together in the

---

1. Kathleen Marie Evans, London Routledge and K. Paul, *Sociometry and Education* (New York, Humanities Press, 1962), p. 13.

same high school for three years) did not know the names of each of their classmates. These students were a class; they were not a group. The teachers couldn't prepare a sociogram since the students were unable to give them three choices! They confessed to their students their inability to construct a sociogram; and in the discussion which followed, the students began to express their feelings of being in classes and knowing so few of their classmates—those of isolation and loneliness. The question put to the students had been to write the names of three persons with whom they would like to form a committee to proofread their transcribed letters (in the shorthand class) and to develop a skit on getting a job (in the retailing class), situations of interest to the students. The choice of the question, or the "criterion," is crucial to the success of the test. If the criterion is not considered a serious or important one, student responses may be adversely affected. Should the teacher pose such a question as, "If you were going to the moon, which three people would you want to have with you?," students might feel this was such a waste of time that they would give silly answers (boys choosing girls) or giving answers with no real thought behind them. It is essential that the teacher act on the responses received and design the committee or the seating arrangements in conformity with the students' expressed choices. Otherwise students feel that their choices had no meaning or that the teacher had another motive than the one stated.

Actually the teacher could have a secondary motive, one which is not shared with the students. Rearranging a class into compatible groups can make teaching more pleasant for the students, and also for the teacher. I have seen teachers randomly assign students to work together for group activities and the dismay reflected in some students' faces as they heard in which group they were being assigned was marked. Little productive work comes from a group in which antagonism or insecurity predominate. A more significant result of interpreting the sociogram than class harmony, however, is alerting the teacher and the counselor to those students who are not accepted by the group.

Terminology of the Sociogram

In interpreting a sociogram, certain terms are used to explain some of the group relationships, including:

stars: students who are highly chosen

isolate: a student who receives no choices

rejectee: a student who receives a majority of negative choices in response to a negative question

mutual choice: two students choose each other

clique: three or more students choose each other and very few other choices outside their own group

neglectee: a student who receives relatively few choices

cleavage: lack of choice between subgroups.

Don Dinkmeyer and Charles Caldwell[2] in their excellent book, *Developmental Counseling and Guidance, A Comprehensive School Approach,* add additional categories, such as *"fringers–*students who get a few second or third choices; *middlers–*who are in the middle or average range; and *lesser stars–*who are highly chosen but would not stand out as stars. Choices between boys and girls are *intersex choices."*

GRAPHING STUDENTS' CHOICES ON THE SOCIOGRAM

In Figure 24 the responses to the question, "Who would you like to work with on a special project?" are shown in the *matrix* or summary sheet of choices. Tabulating may be done by making an "X" or check mark in the appropriate blocks for the chooser and the chosen, or as shown in the illustration, using the letters A, B, C, to designate the first, second, and third choices. Where mutual choices occurred the teacher circled the letter, and where intersex choices occurred, a small 'x" was placed next to the A, B or C. Preparing a matrix can prove quite time-consuming, particularly if there are more than twenty students in the group. With classes of thirty or more, teachers sometimes tabulate the responses but do not prepare the sociogram.

Looking at the "Totals" figure at the bottom of the matrix, it is easy to see that the "stars" in this group are Francis and Annett with six choices each and Donald with five choices. George, Nancy, Kelly are lesser stars; and Paul, though making choices himself, was not chosen by any other student and would be considered by most users of the sociogram as an isolate. The teacher who tab-

2. D. Dinkmeyer and C. Caldwell, *Developmental Counseling and Guidance: A Comprehensive School Approach* (New York, McGraw-Hill, 1970), p. 343.

Chosen → / Chooser	David	Donald	Francis	Fredie	George	John	Paul	Annett	Carol	Kelly	Kimberly	Nancy	Renee	Tina	Torie
David			(B)	A						Cx					
Donald	A		(B)			C									
Francis	(A)	(B)			(C)										
Fredie			B		C	(A)									
George	B		(A)					Cx							
John				(A)	C			Bx							
Paul		A	C		B										
Annett		A	Ax							(B)		(C)			
Carol								A				B			C
Kelly								(A)			(C)	(B)			
Kimberly										(A)					
Nancy		Cx						(B)		(A)					
Renee		Bx							C					(A)	
Tino								A	B				(C)		
Torie											B	A		C	
1st: A's = 3	2	2	2	2		1		3		2		1		1	
2nd: B's = 2	1	2	3		1			2	1	1	1	2			
3rd: C's = 1		1	1		3	1		1	1	1	1	1	1	1	1
Total	3	5	6	2	4	2		6	2	4	2	4	1	2	1
Weighted Total	8	11	13	6	5	4	0	14	3	9	3	8	1	4	1

LEGEND: X — indicates intersex choice

CIRCLE AROUND LETTER — indicates mutual choice

Figure 24. Sample matrix for sociogram.

ulated these choices was surprised by the class reaction to Paul, for she personally had a good relationship with the boy and had not realized that the class had not accepted him. Using the choices expressed, the teacher arranged the work groups, placing Paul with Donald initially, and changing groups to give Paul an opportunity to work with more students. She noticed improvement, particularly in Paul's relationships with the class, but also with other students. Subsequent intervention and reassignment of group members focused on improving the relationships with those students she felt were fringers, Carol, Kimberly, Torie, and Renee, none of whom were the first choice of any other student.

However, the graphic representation of the choices in the form of a sociogram will demonstrate with the greatest clarity the relationships within the class. One type of sociogram, the "target," which uses four concentric circles, is shown as Figure 25.

In the innermost circle, I, are placed the names of pupils who received the most choices, more than would be received if the choices were evenly distributed among all the students. For instance, if three names were asked for, every student receiving more than three choices would have his name placed in the inner circles, with the student receiving the highest number of choices being placed in Circle I. In Circle II would be placed those receiving several choices, while in Circle III, those with few choices, and in the outer Circle, IV, those who received no choices would be placed.

The seventh graders whose choices are graphed in Figure 25 were asked to choose the student they would like to be. The teacher placed those students most often chosen in the inner circle while those chosen less often were placed farther from the center, and those not chosen at all were placed in Circle IV. Only two choices were requested; choices were plotted by using a solid line to indicate first choice and a broken line for second choice. Examining the circles shows that David (11), Chris (7), and Judy (2) are the students whom their peers would like to be if they could be someone else. Mike B. (8) and Roger (3) would be termed "true" isolates since they were not chosen by any students nor did they choose anyone. Reid (1) and Jerry (2), Circle IV, who had been absent on the day the sociometric test was administered, made their choices on the day of their return and chose each other, but no other student in the inner circle. Mutual choices were made by Mindy (1) and Leazette (3); Jody (5) and Marlene (6); Linda (12) and Susan (13); Morris (4) and Don (10).

Another method of preparing a sociogram is to place all the stu-

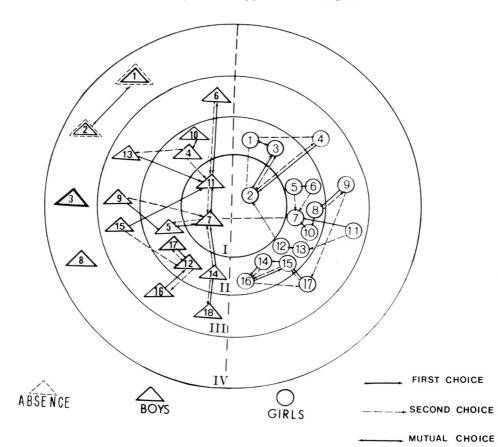

Figure 25. Target sociogram. Criterion question: Choose the person you would most like to be (in this class).

TRIANGLE—BOYS

1. Jerry	5. Karl	9. Mike K.	13. Tom	17. Tony
2. Reid	6. Alan	10. Don	14. Jeff B.	18. Ken
3. Roger	7. Chris	11. David	15. Dan	
4. Morris	8. Mike B.	12. Tim	16. Jeff C.	

CIRCLES—GIRLS

1. Mindy	5. Jody	9. Janice	13. Susan	17. Norma
2. Judy	6. Marlene	10. Robin	14. Dorothy	
3. Leazette	7. Karen	11. Pat	15. Georgia	
4. Jeanette	8. Debbie	12. Linda	16. Maureen	

dents' names on a large sheet of paper and indicate choices by means of connecting lines, as shown in Figure 26, where the first choice was shown by a broken line, second choice by a solid line, and intersex first choice by a dotted line. Circles, triangles, or squares can be used to differentiate sex; in Figure 26, boys' names (represented by a number to facilitate reading the sociogram) were written in squares and the girls were shown in circles. In this class of thirty-three, the teacher plotted only first and second choices since the question was "Which two students would you like to sit with on the bus when we go on our field trip next week?"

Examination of this sociogram shows that Tim (4) and Michelle (9) are stars; Lisa (1), Kathy (3) and Steven (6), lesser stars; mutual choices were made by Tim (4) and Larry (1), Ricky (7) and Lonnie (8), Sherry (16) and Denise (8), Karen (6) and Kim (2). Robert (14), George (13), Jerry (10), and Denny (9) are isolates as are Debbie (17), Pam (18), Yvonne (11), Elizabeth (13), Susan (10), Cindy (15), and Lois (5), totaling exactly one third of this class. Although making choices themselves, they were not chosen. The teacher had been concerned by the lack of social acceptance between students, but he admitted that he was shocked when he saw the completed sociogram. He placed as many of the isolates as possible with their choices and following the field trip administered another sociometric test to arrange work groups for class activities to provide additional opportunities for student interaction.

ARRANGING THE GROUPS

Once the choices have been tabulated, the teacher must act on the students' selections. Students have been told that they may not receive their first choices, so the teacher is free to use his best judgment in determining the most compatible groups. The isolate, chosen by no one, should be given his first choice. Mary Northway[3] feels that the isolate who has made his choice of members

---

3. Mary Northway, *A Primer of Sociometry* (Toronto, Canada, University of Toronto Press, 1967), p. 35.

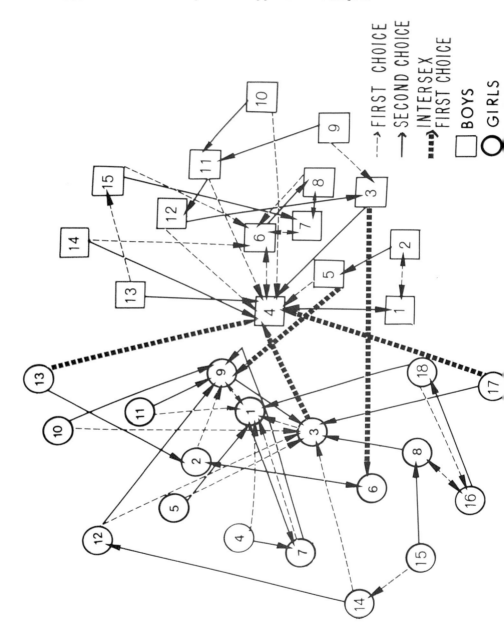

of the class should not be considered a true isolate but should instead be termed "unchosen."

Attempting to evaluate the importance of the choices makes interpreting the sociogram additionally complicated. If a student receives only one or two choices, he could be called a "neglectee." Yet if he had been chosen by "stars," then his selection would give him high status with the rest of the class. Weighing the choices, with three points given a first choice, two points for each second choice received, and one point for a third choice has been tried as a means of underscoring the importance of being chosen. The weighted totals resulting from such choices are shown as the bottom figures of the matrix in Figure 24. However, this additional computation adds further to the time needed to tabulate the choices before making the matrix or preparing the sociogram.

Some teachers who frequently use sociograms report that placing students with their mutual choices often "works out" better than placing with the first choice since these choices are an indication of social aspiration (the people I would like to be with) and not necessarily social fact (the people I actually associate with or who want to associate with me). Once the groups have been formed, the teacher can observe the interaction and note whether the less-accepted students are able to participate. Sometimes readjustment is needed.

Figure 26. Sociogram using connecting lines to plot choices. Criterion question: Which two students would you like to sit with on the bus when we go on our field trip next week?

SQUARES—BOYS

1. Larry	4. Tim	7. Ricky	10. Jerry	13. George
2. Arthur	5. Randy	8. Lonnie	11. Brian	14. Robert
3. Mike	6. Steven	9. Denny	12. Jeff	15. Bobby

CIRCLES—GIRLS

1. Lisa	5. Lois	9. Michelle	13. Elizabeth	17. Debbie
2. Kim	6. Karen	10. Susan	14. Tracy	18. Pam
3. Kathy	7. Brenda	11. Yvonne	15. Cindy	
4. Robin	8. Denise	12. Helen	16. Sherry	

USING THE SOCIOGRAM

Counselors should observe some of the group activities in the classroom to understand better the interaction between students and between students and teachers. Unless the counselor has actually seen how students react with each other, it will be impossible for him to discuss the student's lack of acceptance or the apparent reasons behind real rejection. The counselor should participate with the teacher in initially analyzing the sociogram and discussing possible reasons behind the group's behavior toward certain students. As the sociogram is studied, it must be remembered that the results represent students' choices for one given situation. Given another set of circumstances, a different criterion question, the choices might be very different. Teachers have commented that when students were doing a team project on which they were to be graded, they would usually choose "smart kids, the brains," but when they were going on a social outing, scholarship had little influence. The rapidity with which students switched their choices was further indication that the sociogram measured present interaction. Since the sociogram does not furnish any explanation for the pattern it reveals, be careful in making judgments about what the choices "mean." Neither teacher nor counselor can know with absolute certainty the real motive behind a student's choice. There is also danger of assuming because a student is a "star" he has leadership qualities or that the "neglectee" or "isolate" is maladjusted or withdrawn.

Additional Advantages

Teachers and counselors who use sociometric tests feel one of the greatest advantages lies in providing a means by which the teacher or counselor can check *his* evaluation of students and their group relationships against those expressed by the students themselves. Most teachers admitted they were surprised by the sociograms they graphed, primarily in their failure to notice some students rejected by the group or revealed as "isolates," "neglectees," or "fringers," but for the large majority of their students, their evaluations proved to be accurate. Many teachers also admitted that they would never have thought of the personal combinations revealed by the choices and were somewhat anxious about the possible success of the group arrangements for class work but happily were often surprised with the results. Admittedly, the results were not happy 100 percent of the time. When changes were made because students were unable to work well with their choices, however, the students acknowledged the fairness of the teacher in making the necessary reassignments. One class of middle school social studies students admitted that being on a team project with their friends was just too tempting; "we fooled around instead of getting our work done." Some teachers reported that where the work-activity groups worked successfully, student achievement improved in certain individual instances as well as providing a more relaxed classroom atmosphere.

Statistical studies by Northway[4] indicated that the sociogram has shown relatively high coefficients for validity and reliability, that the sociogram does measure degree of social preference in a group, and that a consistency in choices (for similar types of activities) is maintained over long periods.

Limitations

The sociometric test is certainly a very easy one for the student to take and for the counselor or teacher to administer. It may take a great deal of time, however, to tabulate the choices, draw the sociogram, interpret the choices, and act upon the selections given, especially if the class exceeds twenty and more then two choices are plotted. Since one sociogram represents the choices for only one situation, other sociograms will be needed for varying activities.

Critics of this technique attack the vagueness of the categories for describing the relationships. How many choices, for instance, would distinguish a student as a "star" or a "lesser star"? Would it be the highest number for the group to qualify as a "star" or should the teacher or counselor have a predetermined number in mind? How many choices constitute "few" as in the definition of a "neglectee" and "fringer"?

After interpreting the sociogram and discovering some students

---

4. Northway, *A Primer of Sociometry*, pp. 21-25.

are not accepted by their peers, teachers and counselors often find it difficult to know how to help the student gain greater social acceptance since the reason is not known for the students' choices.

ROLE-PLAYING—SOCIODRAMA AND PSYCHODRAMA

The sociogram provides a pictorial representation of students' acceptance or rejection of each other in the social world of the classroom. Role-playing in the form of sociodrama and psychodrama provides students an opportunity to express their feelings or their interpretation of the feelings of their peers, parents, or teachers in a given social situation.

Definitions

In a spontaneous, unrehearsed (although not unstructured) improvisation of a problem or situation in human relations performed before a group (usually), role-playing "empowers" the participating players to assume the behavior patterns of another person. As a simulated problem is presented, the factors involved reveal themselves more clearly, and following the improvisation, discussion by the entire group analyzes the variables which operated in the drama. As the discussion proceeds, the players become aware of their motivation in responding as they did and develop a better understanding of why other individuals behave as they do.

The difference between psychodrama and sociodrama is well stated by Bennett who says "the educational psychodrama concerns itself with the *individual* involvement of a person with other people . . . whereas the sociodrama deals with problems lodged in a societal situation. Apart from these content differences, the two forms are similar in techniques, goals, and underlying philosophy."[5] She added the word "educational" before the term "psychodrama" to distinguish the form used in schools from the therapeutic psychodrama used by psychiatrists or other clinicians with individuals who have serious emotional problems.[6] When the individual student assumes a role in which he would reenact a situa-

---

5. Margaret E. Bennett, *Guidance and Counseling in Groups* (New York, McGraw-Hill Book Company, Inc., 1963), p. 116.
6. Ibid., p. 116.

tion having real emotional significance for himself (a student recently sent to the principal's office for skipping class selected to play the role of such a student), he would be taking part in a psychodrama.

Concern has been expressed by Cox and Herr[7] that this type of role-playing can probe too intensely into personal feelings of the player-participant and should be attempted only if a skilled and experienced therapist is available. There is also the danger of exploiting the counselee who, once "on stage" (even it be an imaginary one), finds he is revealing more of his emotions than he intended and might feel "stripped" before his peers, teacher, and counselor, with no place to hide. Once the improvisation is completed, he may be further embarrassed, if not more seriously affected, by his peers' analysis of his behavior and the motivations behind his actions. Despite this, he must continue to live with his fellow students and the faculty in the day-to-day relationships of school life, and "it just might be a bit uncomfortable walking the halls in this emotionally naked state."[8]

However, the counselor or classroom teacher, says Chesler and Fox,[9] need not be a psychologist to use role-playing at the instructional and interpersonal levels. Improvisations focusing on the typical roles, problems, or situations that students may ordinarily be expected to face when explored through the role-playing techniques are called *sociodramas*. Topics such as destruction of school property, smoking, stealing, and race relations are good subjects for sociodramas. Relationships between students (students who are dominant or aggressive toward their peers); relationships between students and their teachers (students who cheat, who disrupt class), counselors, and parents (questions of trouble with teachers or the fairness of a grade) also lend themselves well to the sociodrama approach.

---

7. Robert F. Cox and Edwin Herr, *Group Techniques in Guidance* (Harrisburg, Commonwealth of Pennsylvania, Department of Public Instruction, Bureau of Guidance Services, 1968), p. 57.

8. Ibid., p. 58.

9. Mark Chesler and Robert Fox, *Role-Playing Methods in the Classroom* (Chicago, Science Research Associates, Inc., 1966), p. 15.

The Parts We Play

One of the most common causes of conflict between the youth and the adult is misinterpretation of the other's motives and behavior. Misunderstanding the cultural mores of another generation or subculture can lead to misinterpreting words, gestures, and meaning. The teacher who comes into the room to find two boys shoving, pushing, "horsing around," may read their actions as aggressiveness; yet, they may have been indulging in some friendly teasing, nothing more. When the teacher tells them to "stop that fighting this instant," they may be puzzled by such an obvious (to them) misinterpreting of the actual facts. Such students may feel the teacher is prejudiced against them, failing to realize that the teacher's perception of what he saw was inaccurate.

There is a tremendous gap between being told how to act or react and behaving in the appropriate way when the circumstances actually occur. One has only to remember all the great verbal advice received when learning to drive or beginning to play golf, all seemingly to no avail, until sufficient practice developed the skill and confidence to know how to act. As students mature, they must accept new roles and responsibilities. Acquiring these new behaviors may cause feelings of insecurity and inadequacy. The school presents countless opportunities for interaction among individuals with a variety of roles.

Failure to respond properly to an individual's role can mean embarrassment, punishment, even pain, for the student who has miscalculated or misread the "signs." Students expect teachers to behave in certain ways. If the teacher's behavior is inconsistent, the student is confused as to his own role and responses. One day the teacher is "sunny Jim"; tomorrow, he may be "big Chief Thunder Cloud." One day jokes from students seem to be enjoyed, even encouraged; the next day, whispered comments mean a trip to the office. The contradictory behavior of the counselor who yesterday was a sympathetic listener but today tells the counselee to "learn how to get along with your teachers and stop imagining they've got it 'in' for you," causes students to hesitate before returning for future assistance.

Just as students have their expectations of teachers, counselors, and principals, the faculty and administration have definite ideas of the behavior they expect from the students. Although many teachers are very explicit, leaving no doubt in the minds of their students as to how they are to behave, the counselor may be more of an enigma to the students. "He says he's my friend," wonders the student, "but how can he be my friend when he is also a friend of my parents and teachers (and heaven knows parents and teachers are not always friendly)?" Because students are uncertain about the role of the counselor, they may be reluctant to seek out his services. Students frequently become frustrated and puzzled about their parents' expectations (which makes them just about even with their patents, who become hopelessly bewildered at times about their children). Many times my high school counselees would drop by the Guidance Office asking for some simple magic formula for getting along with their parents, with comments like this one, "One day dad says 'son, you're practically a man; you've got to begin thinking about your future' and the next day he takes my privileges away for a week because my stereo was too loud . . . treating me like a little kid; honestly I don't know what he wants of me."

Role-playing can facilitate analyzing behavior by enabling individuals to observe what is said and done in a given situation through the simulated improvisation. This may seem a far cry from the days when you played pirate or cowboys and Indians, or doctor and nurse, but the premise is basically the same: allowing individuals to project themselves into another's role. When you were five, it was fun; at twenty-five, it may be part of a highly sophisticated training program you must complete to satisfy professional or occupational requirements. Manufacturers, retailers, insurance companies, and others in business and industry have found role-playing very efficient for training their sales staffs; the military fight small-scale bloodless battles in war "games"; law schools conduct mock trials, all designed to provide realism not possible through any other technique as they study the effect of interaction among individuals.

The participant in role-playing, as Dinkmeyer and Caldwell[10] remind us, brings to the occasion

> . . . his own personality, values, concepts (or misconcepts), repressions, and learned patterns of response. . . . Moreover, he usually practices these with fewer inhibitions than in his normal behavior, since in the *role* he is not being himself (he believes), but someone else. He will not feel responsible for the acts of the player once the action is at an end. His habitual cover-ups tend to fall away, and his true feelings and emotions begin to emerge. Thus role-playing becomes both a way of being and understanding someone else, and at the same time of being and understanding oneself in a hypothetical social situation.

Uses of Role-playing

The classroom is not a courtroom, battlefield, or salesroom (though at times all three descriptions might be apt as the teacher pleads, fights, and pushes to get the material across to the students), so where would role-playing "fit in" with the curriculum which must be taught? How can the counselor utilize role-playing when he is thought of primarily as an exponent of a one-to-one technique?

A teacher experiencing difficulty with group behavior in one class or finding some minority children not accepted by the other students, for example, may feel that role-playing is a more effective way to explore these problems than "preaching" to students on how they should behave. In the regular curriculum, too, there are numerous opportunities for making teaching more effective by using the role-playing approach. Teaching English and social studies, for instance, should help students understand and appreciate such qualities as compassion, integrity, and courage. Role-playing can project students into such roles as the nineteenth century citizen facing the Fugitive Slave Law or the twentieth century mother facing busing, or trying to disentangle the tortured thoughts of Hamlet by placing the student in a "what would you do if you were so-and-so" position. Such involvement requires emotional as well as intellectual commitment; real learning de-

---

10. D. Dinkmeyer and C. Caldwell, *Developmental Counseling and Guidance: A Comprehensive School Approach,* p. 432.

mands both. Students will see that the problems of twentieth century man–injustice, war, discrimination, famine, disease–existed for countless others before him, and they can examine the decisions used in those times against the needs of their generation today. The classics can be revitalized as students examine morality, freedom, and responsibility from a "You Are There" point of view. Education will then transcend mere memorization of facts and become a study of the philosophies, values, and attitudes of the past and present so the student can develop his own code for today's world.

Certainly the counselor is the key person to assist teachers in conducting role-playing which deals with interpersonal relationships. Situations where group guidance is appropriate, such as a class's rejection of some students in the group or aggressive behavior by some members of the class toward others, could profit from counselor intervention. Sometimes the teacher might feel too close to the situation to want to initiate the role-playing, as in the case of a class whose disruptive behavior is "driving her up the walls."

Preparing for Role-playing

Careful planning is essential for successful role-playing. The problem must be selected, the actors chosen, and the audience-observers instructed as to their responsibilities. Whether the teacher or counselor is concerned with solving a problem in interpersonal relationships in the classroom or discussing behavior or values evolved from the curriculum, the students must clearly perceive the purpose for the improvisation and be willing to participate in the role-playing. The issue chosen must be specific, not too complex, and one that can be "solved" by the group. Students must also understand that the dramatization itself is not the important aspect, but rather the discussion and analysis of the behaviors presented which *follows* the role-playing episode. Participants should either be volunteers or chosen by the teacher or counselor, taking special care not to place any student in his usual life role. Students should, of course, feel free not to participate if they feel uncomfortable in doing so.

When role-playing is attempted for the first time, some "warm-up activities" may be needed to relax both players and audience by providing practice which will lead to a feeling of security when the performance occurs. Depending upon the age group, warm-up activities can include those requiring a varying degree of emotional involvement (show how you feel when you get a phone call breaking a date; show how you feel when you open a box and it is a present you wanted; show how you feel when you learn you've just failed your final exam in your worst subject) to those requiring more skill in expressing one's feelings (You are a teenager with long hair. As you are walking down the street, a man passes you and mutters, "you dirty hippie." What's your reaction?).

The actors selected for the role-playing may be given a written description of their feelings or background information needed to portray the character, or the counselor or teacher may "fill them in" orally, as shown below.

> *Teacher or Counselor:* Chuck, you've just gotten your report card and you've gotten a D in English. You don't think it's a fair grade. You think that the teacher has it "in" for you. He's always calling you down for things that happen in class and you feel the grade is in retaliation for your behavior.

> *Teacher or Counselor:* Bill, you're going to play the teacher. You don't dislike Chuck and you don't think that you've been unfair to him. You believe that you have based your grade for him fairly on the work he has done.

Once the role-players have been briefed on their roles, instructions to the students who are acting as the audience-observers are needed. The teacher or counselor briefly explains the situation to them. For example, for the improvisation which Chuck and Bill are going to act out, the explanation to the class might go like this.

> *Teacher or Counselor:* We've been talking about injustices and how some people treat others unfairly because they dislike their race, their religion, or how they look or act. Sometimes we feel others dislike us for any of these reasons, but we are wrong. This situation can occur between a teacher and a student. Chuck is going to play a student who feels a teacher gave him

an unfair grade, and Bill is going to play the teacher who does not feel the grade is unfair, nor that he dislikes Chuck.

There may be occasions when the teacher or counselor would not set the stage before the dramatization. Only the individual players are briefed, and the improvisation is presented to an unprepared audience. Then the postpresentation discussion would serve to define the problem, identify the sources of conflict as projected, and determine the solution.

The Role-play Goes On

Students must be cautioned to focus on the *problem* during the presentation and not on the personalities of the players. The atmosphere toward the improvisation must be a serious one. If the role-playing is not going well, the teacher or counselor should not hesitate to stop the action; ask the class "is this the way we see the problem?"; refocus, and begin again. If necessary, a student who cannot perform his role satisfactorily should be removed (tactfully, of course). The improvisation itself will probably last only a few minutes, but the analysis which follows could easily require the remaining minutes of the class period.

It is very important to stop the action once the problem has been clearly projected, but the participants should remain where they were when the action stopped so that the scene remains clear in the minds of the audience. If an audio- or video-tape recorder could be used, the improvisation could be replayed while the discussion was ongoing. Once the action has stopped, the class should explore the feelings of each of the players involved. First, have the class react to what they saw; have them evaluate who was responsible for the problem. How could the conflict have been avoided? Why do people behave as they do sometimes? Then have the actors indicate what they were trying to portray. Students will quickly discover that sometimes what they meant to express was misinterpreted by the audience and their fellow actors. Once an individual steps into someone else's shoes, so to speak, and sees himself as others see him, he may attain a clearer understanding of how he affects others and why they behave toward him as they do.[11]

---

11. Chesler and Fox, *Role-Playing Methods in the Classroom*, p. 7.

Variations within the role-playing structure include the use of soliloquy, described as "providing a player with an opportunity to say something which might not be revealed during the ordinary course of the improvisation. The participant simply raises his hand; all action stops and others wait while the player tells how he feels at that moment. . . ."[12] Chesler and Fox[13] suggest an alternative to the soliloquy, the "double," a type of identifier, as a good means of providing material for the exploration of motives, feelings, and concerns. The "double" is involved right along with the actor and enters the conversation when the play is stopped; he expresses his impressions of the character's private thoughts and reactions rather than his observable actions and statements. There are also "consultants" who may meet with the actors prior to the role-playing session and suggest how best to carry out the role. They do not, however, appear during the improvisation. The technique of *role reversal* may also be used where the player must suddenly switch to the opposite or adversarial role, where he finds he must adopt the other person's viewpoint and attempt to solve the very problems he himself created.

Although role-playing occurs primarily in a classroom setting, counselors can make effective use of the technique to help students solve individual problems (such as the student too shy to ask a teacher for help, or one afraid to discuss plans for the future with parents). Such issues lend themselves readily to role-playing in which the counselor assumes first the role of the other individual and then reverses and assumes the role of the student. Thus, the student is able to try out a variety of behaviors to meet the troubling situation in a protected setting and without fear of consequences.

So What Does It Prove?

How can the counselor or teacher assess the worth of role-playing? Is this technique worth the time and energy involved? How much do students profit from this type of experience? Evaluating role-playing improvisations can be done through informal ques-

---

12. D. Dinkmeyer and C. Caldwell, *Developmental Counseling and Guidance: A Comprehensive School Approach,* p. 441.
13. Chesler and Fox, *Role-Playing Methods in the Classroom,* p. 40.

tioning of the class as to whether they feel this technique is the best procedure for investigating a particular problem and by written questionnaires on which students indicate how effectively they think each of the actors has played his role, how profitable the discussions following the dramatization are to the students, and whether they wish to consider this procedure for future analyses of interpersonal problems.

During the role-playing, the teacher or counselor can make notes indicating how many students seem actively interested in the dramatization and the amount and depth of participation in the discussions which follow. If the goals are set prior to the improvisation, the evaluation should serve as a check on how effectively these goals have been met. If the role-playing is directed toward improving interpersonal relationships among students, however, it may be some time before observable results can be noted.

Advantages of Using Role-playing

Used properly, role-playing can provide a forum for clarifying an individual student's personal and societal expectations, improving interpersonal relationships, and making academic tasks and the school's curriculum more relevant to the student's daily life. Also, during role-playing improvisations, students have a chance to identify and feel with others–to put themselves in the other person's place–and to act out their feelings without fear or inhibition. In the course of the discussions which follow the role-playing, students begin to realize that there are many ways to resolve social conflicts. Every individual, each with his own set of values, responds differently to the same problem. The counselor or teacher observing the improvisation and listening to the discussions gains insights into the causes of pupil behavior difficult to secure by any other means. Information obtained from watching a sociodrama may verify or contradict data from other objective sources.

Bonney and Hampleman[14] suggest that observations made during a sociodrama could provide a basis for conferences between students, teachers, and counselors. A reduction of tension and

14. Merl E. Bonney and Richard S. Hampleman, *Personal Social Evaluation Techniques* (Washington, D. C., The Center for Applied Research in Education, Inc., 1962), p. 41.

friction within the class may also occur when individuals are allowed to act out their true feelings,[15] as well as developing flexibility to handle situations by testing one's resources to face unanticipated circumstances by providing a sheltered setting where mistakes can be made without fear of consequences.[16]

Disadvantages of Using Role-playing

It seems for every champion of a cause there is a critic. Those who have reservations about the role-playing approach cite these dangers: (1) the difficulty of interpreting such self-expression techniques as role-playing without the interpreter's projecting his own background into his interpretation;[17] (2) teachers and counselors untrained in this technique lack confidence and skill sufficient to plan and conduct sociodramas, since practice cannot be accomplished in private but requires interaction between individuals (reading a book on role-playing won't make you an expert on improvisation). Other cautions include a warning to teachers and counselors who do not have good rapport with their students and counselees: don't try it! A poorly motivated role-playing demonstration will surely degenerate into a silly farce which loses sight of the real purpose of the improvisation. Situations which suddenly become too emotionally charged can also prove damaging to individual students or to the entire class.

SUMMARY

Counselors and teachers seeking clues to students' perceptions about themselves and how others see them use the sociogram to measure peer acceptance and rejection. Role-playing provides a method for students to express their feelings or their interpretation of how they believe their peers, parents, or teachers would act in certain situations. Each device demands good rapport between teacher, counselor, and students; although each has limitations stemming primarily from the subjective nature of the technique

15. R. N. Hatch and J. W. Coster, *Guidance Services in the Elementary School* (Dubuque, Wm. C. Brown Company Publishers, 1961), p. 343.

16. Bennett, *Guidance and Counseling in Groups*, p. 41.

17. Bonney and Hampleman, *Personal Social Evaluation Techniques*, p. 41.

but also from the lack of training in the use of these approaches (particularly of teachers and to a lesser degree, of the counselor), these sociometric tools provide an excellent opportunity for co-operative involvement by counselors and teachers with the joint aims of studying student behavior and improving the effectiveness of the teacher or counselor presentation of the devices. The insights into student behavior revealed are not available through any other means.

SUGGESTED READINGS

Chesler, Mark, and Fox, Robert: *Role-playing Methods in the Classroom.* Chicago, Science Research Associates, 1966.
  Comprehensive, thoroughly readable, filled with examples describing steps for planning, conducting, and evaluating role-playing improvisations.

Fox, Robert, Luszki, Margaret B., and Schmuck, Richard: *Diagnosing Classroom Learning Environments.* Chicago, Science Research Associates, 1966.
  Relates questionnaire evaluation of students by peers and the use of sociograms to graph the data. Practical suggestions with good illustrations; worth reading.

Moreno, J. L.: *The Sociometry Reader.* Glencoe, Free Pr, 1960.
  The author of this classic in sociometry updates information on methods of sociometric measurement, validity and reliability of sociometric measures, sociometric status.

Northway, Mary: *A Primer on Sociometry.* Toronto, The University of Toronto Press, 1967.
  Concise handbook for designing and administering the sociometric test, and the organization and interpretation of results.

Reichert, Richard: *Self-awareness through Group Dynamics.* Dayton, Pflaum/Standard Pr, 1970.
  Offers exercises that aid the student in developing awareness of himself in the group setting.

signed to advise the student, the parents, and his teachers what information developed from the student's performance. It seems unbelievable that sometimes students are not told of their standing on standardized tests. If the student is in the early elementary grades, it may not be possible for him to understand an explanation of the results. The parents, however, should be fully informed. Sad to say, this is not always the case. Yet evaluating the achievement of the individual student is one of the prime reasons for having a testing program. Determining the individual's potential or aptitude for further learning and diagnosing learning difficulties are other important uses of standardized testing.

Standardized test results can also be used for comparison purposes. Students of the same age and grade can be compared nationally and locally (for example, all ninth grade students in the same school or all ninth graders in all the junior high schools of the district). Scores are used to predict whether a student who has achieved a given score is a good prospect for successfully completing advanced courses in mathematics (algebra, geometry), science (chemistry, physics, biology), or foreign languages, or whether he is likely to be admitted to a specific college.

Some administrators use comparative data as a means of evaluating the effectiveness of the curriculum and instruction in their schools, a practice which has caused deep concern by teachers, particularly if the results of the standardized tests are the only methods for evaluating the staff and the programs of study. Teachers fear that if students at School X should fall below grade level on standardized tests, "heads will roll," if the superintendent reasons that the students' poor showing is evidence that the teachers have not taught. Now, of course, this may be true, but the test results alone cannot provide "proof positive." Since the answer sheets are rarely returned with the test scores, it is impossible to determine which items were answered incorrectly. Such information is essential to substantiate the charge that the material (1) wasn't taught or (2) if taught, it wasn't mastered by the students.

Other variables also affect test results—the motivation of the students while taking the test, physical conditions in the room where the test is administered (have you ever tried taking a three-hour test in a room with the temperature crowding 90°?), the attitude of those administering the tests, and the resulting emotional atmosphere in the room.

The students were concluding an achievement test battery started two days earlier. As they were sitting in the cafeteria waiting for the counselor to distribute the test booklets, the principal's voice came over the intercom.

"I'm sorry to interrupt but I thought you should know that Mrs. Lizowski (one of the most popular of the school's teachers) had an automobile accident on the way to school this morning. She's been taken to Mercy Hospital. We don't know anything more at this time. Those who have classes with Mrs. Lizowski, report to your regularly assigned room; there will be a substitute for her."

One or two of the girls started to cry and several students appeared quite upset. Mr. March, the counselor, started handing out the booklets saying, "Now, boys and girls, there's nothing we can do to help Mrs. Lizowski, so let's get on with our work."

It would not seem remarkable for such an incident to affect the students' ability to concentrate and thus their performance on this section of the achievement battery, but there will be no way to assess its impact. Therefore, the use of test scores as the single measure of the curriculum or the instruction cannot logically be defended.

Beyond evaluating individual student's progress, diagnosing learning difficulties, and comparing students and classes, standardized tests provide data which the administration can use in determining whether adaptations and changes in the present curriculum are justified. Teachers and counselors should examine the items on achievement tests and decide whether the test does measure what is actually being taught in the school. If the test emphasizes areas not taught, then the faculty should decide whether such material is of sufficient importance to be added to the curriculum. Conversely, if the school stresses certain topics not included in the tests, should these be cut or retained? Test-makers admit that the content of their tests frequently lags behind curricular change in the schools. The faculty, then, has the responsibility to see that the tests administered in the school accurately measure the content which they as professional educators have determined meet the educational goals of that school system.

THE TESTING COMMITTEE

The significance of such analysis of tests by a school's faculty reinforces the importance of cooperation between administrators, teachers and counselors in the testing program. Some writers on educational tests recommend that a committee representing the administration, guidance, teachers, students, and parents cooperatively decide the objectives of the school's testing program, which tests will be used, when and by whom they will be administered, and what system will be used to record and disseminate the results. I applaud the premise and the optimism of those who champion such a committee. Admittedly, administrators, teachers, counselors, students, and parents have a real stake in the testing program. The knowledge exchanged by such a group could greatly lessen the suspicion surrounding test-taking and give important support to an effective testing program within the school. But the likelihood of such a committee's determining testing policy is virtually "the impossible dream," in my opinion. In actual fact, tests selected for use in all the schools of a given system are chosen by individuals in the central administrative office of the district or, where statewide plans exist, from the State Department of Education's administrative office. Thus, few counselors *or* parents *or* teachers *or* students have an opportunity to suggest tests particularly suited to a specific school, since each test approved must usually be used by all the schools in the system. However, such a committee within each school could cooperatively evaluate the present testing program to see how well the tests meet curriculum goals, as well as learning the purposes of each test and providing an opportunity for students, parents, and teachers to express their apprehensions and concerns about the program or about the use of test results. This could prove a valuable service to other parents, the student body, and the faculty by correcting misinformation and helping to develop a supportive climate for the testing program.

COMPONENTS OF A COMPREHENSIVE SCHOOLWIDE TESTING PROGRAM

Testing begins in the kindergarten and ends in the twelfth grade for many students, although it continues for many more through college, graduate school, and even on the job. Usually a student's first test is one evaluating reading readiness or assessing general learning readiness. Subsequently, tests of general intelligence, achievement, aptitude, and interest are administered. Spread throughout the school years, a typical testing program might look like Table V.

TABLE V

Grade	Type of Test
K	Reading readiness
1 or 2	Learning readiness Reading ability Mental ability (general intelligence)
3 or 4 or 5	Achievement battery (language skills, including reading, mathematics, social studies, science)
6 or 7 or 8	Mental ability (repeated at entrance to middle school or junior high) Multifactor aptitude
9 or 10 or 11	Achievement battery
11 or 12	College aptitude Interests—personal Interests—vocational

It is beyond the scope of this chapter to list all the available tests applicable to such a testing program, but presented below is a brief description of a few standardized tests, randomly selected, which are illustrative of each type mentioned in the table above. More complete information, as well as critical evaluations of each test, can be found in Buros' *Mental Measurement Yearbook* published by Gryphon Press.[5]

---

5. Oscar K. Buros (Ed.), *The Seventh Mental Measurement Yearbook* (Highland Park, New Jersey, The Gryphon Press, 1972).

TESTS

Readiness

Lee-Clark Reading Readiness. Publisher: California Test Bureau, Monterey, California, 1962. K-1. Four-part tests–recognizing similarities and differences in printed letters, demonstrating ability to mark pictures and letters, and words that match given ones.

Murphy-Durrell Reading Readiness Analysis. Publisher: Harcourt, Brace, and World, New York, 1964-65. K-1. Identifying separate sounds in spoken words, identifying capital and lower-case letters named by the examiner, and recognizing sight words one hour after they have been taught.

Primary Mental Abilities. Publisher: Science Research Associates, Chicago, 1962. K-12. Four- or five-part score and a total IQ score are derived. Scores reflect ability in verbal meaning, number facility, reasoning (omitted on two lower levels), perceptual speed (omitted on two highest levels), and spatial relations.

Metropolitan Readiness. Publisher: Harcourt, Brace, and World, New York, 1965. K-1. Group tests that assess six important aspects of readiness for formal first grade instruction: word meaning, listening, matching (visual perception), alphabet (knowledge of names of lower case letters), numbers, and copying.

Mental Ability, Mental Aptitude, Intelligence

Otis-Lennon Mental Ability. Publisher: Harcourt, Brace, and World, New York, 1967. K-12. Six levels. Test items, lower level, are pictorial type to sample the mental process of classification, following of directions, quantitative reasoning, and comprehension of verbal concepts. At upper levels, eighty items arranged in spiral omnibus form, various types of verbal and nonverbal items, emphasis upon the measurement of mental processes and abstract reasoning ability.

California Short Form Test of Mental Maturity. Publisher: California Test Bureau, Monterey, California, 1963. K-12. Six levels measure logical reasoning, numerical reasoning, verbal concepts and memory (grouped into two sections, language and non-language). Separate mental age and IQ are obtained for each of these sections, also yielding a total MA and IQ.

Lorge-Thorndike Intelligence Tests. Publisher: Houghton-Mifflin Company, Boston, 1964. K-13. Tests of abstract intelligence, five levels. Two lower levels require no reading through comprehension of oral language; three higher levels provide a verbal and nonverbal battery, separate verbal and nonverbal IQ, and composite IQ are obtained.

Achievement

Stanford Achievement Tests. Publisher: Harcourt, Brace, and World, New York, 1964 and 1969. K-12. One series, the Early School Achievement Test (1969) for K.1-1.1 measures environment in meaning of words taken from both social and natural environment; also mathematics, numbers, measurement, letters and sounds, aural comprehension. The 1964 revised achievement series covers Grades 1-12 at five levels and measures content and skills in reading, language arts, and arithmetic, and at Grade 4 and above, science and social studies.

Iowa Tests of Basic Skills. Publisher: Houghton-Mifflin Company, Boston, 1971. 3-8. Tests vocabulary, reading comprehension, spelling, capitalization, punctuation, map reading, reading graphs and tables, knowledge and use of reference materials, mathematical concepts, and problem solving.

Sequential Tests of Educational Progress. Publisher: Cooperative Test Division, Educational Testing Service, Princeton, New Jersey, 1969. 4-14 (college). Measures students' verbal, mathematical, and general abilities through a series of tests in verbal ability, mechanics of writing, English expression, and reading comprehension. Mathematical abilities and understandings assessed through three tests in quantitative ability, mathematical concepts and computation. Other content areas include science and social studies.

Comprehensive Tests of Basic Skills. Publisher: CTB/McGraw-Hill, Del Monte, California, 1973. K-12. Four levels; content areas tested are reading vocabulary, reading comprehension, spelling, language mechanics and expression, mathematics computation and concepts and applications, reference skills, science, and social studies. Publisher states research conducted to reduce ethnic and cultural bias in test items.

Aptitude

Differential Aptitude Tests. Publisher: The Psychological Corporation, New York, 1972. 8-12. Eight aptitude tests covering verbal reasoning, numerical ability, abstract reasoning, space relations, mechanical reasoning, clerical speed and accuracy, spelling, and sentences (grammar, punctuation, and word usage used in sentences).

School and College Ability Test. Publisher: Cooperative Test Division, Princeton, New Jersey, 1967. 4-14 (college). Designed to provide estimates of basic verbal and mathematical ability. Scores can be used for comparison purposes and predicting success in related activities; reported in percentiles.

College Aptitude

Scholastic Aptitude Test. Publisher: College Entrance Examination Board, New York, issued annually. 11-12. SAT gives two scores—verbal, based on paragraph comprehension and vocabulary, and mathematical which requires mathematical reasoning, drawing conclusions from tables. Test is essentially a job sample; uses standard-score scales.

American College Testing Program. Publisher: American College Testing Program, Iowa City, Iowa, issued annually. ACT measures what has been learned in high school: mathematical reasoning, language skills, reading, comprehension, evaluation of science, and social studies. Samples skills and knowledge required in college; uses standard-score scales.

Although hundreds of tests are available in a large variety of areas, "only some twenty-five tests or series of tests account for three-fourths or more of all testing in American education,"[6] and this multimillion dollar business is shared by Houghton-Mifflin

6. Gene R. Hawes, *Educational Testing for the Millions* (New York, McGraw-Hill Book Company, Inc., 1964), p. 7.

Company, California Test Bureau, Psychological Corporation, Educational Testing Service, Harcourt, Brace, and World, and Science Research Associates, called by Gene Hawes[7] "the big six."

TERMINOLOGY NECESSARY FOR INTERPRETING TEST SCORES

Counselors skilled in the jargon of testing are apt to forget how confusing the terminology is to the uninitiated. Although the very useful glossary of measurement terms issued by Harcourt, Brace, and World publishers numbers an even 100, mastery of somewhat fewer items will enable teacher, student, and parent to understand the meaning of test results. The definitions shown below have been taken from this glossary. I have found these most used in explaining test scores.

A SHORT GLOSSARY OF MEASUREMENT TERMS*

Academic aptitude. The combination of native and acquired abilities that are needed for school learning; likelihood of success in mastering academic work, as estimated from measures of the necessary abilities. (Also called scholastic aptitude, school learning ability, academic potential.)

Achievement test. A test that measures the extent to which a person has "achieved" something, acquired certain information, or mastered certain skills—usually as a result of planned instruction or training.

Arithmetic mean. A kind of average usually referred to as the *mean*. It is obtained by dividing the sum of a set of scores by their number.

Battery. A group of several tests standardized on the same sample population so that results on the several tests are comparable.

---

7. Ibid., p. 7.

* All terms listed except for "intelligence test," are taken from Mitchell, "A Glossary of Measurement Terms," (n.d.) pp. 1, 2, 4, 5, 6, 7, 8.

(Sometimes loosely applied to any group of tests administered to-gether, even though not standardized on the same subjects.) The most common test batteries are those of school achievement which include subtests in the separate learning areas.

Coefficient of correlation. A measure of the degree of relationship between two sets of measures for the same group of individuals. The correlation coefficient most frequently used in test develop-ment and educational research is that known as the Pearson or *product-moment r.* Unless otherwise specified, "correlation" usu-ally refers to this coefficient, but *rank, biserial, tetrachoric,* and other methods are used in special situations. Correlation coeffi-cients range from .00, denoting a complete absence of relationship to +1.00, and to −1.00, indicating perfect positive or perfect nega-tive correspondence, respectively.

Deviation IQ (DIQ). An age-based index of general mental abili-ty. It is based upon the difference or deviation between a person's score and the typical or average score for persons of this chrono-logical age. Deviation IQs from most current scholastic aptitude measures are standard scores with a mean of 100 and a standard-ized deviation of 16 for each defined age group.

Intelligence quotient (IQ). Originally, an index of brightness ex-pressed as the ratio of a person's mental age to his chronological age, MA/CA, multiplied by 100 to eliminate the decimal. (More precisely—and particularly for adult ages, at which mental growth is assumed to have ceased—the ratio of mental age to the mental age normal for chronological age.) This quotient IQ has been gradually replaced by the deviation IQ concept.

Intelligence test.[8] A test designed to infer future learning, usually some combination of verbal and numerical and/or abstract rea-soning measures; also called scholastic aptitude test or mental abil-ity test.

---

8. Harold G. Seashore (Ed.), "Test Service Bulletin Number 51" (New York, Psychological Corporation, December, 1956), p. 5.

Mean. See **Arithmetic mean.**

Median (Md). The middle score in a distribution or set of ranked scores; the point (score) that divides the group into two equal parts; the fiftieth percentile. Half of the scores are below the median and half above it, except when the median itself is one of the obtained scores.

Mental age (MA). The age for which a given score on a mental ability test is average or normal. If the average score made by an unselected group of children six years, ten months of age is 55, then a child making a score of 55 is said to have a mental age of 6–10. Since the mental age unit shrinks with increasing (chronological) age, MAs do not have a uniform interpretation throughout all ages. They are, therefore, most appropriately used at the early age levels where mental growth is relatively rapid.

Normal distribution. A distribution of scores or measures that in graphic form has a distinctive bell-shaped appearance. Figure 27 shows graphs of such a distribution, known as a normal, normal probability, or Gaussian curve. In such a normal distribution, scores or measures are distributed symmetrically about the mean, with as many cases up to various distances above the mean as down to equal distances below it. Cases are concentrated near the mean and decrease in frequency, according to a precise mathematical equation, the farther one departs from the mean. *Mean* and *median* are identical. The assumption that mental and psychological characteristics are distributed normally has been very useful in test development work.

Norms. Statistics that supply a frame of reference by which meaning may be given to obtained test scores. Norms are based upon the actual performance of pupils of various grades or ages in the standardization group for the test. Since they represent average or typical performance, they should not be regarded as standards or as universally desirable levels of attainment. The most common types of norms are deviation IQ, percentile rank, grade equivalent,

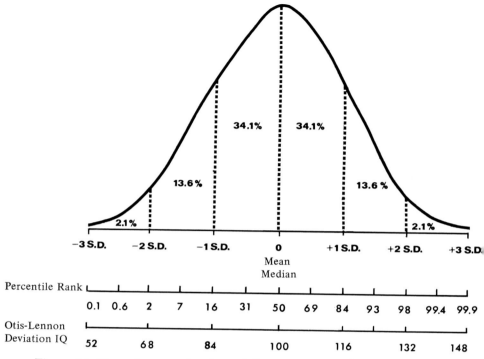

Figure 27. Normal curve, showing relations among standard deviation distance from mean, area (percentage of cases) between these points, percentile rank, and IQ from tests with an S.D. of 16. (Reproduced with permission from Blythe C. Mitchell [consultant], "A Glossary of Measurement Terms," *Test Service Notebook 13* [New York, Harcourt Brace Jovanovich, Inc., Test Department, n.d.].)

and stanine. Reference groups are usually those of a specified age or grade.

Percentile (P). A point (score) in a distribution at or below which fall the percent of cases indicated by the percentile. Thus, a score coinciding with the 35th percentile (P_{35}) is regarded as equaling or surpassing that of 35 percent of the persons in the group, and such that 65 percent of the performances exceed this score. "Percentile" has nothing to do with the percent of correct answers an examinee makes on a test.

Quartile. One of three points that divide the cases in a distribution into four equal groups. The lower quartile (Q_1), or 25th percentile, sets off the lowest fourth of the group; the middle quartile (Q_2) is the same as the 50th percentile, or median, and divides the second fourth of the cases from the third; and the third quartile (Q_3), or 75th percentile, sets off the top fourth.

Raw score. The first quantitative result obtained in scoring a test (usually the number of right answers, number right minus some fraction of number wrong, time required for performance, number of errors, or similar direct, unconverted, uninterpreted measure).

Readiness test. A test that measures the extent to which an individual has achieved a degree of maturity or acquired certain skills or information needed for successfully undertaking some learning activity. Thus, a *reading readiness* test indicates whether a child has reached a developmental stage where he may profitably begin formal reading instruction. *Readiness* tests are classified as *prognostic* tests.

Reliability. The extent to which a test is consistent in measuring whatever it does measure: dependability, stability, trustworthiness, relative freedom from errors of measurement. Reliability is usually expressed by some form of *reliability coefficient* or by the *standard error of measurement* derived from it.

Standard deviation (S.D.). A measure of the variability or dispersion of a distribution of scores. The more the scores cluster around the mean, the smaller the standard deviation. For a normal distribution, approximately two thirds (68.3%) of the scores are within the range from one S.D. below the mean to one S.D. above the mean. Computation of the S.D. is based upon the square of the deviation of each score from the mean. The S.D. is sometimes called "sigma" and is represented by the symbol σ. (See Fig. 27.)

Standard error (S.E.). A statistic providing an estimate of the possible magnitude of "errors" present in some obtained measure, whether (1) an *individual* score or (2) some group measure, as a mean or a correlation coefficient. (1) Standard error of measurement (S.E. Meas.): As applied to a single obtained score, the amount by which the score may differ from the hypothetical true score due to errors of measurement. The larger the S.E. Meas., the less reliable the score. The S.E. Meas. is an amount such that in about two thirds of the cases the obtained score would not differ by more than one S.E. Meas. from the true score. (Theoretically, then, it can be said that the chances are 2:1 that the actual score is within a band extending from the *true score minus 1 S.E. Meas.* to *true score plus 1 S.E. Meas.;* but since the true score can never be known, actual practice must reverse the true-obtained relation for an interpretation.) Other probabilities are noted under (2) below.

(2) Standard error. When applied to group averages, standard deviations, correlation coefficients, etc., the S.E. provides an estimate of the "error" which may be involved. The group size and the S.D. are the factors on which these standard errors are based. The same probability interpretation as for S.E. Meas. is made for the S.E.s of group measures, i.e. 2:1 (two out of three) for the 1 S.E. range, 19:1 (ninety-five out of 100) for 2 S.E. range, 99:1 (ninety-nine out of 100) for a 2.6 S.E. range.

Standard score. A general term referring to any of a variety of "transformed" scores, in terms of which raw scores may be expressed for reasons of convenience, comparability, ease of interpretation, etc. The simplest type of standard score, known as a Z-score, is an expression of the *deviation* of a score from the mean score of the group *in relation to* the standard deviation of the scores of the group. Thus:

$$\text{standard score } (Z) = \frac{\text{raw score } (X) - \text{mean } (M)}{\text{standard deviation } (S.D.)}$$

Adjustments may be made in this ratio so that a system of standard scores having any desired mean and standard deviation may be set up. The use of such standard scores does not affect the relative standing of the individuals in the group or change the shape of the original distribution. T-scores have an M of 50 and an S.D. of 10. Deviation IQs are standard scores with an M of 100 and some chosen S.D., most often 16; thus a raw score that is 1 S.D. above the M of its distribution would convert to a standard score (Deviation IQ) of $100 + 16 = 116$. (See Fig. 27.)

Standard scores are useful in expressing the raw scores of two forms of a test in comparable terms in instances where tryouts have shown that the two forms are not identical in difficulty; also, successive levels of a test may be linked to form a continuous standard-score scale, making across-battery comparisons possible.

Standardized test (standard test). A test designed to provide a systematic sample of individual performance, administered according to prescribed directions, scored in conformance with definite rules, and interpreted in reference to certain normative information.

Stanine. One of the steps in a nine-point scale of standard scores. The stanine (short for standard-nine) scale has values from 1 to 9, with a mean of 5 and a standard deviation of 2. Each stanine (except 1 and 9) is ½ S.D. in width, with the middle (average stanine of 5 extending from ¼ S.D. below to ¼ S.D. above the mean.

Validity. The extent to which a test does the job for which it is used. This definition is more satisfactory than the traditional "extent to which a test measures what it is supposed to measure," since the validity of a test is always specific to the purpose for which the test is used. The term validity, then, has different connotations for various types of tests, and, thus, a different kind of validity evidence is appropriate for each.

CAUTIONS ABOUT STANDARDIZED TESTS

Whether the counselor or the classroom teacher uses test results with students or parents, certain considerations about tests should be clearly understood by all parties before any decisions are made based on the test results.

First, any standardized test (or any test) measures the student's performance at one given time based on a specific set of items, usually multiple choice questions. Before discussing the results of

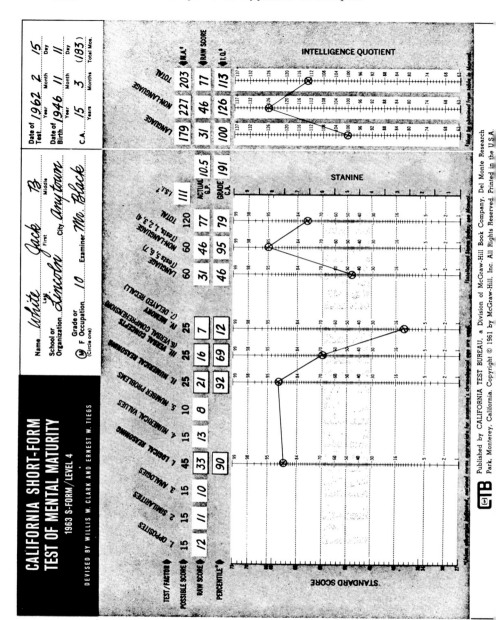

cannot rely on a single number when it hides so much meaningful information when a study of the profile can yield so much. Figure 28 is an example of such a Profile Sheet prepared by the California Test Bureau of McGraw-Hill Book Company to accompany results on the California Short Form Test of Mental Maturity.

WHAT DOES IT ALL MEAN? USING THE TEST RESULTS WITH STUDENTS AND PARENTS

Teacher Use of Test Results

Teachers frequently condemn standardized tests as "a waste of time," "totally invalid" (perhaps victims of too many standardized tests themselves, they are wary and suspicious). Yet sometimes these same teachers will use a score on a mental ability or achievement test as justification for a low grade. Studies have shown that teacher expectations and treatment of students believed to possess high IQ's and thus considered capable of high school achievement are far different than for those believed to have low IQ's and ipso facto unable to achieve academically.[12, 13]

Mrs. Kurtz had requested a conference with all Allen's seventh grade teachers to discuss his poor grades on the first quarterly report card. The counselor had begun the conference with her when Mrs. Hemmett, Allen's English teacher arrived.

"I can't understand why Allen doesn't do better in English," his mother told Mrs. Hemmett. "He always does his homework; I check on that every night. We tell him he should try to do his best on

---

12. Robert Rosenthal and Lenore Jacobson, *Pygmalion in the Classroom* (New York, Holt, Rinehart and Winston, Inc., 1968).

13. W. B. Brookover, et al., *Self-Concept of Ability and School Achievement II: Improving Academic Achievement through Students' Self-Concept Enhancement* (East Lansing, Mich.: Office of Research and Publications, Michigan State University, Cooperative Research Project No. 1636, U. S. Office of Education, 1965).

Figure 28. Profile sheet for California Short Form Test of Mental Maturity. (From Examiner's Manual, California Short-Form Test of Mental Maturity devised by Willis W. Clark and Ernest W. Tiegs. Copyright © 1963 by McGraw-Hill, Inc. Reprinted by permission of the publisher, CTB/McGraw-Hill, CA 93940. All Rights Reserved. Printed in the United States.)

every assignment. We want him to go to Princeton; his father is a graduate of Princeton, you see."

"Go to Princeton with D's in English?" exclaimed Mrs. Hemmett.

"Well, if he can't make Princeton, at least State University," countered Mrs. Kurtz.

"The University? Why, with an IQ of 86, I can't even justify a C in seventh grade English! Go to the University? You must be joking," retorted Mrs. Hemmett.

Mrs. Kurtz looked as if someone had struck her. She turned to the counselor and said, "Is it true? Is Allen's IQ really only 86? He can't ever go college now, can he?" She then proceeded to have hysterics.

As the counselor in that situation my first impulse was to strangle the teacher (which I did not follow) and my second was to calm the distraught mother (which I tried to do but with small success). This disclosure was the beginning of a long, sad transition for both parent and child. True, the parents had been unrealistic about the boy's ability, yet once the IQ was revealed, it was difficult to convince the mother (and the father) that their boy could learn anything! Surely no test score should have such an impact. The parents' misconception about the significance of that single number and the teacher's stupidity in blurting it out without a complete explanation did tremendous harm. Certainly the "shock treatment" given the parents was a gross misuse of test results, but what are legitimate and beneficial ways in which a teacher can utilize test data?

Assume for a moment you are a twelfth grade government teacher looking over Denise's permanent record in the middle of the fall semester. Denise has failed the first two quizzes in government and appears unable or unwilling to participate in the class discussions. You are hoping to get some clues about her ability and aptitude in social studies.

The first entry on her Test Record card reported the results of the California Short Form Test of Mental Maturity taken at the beginning of the seventh grade when she was twelve years, three months of age. These results have been reproduced in Figure 29.

What do these scores mean? The abbreviations "C.A." "Lang. M.A.," and "Nonlang. M.A." stand for "chronological age," "lan-

CTMM Jr Level	DATE 09/64	C. A 147	LANG. M.A. 204	NONLANG. M.A. 184	TOTAL M.A. 194	L IQ 139

NL IQ 125	T IQ 132	L 99	NL 90	T 98

Figure 29. Test score for California Short Form Test of Mental Maturity for Denise.

guage mental age," and "nonlanguage mental age," all reported in months. Denise's language and nonlanguage mental ages exceeded her chronological age of 147 months (12 years, three months). Her language mental age of 204 months equals the average score that would be made by an unselected group of students of seventeen, 204/12, on the language subtests. Students aged fifteen years and three months would make an average score of 184 months on the nonlanguage subtests. To determine the language IQ, simply apply the formula CA/MA × 100 (204/147 × 100); 184/147 × 100 to secure the nonlanguage IQ and 194 (the average of the language and nonlanguage M.A.'s)/147 × 100 to determine the total IQ. We would come up with 139 language IQ; nonlanguage IQ of 125 and a total IQ of 132. Remember, when using these figures, allow for the standard deviation of sixteen points; thus, the true language IQ will fall between 123 and 155; the language IQ between 109 and 141, and the total IQ between 116 and 148.

The three figures, L 99, NL 90, T 98, are percentiles, still another way of expressing test scores. On the language subtests, Denise's score placed her at the 99th percentile (99%ile); she did better than 99 percent of all the seventh grade students who formed the norming population on which the test was standard-

DIFFERENTIAL APTITUDE TESTS					
	Verbal Reasoning	Numerical Ability	VR + NA	Abstract Reasoning	Clerical Speed & Acc.
Raw Score	38	28	66	40	65
Percentile	95	90	97	90	99

Figure 30 and Figure 31. Test score for Differential Aptitude Test for Denise.

ized; 90 percent better than all those seventh graders tested in the nonlanguage areas, for a total of the 98th percentile (98%ile) placing her above 98 percent of all the seventh grade students used for standardizing this test; an indication of high scholastic aptitude.

The Differential Aptitude Test (DAT) administered in the eighth grade revealed the results found in Figures 30 and 31.

Looking at the percentiles, Denise scored in the top quartile in every section. Again, she has shown high aptitude for academic studies. A check of her eighth grade marks shows an almost perfect A average (English, math, history, science, physical education); the only B received was in a one-half credit course in art. At that point in her academic career, Denise's test scores were an accurate barometer of her in-class performance.

At the beginning of the ninth grade, Denise took the Sequential

	Space Relations	Language Usage		
		Spelling	Grammar	
Raw Score	31	76	43	
Percentile	80	80	95	

Figure 31. Test score for Differential Aptitude Test for Denise, concluded.

S	TEST FORM 3B	CONV SCORES	MATH 292	SCIENCE 302	SOC STUDIES 298	READING 301
T	NATL NORMS 09 F					
E		%ILE BANDS	97-99	96-99	94-99	89-99
P						

Figure 32. Test score for Sequential Tests of Educational Progress for Denise.

Tests of Educational Progress (S.T.E.P.), an achievement battery, with the results shown in Figure 32.

Her achievement in math, science, and social studies and reading, as expressed by the percentile bands, placed her among the top quarter nationally (note the block indicating that the norms used were for ninth grade students, fall 09 F) of all the ninth graders tested in setting the norms for this battery. The figures opposite the words CONV SCORES (converted scores) represent a weighted raw score for each subtest from which the percentiles were determined. (There are two other sections of this battery, Listening and Writing, but Denise was absent for these subtests.)

Denise also took the School and College Ability Test (S.C.A.T.) at the same time with results shown in Figure 33.

The S.C.A.T. is a "predictor," indicating aptitude for future learning. Denise's 99%ile total score exhibits the highest aptitude. Her final grades for the ninth grade include A's in science, world geography, algebra, and physical education and B's in English and French II. Again, her test scores proved accurate indicators of her

S	TEST FORM 3B	VERBAL		QUANTITATIVE		TOTAL	
C	NATL NORMS 09 F	309	99-00	323	98-99	316	99-00
A		CONV SCORE	%ILE BAND	CONV SCORE	%ILE BAND	CONV SCORE	%ILE BAND
T							

Figure 33. Test score for School and College Ability Test for Denise.

school performance. In the tenth grade, her final grades included four A's (English, biology, geometry, and journalism); one B, physical education; and one D (French III).

The S.T.E.P. and S.C.A.T. tests were repeated in the eleventh grade, using Form 2B, a level specifically designed for this grade. There was virtually no change in any of the test scores or percentiles; Denise still scored in the top quartile on every subtest. She was absent for the social studies and the listening subtest but did take the writing test, which she had missed as a freshman, and scored at the 99% ile. Her total score on the Form 2B for the S.C.A.T. was at the 97 to 99% ile band. Her courses as a junior included English III, U.S. history, advanced algebra, trigonometry, chemistry, German, physical education, and personal typing. She maintained a B average with this rigorous program, with A's in German, chemistry, and personal typing.

At the beginning of her junior year, she took the P.S.A.T. (Preliminary Scholastic Aptitude Test, often called the "baby" college boards), scoring at the 99% ile in both the verbal and quantitative sections, and at the end of the same year, she tried the college boards themselves, the Scholastic Aptitude Test, receiving 675 on the verbal and 662 on the math (on the S.A.T., 450 plus or minus 50 is considered an "average" score).

Yet this same student, in the fall of her senior year, was failing government! A check with her other teachers revealed that she was also failing physics and analytic geometry. Even a cursory review of her test record rejects the premise that she has shown no aptitude or achievement in these areas in the past. Her previous test scores and grades offer a far different conclusion. The teacher or counselor must look for other causes preventing Denise from performing as she has already proven herself capable of doing. An accurate analysis of a set of test scores can reveal a pattern of student potential and performance; deviations from this pattern should alert teachers and counselors to search for factors adversely affecting the student. Drug addiction proved the tragic reason for Denise's sudden scholastic breakdown.

Teachers may also check on the standings on achievement tests to get some idea of the extent of their students' preparation in the

DIFFERENTIAL APTITUDE TEST					
FORM L	GRADE 08	Sex M		Numerical Ability	Abstract Reasoning
			Raw Score	11	23
			Percentile	15	25

Figure 34. Test score for Differential Aptitude Test for Ernie.

subject, keeping in mind the variables which may affect the reported results. The teacher should examine the items comprising the test to be sure that the questions accurately assess the kinds of knowledge he feels are important.

Take the case of Ernie, for example, who was talking with his math teacher in mid-October wondering whether he should drop algebra. Figure 34 shows the test results the math teacher found on his record relating to math (other scores have been omitted).

In talking with the counselor, the teacher also learned that based on the above D.A.T. scores and a C— in Math 8, the counselor had advised Ernie in the spring when he was making out his ninth grade schedule that he might have real difficulty in algebra, but Ernie said his father insisted he take algebra since he would need it to get into college. Ernie had just completed taking the S.T.E.P. battery; his math scores on this achievement battery were as follows in Figures 35 (only math scores shown).

Based on the aptitude test (D.A.T.) and the achievement test scores (S.T.E.P.) in math, Ernie's chances of succeeding in algebra were not too hopeful. However, no counselor or teacher would decide this issue with a student based on these scores alone. Are these tests an accurate measure of potential required and the skills needed for algebra? Does Ernie want to stay in the course? What are his present grades in algebra? Has he understood the work so far? Has he been doing his homework? Could a tutor help? Answers to these questions must also be sought before any action is taken. Should the teacher be fortunate enough to have the answer

S	TEST FORM 3B NATL NORMS 09 F	CONV SCORES	MATH 251
T			
E		%ILE BANDS	07-27
P			

Figure 35. Test score for Sequential Tests of Educational Progress for Ernie.

sheets from the D.A.T. and the S.T.E.P. math subtests, it would be possible to see which items were answered incorrectly, thus determining the weaknesses in Ernie's background and the limitations he has shown which are likely to prevent his succeeding in advanced mathematics.

If the teacher does a similar analysis of the answer sheets for all his students, he will have a rich body of data to use in deciding remedial work needed by the entire class as well as by each student. This, however, is no small undertaking for the teacher. Unfortunately, too, as stated earlier, the availability of answer sheets for such analysis is rather rare, in my experience. In some schools, even the copies of the tests are returned to the central school board office immediately after the test has been administered, making it impossible for the teachers or counselors to examine test items.

Counselors' Use of Test Results

In interviews with students and parents, counselors should include a thorough discussion of test scores whenever educational or vocational decisions are to be made. Although the logic of this statement seems obvious, some counselors are reluctant to share all test data with students or parents, fearing they will be unable to understand or may misunderstand the significance of any given score.

A survey of state policy on releasing such information indicates that there is still substantial hesitancy about sharing such information.

In completing the questionnaire from which the data in Table VI were drawn, some respondents voiced a need for great caution and care in releasing the IQ scores, urging that all scores be interpreted by appropriate professional personnel. The role of the counselor in interpreting the scores completely and clearly cannot be minimized; it is a responsibility of crucial importance.

Since the counselor usually administers all the tests, he must accept full responsibility that correct testing procedures are followed, test security is maintained, and the students are fully informed of the purposes of each test. Attention to detail can save much irritation on test day. Before administering the test, the test manual should be reread, checking particularly the verbal directions to be read. Those teachers who will be assisting as proctors should understand their duties and be informed how to complete identifying information on the answer sheets and handle student questions. Bring extra pencils and verify that the correct test booklets and answer sheets have been distributed before the test actually begins.

Mr. Raylor was collecting the answer sheets following the morning administration of the first three subtests on the S.T.E.P. battery. He was stacking the answer sheets when suddenly he started groaning, "Oh, NO, no, no."

TABLE VI

NUMBER OF STATES WITH POLICIES AND PRACTICES FOR TELLING PARENTS ABOUT THE ABILITY TEST SCORES OF THEIR CHILDREN

How Many School Districts in the State Report Scores at Parents' Request	For Achievement Tests		For IQ and Other Tests of General Mental Ability	
	Number	%	Number	%
All	6	10	5	8
Many	30	60	13	26
Some	10	20	14	28
Few	3	5	12	24
Few to none	—	—	3	5
None	—	—	2	4
No answer	2	5	2	5
Total	—	—	—	—
	51	100	51	100*

* Figures include the District of Columbia as well as the 50 states.
(Reprinted with permission from Gene R. Hawes, *Educational Testing for the Millions* [New York, McGraw-Hill Book Company, Inc., 1964], p. 273.)

"What is it?," Miss Prentis, the ninth grade counselor, asked him. "I gave those kids the wrong answer sheets!"

Mr. Raylor and Miss Prentis (and any unwary teacher who happened to be seen during a free period near the Guidance Office) spent the entire afternoon recopying every answer onto the correct set of answer sheets. Mr. Raylor then took all the used answer sheets home and paid his three sons a penny a sheet to erase them. A very embarrassed Director of Guidance explained his error to the freshmen (who roared) when he had to redistribute the erased forms for the appropriate subtests later in the week.

Teachers must also be acquainted with the goals of the testing program as well as their role in test administration, and the results of the tests must also be shared with them. One can easily sympathize with teachers who "lose" several teaching days because their classes are taken to the library or cafeteria or multipurpose room for testing, who may be "volunteered" into proctoring such tests, and then never hear another word about the outcome. Teachers have as much "right" as students to know the levels of ability and achievement demonstrated by their pupils, and counselors have a serious obligation to see that such information is disseminated and fully explained to them.

Fortunately, more and more counselors are sharing data, and more and more teachers, students, and parents, realizing that "ignorance is *not* bliss," are making the effort to understand the meaning locked inside test scores. Perhaps the chief use of test results by the counselor is in counseling (individual and group) with students and parents when decisions are to be made about future schooling or career choice. More and more schools are inviting parents and students to come to the school, often in the evening, for a group meeting and discussion of achievement or aptitude test results. Following the large-group presentation, counselors are available in their offices for individual conferences to answer questions and clarify issues not developed in the group presentation. Thus, the initial session might explain the purpose for giving the Iowa Test of Basic Skills or the uses of the Scholastic Aptitude Tests by colleges, and in the individual conferences, parents and students could ask how the results will personally affect them.

When discussing test results with students, some counselors

have the tests available so that the student may look them over again. An achievement battery taken in the early part of the school year may be completely forgotten by April. Sometimes when the student sees the test, he may remark, "Oh, that one. Yeh, I remember. That was the test that we took for five days straight. By Wednesday I was so tired of the whole thing, I just marked down any answer that came into my head."

If there is no correlation between the achievement reported as a result of the standardized test and the student's current grades, his description of his attitude and resulting performance during the test may have a real bearing on the scores. Another student might say she wasn't feeling well or was worried about something else and didn't put forth her best effort. Sometimes seeing the test provides an opportunity for the student to relate feelings about test-taking in general: "I get so nervous, I think I'm going to die; I just can't think at all." Of course, the student may simply be trying to alibi or rationalize his poor performance.

The counselor must explain the test scores simply and thoroughly and provide ample opportunity for questions. If the student insists that the test score is not accurate, accept that possibility. Look with him at his present achievement not only in relation to the standardized aptitude and achievement scores but also as measured by his teachers' evaluation of his progress, his grades. Students are quick to point out that grades can be biased and distorted; all of which may be true. Yet the student must realize that decisions about him will be made by colleges, vocational-technical schools, and employers on the basis of the only records available. Certainly there *are* students who do not do well on standardized tests and do not get good grades, and yet become eminently successful in business, the professions, in the world of sports and entertainment. Let's not forget these students; never be lulled into such dependence on test results or grades that such data alone become the decision-makers.

But often there is a relationship between aptitude and achievement which can be shown to the student.

Isabel, an eighth grader, was planning her program for the next year with her counselor, Mrs. Correlli.

"I'm going to be a nurse, Mrs. Correlli, what courses do I have to take? I watch all the medical shows on TV; I just know I'd love to work in a hospital."

Isabel had transferred to Ricker Junior High in November of her seventh grade, so she missed the Otis-Lennon Mental Ability test given at the entrance to junior high. She did not have a mental ability score from her previous school. Her grades fluctuated between C's and D's. On the Sequential Tests of Educational Progress, her science score fell between the 5 to 18th percentile band. Mr. Dobrowski, her present science teacher, had sent her two deficiency warnings and her grade was presently hovering close to a D. If Isabel was serious about nursing, she would probably have to complete biology and chemistry, a possibility which seemed doubtful on the basis of previous performance in science. Mrs. Correlli felt Isabel's choice of nursing was based solely on television glamour; she had no realistic idea of the duties and demands of nursing. She went over the test score and Isabel's grades in science and mentioned the courses required to become a nurse. Isabel agreed she really had no interest in science nor did she realize how long you had to study in order to become a nurse.

"Do nurses really have to know about that kind of stuff just to help people get better?," she asked Mrs. Correlli.

The counselor then suggested she consider practical nursing and some other jobs in the field of health care and urged her to join the student-volunteers at the local hospital so that she might gain a more realistic picture of this career.

Students with poor math grades and low aptitude and achievement in mathematics who announce an interest in engineering; the student who decides to become a lawyer but whose reading scores imply trouble ahead should be informed of the possibilities of disappointment and defeat if they choose programs of study which their previous performance, via tests and/or grades, suggests are inappropriate. If the student persists in his choice, the counselor has met his obligation of bringing all the facts available to his attention. It should never be forgotten that since grades and tests are not perfect measures, the student's ambition and perseverance may enable him to succeed in the face of negative prospects according to the statistics.

These uses of test scores can be defended and for the most part are endorsed and encouraged. But let us examine using standardized tests as the basis for *ability grouping,* for placing students in classes based on their standing on these tests. Many teachers and counselors are convinced that homogeneous grouping is the only way to organize classes for optimal learning. Recent surveys indicate that "ability grouping . . . is (a) presently one of the predominant methods for organizing or classifying children into classroom units on both the elementary and secondary levels, (b) becoming more and more prevalent and is likely to be more widespread in the near future and (c) occurs more and more frequently as a child progresses each year through the elementary and secondary grades."[14] Such a pattern, its proponents contend, takes individual differences into account by allowing pupils to proceed at their own pace, enables teachers to use methods and materials especially geared to the learning style of each group, permits more individual attention to each pupil, and challenges students to do their best in their own group within realistic ranges of competition.[15] But research has *not* shown these excellent results occurring from such grouping. Rather, research indicates that "ability grouping in itself does not produce improved achievement in children . . . grouping may be detrimental to children in average and lower ability groups. These children appear to suffer from deprivation of intellectual stimulation when brighter children are removed from the classroom."[16]

The principal finding of an extensive study of ability grouping of some 3,000 fifth and sixth grade students reported by Goldberg, Passow, and Justman was that ability grouping per se produces no improvement in achievement for any ability level.[17] The students' self-concept and attitude toward peers were also assessed. The re-

---

14. Dominick Esposito, "Consequences of Ability Grouping: Ethnic and Socio-Economic Separation of Children," The National Center for Research and Information on Equal Education Opportunity TipSheet No. 4 (May, 1971), p. 1.

15. Ibid., p. 4.

16. Miriam L. Goldberg, A. Harry Passow, and Joseph Justman, *The Effect of Ability Grouping* (New York, Teachers College Columbia, 1966), p. 9.

17. Goldberg, et al., *The Effect of Ability Grouping,* p. 163.

searchers reported that what children experience within the class-room makes more difference in how they view themselves than does the organizational pattern of the class.[18]

Borg[19] also found that self-concept scores were consistently lower in the ability-group samples in his study of 4,000 elementary and secondary students. His research revealed no consistent general effects on achievement at any grade level. What few differences were found favored ability groups at the superior level. These students seemed to recognize their achievement potential more completely. However, this attitude did not reach down to the slow or average pupils.

Youngsters who perform below the school's predetermined level of performance on a given standardized test and placed in a special class section labeled "low," "basic," "slow," or indicated by a supposedly unidentifying number or letter of the alphabet are quick to realize that they have been singled out as "stupid." Despite every ploy to disguise ability grouping, students soon break any administration-devised code and can tell you that 9-K's are "dummies" or that the 12-7's are the "brains." Too often teachers assigned these students have little sympathy and less understanding for them. Nor do they make any special efforts to reach these pupils, already stigmatized as less able, until in some cases, the instruction can only be termed glorified baby-sitting. Frequently, the first-year teacher, fresh from the protective college cloister will be assigned the slower students. The experienced teachers, with seniority and battle fatigue, may have "served notice" on the principal that "we've suffered long enough with those kids; let someone else try to teach them. We've earned a chance to work with the brighter students." The new teacher is usually untrained and emotionally unprepared to teach students who feel learning is a vicious game they have no hope of winning. Meeting apparent student antagonism and resistance (which may be their pathetic defense, a barrier these students use to shield their feelings of inadequacy), the teacher may simply "throw in the towel," and attribute *his* inabili-

18. Ibid., p. 105.

19. Walter R. Borg, *Ability Grouping in the Public Schools* (Madison, Wisconsin, Dembar Educational Research Services, 1967).

ty to reach and teach these pupils to *their* intellectual inferiority. Realizing that the teacher's expectations of their ability to succeed are nil, the students make little effort to learn. Thus, the grim self-fulfilling prophecy of failure is realized. What expectations can these students have for themselves when the school communicates to them, loud and clear, such doubts on their chances for academic success? How welcome will they feel in such a school; how likely will they be to work hard to achieve after having been "put down" so thoroughly?

Teachers often complain bitterly when they are assigned a section of slow students, yet they are extremely reluctant to have heterogenous grouping, perhaps convinced that coping with thirty or thirty-five of the slow students once a day is preferable to having them "sprinkled" throughout every class.

If the standardized test is biased, as some critics claim, or if the student has not performed at his real ability level due to any number of influencing variables already discussed, his plight is even more tragic. Once labeled "slow," it is exceedingly difficult in many schools to have the student placed in a higher section. There is also the indefensible practice of using an "across-the-board" grouping for students so that once placed in a high section in one or more courses, they find themselves in top sections in every subject. This frequently puts great pressure upon students who simply are not equally proficient in every subject they are taking. It is hard enough on the strong history student, for example, who finds himself struggling in the top math section, but it is even more tragic for the student who is placed in low sections in every course when in reality he may be weak in perhaps one area.

The superior student, best served by ability grouping, constitutes approximately 15 percent of the student population. The remaining 85 percent of the student body, the vast majority, are badly short-changed by this method. The "average" student, and particularly the noncollege bound, also suffer from the lower teacher expectations inherent in ability grouping. "After all, you can't expect too much, these kids are only average; they aren't going to college, so why push them," is a common reaction of many teachers. The students are quick to sense this; they consequently do not exert themselves to reach their academic potential. Students learn from each other as well as from the teacher. The college-bound can benefit from the practical and perhaps more realistic views of his noncollege-bound peers. Segregating students develops in the brighter students a sense of intellectual elitism, an inability to accept or understand those rated less able than themselves; and in those labeled "slow," a sense of frustration, despair, and bitterness. Yet these attitudes are both false. All aspects of intelligence and achievement cannot be measured by paper-and-pencil tests. The student who is superior on a standardized test may be limited in areas not tested where the so-called dull student may excel.

Ability grouping, whether based on standardized test scores, grades, teachers' evaluations, or a combination of these, says the researchers inflict serious damage on students' self-concepts and on their achievement. In the face of such charges, the counselor should risk assuming the role of "agent of change" and reexamine with teachers and administrators the consequences of such a policy.

A final use of standardized test data by counselors, and one which also causes occasional controversy, is the compilation of statistics on test performance requested by the school board or the State Department of Education. For example, counselors may be asked to determine the mean IQ for each grade; report how many students were tested at each grade level, in what areas, and on what types of tests; compute the average quantitative and verbal scores for seniors who took the college board exams. Data comparing IQ, grade average, and achievement test scores are also possible areas for counselor-computation. The dangers of making judgments about the quality of the school's program or staff by individuals unacquainted with the limitations of such data (as some school board members are) have raised justifiable criticism. Here, again, the counselor's role must extend beyond that of mere reporter. Particularly in preparing materials for the use of local school board members, the counselor should assume leadership in suggesting appropriate types of data and the best methods of presenting such material. Even so, a written summary of the information requested is rarely sufficient. The counselor must be on hand when comparative statistics are discussed in order to clarify any points in question and to instruct those seeking to find meaning within medians, means, percentile bands, and stanines.

Using test data to help individual students and their parents in making realistic educational and vocational choices, working with teachers in understanding the strengths and limitations of individuals and groups of students, and disseminating test data in an understandable manner to the school board and the community at large are perhaps the key responsibilities of the counselor in this sensitive area.

SUMMARY

The last component in self-understanding and awareness by the student and his parents is an accurate assessment of the individual's potential and achievement. Standardized tests constitute the most widely used means of securing such evaluation.

Testing programs administered by the public schools, extending from the kindergarten to the twelfth grade, include mental ability (IQ), aptitude, achievement, and interest tests; the resulting scores should be used by counselors and teachers in conferences with students and parents whenever educational or vocational decisions are to be made.

Cautions listed in the chapter regarding the limitations of standardized tests should be remembered in making judgments based on test data. Interpretation of test scores and their implication for the student are the responsibility of both counselor and teachers, so all faculty must be fully conversant with the terminology surrounding standardized tests. For this reason, a brief glossary of most-used measurement terms is included.

Misuse of test data and the danger of incorrect test interpretation have also been explored.

SUGGESTED READINGS

Cronbach, Lee J.: *Essentials of Psychological Testing.* New York, Har-Row, 1970.
Thorough discussion of purposes of tests, administering, scoring, test validation, errors in testing plus description of many of the psychologi-

cal tests now available. "Must" reading for those who wish to understand this field.

Black, Hillel: *They Shall Not Pass.* New York, Morrow, 1963.

The "other side" of the story; an indictment of the misuses of standardized testing; very readable.

Hawes, Gene R.: *Educational Testing for the Millions.* New York, McGraw, 1964.

Provides brief description with illustrations of most-used standardized tests. A useful guide for teacher, parent and student, assembled by the former editor of the College Entrance Examination Board.

Manuel, Herschel T.: *Taking a Test—How to do Your Best.* Yonkers-on-Hudson, World Book, 1956.

Intended for those who must take tests; presents purposes of the test, tips for most effective test-taking. Although written in 1956, it would be useful for those about to take their first plunge into standardized test-taking.

CHAPTER 12

SUMMING UP

IF I HAVE ACCOMPLISHED my aim now that you have reached these final pages, you accept my premise that understanding the individuality of each of your students or counselees is essential to effective teaching or counseling. Furthermore, you see the counseling relationship not as the exclusive province of the counselor but rather a joint association of counselor, teacher, and parents working cooperatively to help students better understand themselves so that they can function to their optimal advantage in the academic setting and develop strategies for coping successfully with problems of adjustment and educational and vocational choice.

From mutual sharing by counselors and teachers of information in the students' permanent files, through participation in case conferences, in planning and analyzing sociometric devices for classroom use, in conducting observations and preparing anecdotal records, in analyzing rating scales and questionnaires will come awareness, understanding, and empathy by the faculty member for his students. At times the teacher will become a counselor and the counselor will become a teacher as each helps the other in his efforts to help his students.

Other nontest appraisal devices such as the autobiography and the fact-finding interview, whether used by the counselor or the teacher, will build still other bridges of communication between students and faculty.

Counselors and teachers must realize the impact that standardized tests exert on students and their parents. Too many decisions affecting students are made on the basis of test data for any faculty member to remain uninvolved or uninformed about them.

Those of you entering the profession as teachers, or presently in the field, will, I hope, accept the roles I've described; roles

241

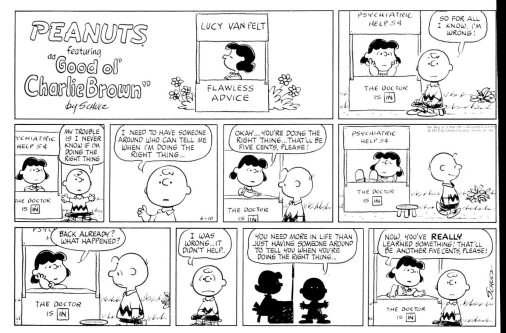

Figure 36. © 1973 United Features Syndicate, Inc. Adapted from Charles Schultz's "Peanuts" comic strip.

which will extend your influence beyond that of instructor. To those preparing for counseling, or now acting as counselors, I urge you to remember you have an obligation to each of your counselees, his teachers, parents, and administrators. You can serve none effectively if you fail to serve them all.

Counselors and teachers willing to push back the barriers separating them and their students will be rewarded a thousand-fold in the satisfaction gained by providing vitally needed services more effectively. I have been fortunate in experiencing these gratifications both as teacher and counselor. Don't miss them. They are worth every bit of effort you expend. Take my word for it.

AUTHOR INDEX

243

SUBJECT INDEX

A

Ability
  mental, 209-211
  reading, 209, 210-211
Ability grouping, 235-237
Academic aptitude, 213
Academic information, 34, (form) 36
Achievement
  battery, 209, 211-212
  expectations, minorities, 28-29
  test, 209, 213
Activities
  student record, 34, (form) 43
ACT, 203
American College Testing Program, 203
Anecdotal record, 114
Anxiety
  boys, 25-26
Aptitude
  college, 209
  multifactor, 209
  tests, 212
Arithmetic mean, 213
Attitude scales, 88-89, 91-92
Attitudes, school, 91-92
  (see also Bias)
Autobiographies, 56-86
  advantages, 79-80
  analysis, 66
  appearance, 65
  benefits, 60-61
  depth of expression, 71
  disadvantages, 80
  distortions, 74
  emphasis, 73-74
  forms, 61-63
  gloss, 73
  language, 69
  length, 67
  lies, 74
  omissions, 73
  organization, 75-76

purposes, 58-59
quality, 71
reading, 63
semantics, 69
tape recording, 81-82
tone, 72
types, 61-63, 81
unconscious error, 74

B

Basic classes, 236
Battery, 213
Behavior, disruptive, 7
  boys, 20
  causes, 23-24
  teacher reaction, 23
Bias, 13
  boys, 23
  education, 15, 19
  interview, 163
  jobs, 19
  rating scales, 139-140
  teacher, 19, 23
  test, 18, 212
Biographical data, 33, (form) 36
Blocks, communication, 155-156
Body language, 112-113

C

California Short Form Test of Mental
    Maturity, 210-211
Case conference, 166-176
  counselor role, 166-168
  follow up, 172
  limitations, 171-172
  parent participation, 174-175
  purposes, 166
  scheduling, 172
  student involvement, 175
  teacher responsibility, 170-171
Case study, 166
Central tendency, 140

You Will Be Interested Also In These . . .

Henry E. Adams & Irving P. Unikel – ISSUES AND TRENDS IN BEHAVIOR THERAPY. 288 pp., 38 il., 14 tables, cloth $10.95, paper $7.95

(10 Contributors) An evaluation of selected current and significant issues and trends in behavior therapy. Part I is concerned with issues and theoretical developments. Included is discussion of the necessity for the study and integration of consumer requirements and reactions in behavior therapy systems. Part II give evidence of major trends in behavior therapy.

Lloyd Keith Daniels – THE MANAGEMENT OF CHILDHOOD BEHAVIOR PROBLEMS IN SCHOOL AND AT HOME. 480 pp. (7 x 10), 75 il., 22 tables, $22.50

(108 Contributors) The application of principles of behavior modification is described for numerous problem situations, and solutions are presented for the teacher and parent that can be conveniently used as a ready source of reference in either the classroom or at home. The book is concerned with three major issues: the modification of avoidance problems by the classroom teacher, the modification of approach problems by the classroom teacher, and the role of parents in the remediation process.

Robert Friedman – FAMILY ROOTS OF SCHOOL LEARNING AND BEHAVIOR DISORDERS. 360 pp., cloth $14.75, paper $9.50

(12 Contributors) Provides educators and mental health clinicians for the first time with a comprehensive overview of the family aspect of school-related problems. The chapters combine theory and practice in dealing with learning and behavior disorders in preschool through high school. Parental values and attitudes, parent-child relationships, and family interactional systems are related to cultural diversity and social change.

Roger D. Klein, Walter G. Hapkiewicz & Aubrey H. Roden – BEHAVIOR MODIFICATION IN EDUCATIONAL SETTINGS. 568 pp., 77 il., 27 tables, $14.95

(69 Contributors) The major portion of this book of readings is devoted to a sampling of articles which illustrate the rationale behind and the utilization of operant principles in classroom behavior modification. The four sections of the book cover operant principles in education, respondent principles of education, teacher training, issues and problems.

James M. Stedman, William F. Patton & Kay F. Walton – CLINICAL STUDIES IN BEHAVIOR THERAPY WITH CHILDREN, ADOLESCENTS, AND THEIR FAMILIES. 412 pp., 77 il., 24 tables, cloth $18.50, paper $14.95

(59 Contributors) This book offers selected readings in behavior therapy techniques which present both the principles of applied learning and sufficient case detail for clinical application by the practitioner. The material is useful in understanding deviant behavior and formulating treatment plans. The confusing terminology of behavioral psychology is explained with concrete examples illustrating use of these terms and concepts. An annotated bibliography is provided.

Constance Tarczan – AN EDUCATOR'S GUIDE TO PSYCHOLOGICAL TESTS: Descriptions and Classroom Implications. 128 pp. (5 3/4 x 8 3/4), 2 il., 5 tables, cloth $6.95, paper $3.95

Foreword by Robert E. Hemenway. A unique, compact and handy reference guide to interpreting psychological data. Includes a wealth of information concerning intelligence, mental age, psychometric terminology, and descriptive material regarding over sixty types of psychological, achievement, reading, projective, social, infant and preschool measures. Provides examples of questions asked, what the text proports to measure, standardization and reliability norms and examples of remedial techniques.

CHARLES C THOMAS • PUBLISHER • SPRINGFIELD • ILLINOIS